Participatory Rural Development Methodology and Applications

Participatory Rural Development Methodology and Applications

Sonia Mahajan

RANDOM

RANDOM PUBLICATIONS

NEW DELHI (INDIA)

ISBN 978-93-5111-482-6

Published in 2015 in India by
RANDOM PUBLICATIONS
4376-A/4B, Gali Murari Lal, Ansari Road
New Delhi-110 002
Phone : +9111-43580356, 011-23289044, 011-43142548
e-mail: sales@randompublications.com,
info@randompublications.com, randomexports@gmail.com

Reprinted 2026

Type Setting by : Friends Media, Delhi-110089

Preface

People's participation as a concept was formulated – or rediscovered – in the 1970s, in response to the growing awareness that the various approaches then employed for rural development, such as community development, integrated rural development or basic needs did not often lead to significant rural development and especially poverty reduction, largely, as was then thought, because there was little involvement in development projects of those undergoing 'development', and particularly the poor.

The main tenet of participative approaches to rural development is that the community and stakeholders are collaborators in activities at every stage of development process. Thus, participative methods are meant to generate a sense of ownership of decisions and actions. This is in contrast to the alternative model of development where project conceptualization, objectives and design are imposed on the community by people external to the community who are characterized as experts. Participatory approaches can also challenge perceptions, leading to a change in attitude and agendas. They can also provide new and sometimes surprising insights.

This book makes significant contribution to the understanding of the actual status of participatory rural development. It discuss the issues of people's participation in the rural development planning and governance with case studies from different countries. It examines rural experience and provides brief overviews of past interpretations and practices and of current debates. Its main purposes are to identify the methodologies, applications and challenges facing the use of participatory approaches to rural development, and to propose a number of topics for discussion. The book will be immensely valuable for students, researchers and academicians working in the areas of social work, rural development, agriculture, and environmental science, and also for NGO workers and trainers and researchers in the development field.

Author

Preface

Contents

1

Participatory Approaches in Rural Development

People Participation is a process through which stakeholders influence and share control over development initiatives and the decisions and resources which affect them. Unless the poor are given an opportunity to participate in the development of interventions designed to improve their livelihoods, they will continue to miss the benefits of any intervention.

The need for stakeholder ownership is now well established in the donor community. Ownership of a project by stakeholders involves ensuring the widest possible participation of those who are supposed to be the beneficiaries of the project. The essence of ownership is that the recipients drive the process.

The main tenet of participative approaches to development is that the community and stakeholders are collaborators in activities at every stage of development process. Thus, participative methods are meant to generate a sense of ownership of decisions and actions. This is in contrast to the alternative model of development where project conceptualization, objectives and design are imposed on the community by people external to the community who are characterized as experts. Participatory approaches can also challenge perceptions, leading to a change in attitude and agendas. They can also provide new and sometimes surprising insights.

Development of Participatory Approaches

The development paradigms of the 1960s and 1970s derived from the legacy of colonial rule, especially the planning systems of the late 1930s and post World War II period. The conception was top down (development was something governments did for or to people), and the language military-bureaucratic. There was little stakeholder involvement of those undergoing "development", a fact which must rank high among the causes of the failures of development to improve the lives of the majority poor of the "developing" world. Participatory development arose as a reaction to this realization of failure, popularized particularly by Gordon Conway and Robert Chambers (1992), and more recently by David Korten (1996).

Another guiding principle therefore is that research is participatory, a much abused word that encompasses several virtues and vices. As with all methods, its merits vary with the research situation and the practitioner. At its best, the process can be liberating, empowering and educative, a collegial relationship that brings local communities into the policy debate, validating their knowledge. At its worst, it can degenerate into a process of co-option of local communities into an external agenda, or an exploitative series of empty rituals imposing fresh burdens on the community's time and energy and serving primarily to legitimize the credentials of the implementing agency as "grassroots oriented". While participation must be integral to the research process, it must be understood and practiced as a genuine process.

Despite a wealth of alternative and often confusing names, participatory research methods can be conveniently classified into four main types, each with a distinctive style and ethos.

- Participant Observer
- Rapid Rural Appraisal (RRA)
- Participatory Rural Appraisal (PRA)
- Participatory Action Research (PAR)

Participatory Rural Development

Participatory approaches have been used in several settings in development both in rural and urban areas. In particular, participatory approaches allow a community to:

- Express and analyse the realities of their lives;
- Plan themselves what action to take to change the situation;
- Monitor and evaluate the results themselves.

However, the rationale for using participative methods is a pragmatic one. A problem with non-participative methods is that they often impose a commitment on the community to do certain things even though they were not involved in the project. Where the community has not been involved in a project, they are not equipped to fully understand the nature and rationale of the commitments they are being asked to make. It is futile for the community to give its commitment only for it to be demonstrated that in practice, they are unable to fulfill their commitment. Conversely, it has been found that where communities have been involved, projects have a better chance of surviving through shocks, as the commitment is there to ensure that the project does not fail.

In the area activities, it may well be the case that interventions reliant upon behavior change may fail if the community was not involved in designing these. However, when communities are involved, such messages are much better understood and are therefore taken on board. A secondary benefit is that members of the community will subsequently be better placed to act as change agents.

It must be said that it is important that all stakeholders are involved in the development of projects and not just direct beneficiaries. Three levels of stakeholder defined to include beneficiaries can be considered:

- Direct beneficiaries (end users, farmers, urban poor etc.)
- Intermediaries (e.g. professionals, advisers, practitioners, consultants, experts etc.)
- Decision, policy makers (politicians, senior civil servants, etc.)

All three groups are important to have represented on the project as stakeholders if the necessary commitment is to be achieved. Care must be taken however to ensure that when a diverse range of stakeholders such as those listed above are engaged in a project, account is taken of the huge differentials in power relationships which could negate the value of a participatory approach. The danger is in a powerful stakeholder group hijacking the entire project with other groups being relegated to passive conspirators at best.

Advantages of Participatory Approaches

Participatory approaches are particularly useful in providing feedback to policy-makers.

- *Economies of scale:* Participatory groups constitute a grassroots "receiving system" that allows development agencies to reduce the unit delivery or transaction costs of their services, thus broadening their impact.
- *Higher productivity:* Given access to resources and a guarantee that they will share fully in the benefits of their efforts, the poor become more receptive to new technologies and services, and achieve higher levels of production and income. This helps to build net cash surpluses that strengthen the groups' economic base and contribute to rural capital formation.
- *Reduced costs and increased efficiency:* The poor's contribution to project planning and implementation represent savings that reduce project costs. The poor also contribute their knowledge of local conditions, facilitating the diagnosis of environmental, people and institutional constraints, as well as the search for solutions.
- *Building of democratic organizations:* The limited size and informality of small groups is suited to the poor's scarce organisational experience and low literacy levels. Moreover, the small group environment is ideal for the diffusion of collective decision-making and leadership skills, which can be used in the subsequent development of inter-group federations.
- *Sustainability:* Participatory development leads to increased self-reliance among the poor and the establishment of a network of self-sustaining rural organisations. This carries important benefits: the greater efficiency of development services stimulates economic growth in rural areas and broadens domestic markets, thus favouring balanced national development; politically, participatory approaches provide opportunities for the poor to contribute constructively to development.

Difficulties in Implementing Participatory Approaches

There are two potential pitfalls to take into account when implementing participatory approaches. The first of these is that engaging the poor is often a far more difficult task than engaging the more powerful stakeholder groups. It is fairly easy to demonstrate to government officials for instance why their participation in a particular initiative would be valuable. It is not the same for the poor and therefore different techniques are required to achieve one?s aim. Examples of techniques used include:

- maps, flow diagrams, seasonal calendars, matrices and so on;
- Visual techniques are a good way to engage the poor especially where local materials are used for preparation of resources.
- Visual techniques also encourage creativity and the exchange of ideas.

A second thing to bear in mind is that for participatory techniques to work effectively, the implementing agency must itself be prepared to change and learn to accept change. The main changes are:

- Loss of power. The agency should be prepared to accept a loss of power;
- Learn to listen. The agency should be prepared to listen actively and not pay lip service.
- Loss of control. The agency should be prepared to cede control to the community so that they own the project or initiative.

Issues in People Participation

What real voice do people with direct experience of poverty have in research and inquiry into poverty? This study, by Fran Bennett with Moraene Roberts, gives an overview of important of people participation in rural development through participatory approaches. The Participatory approaches respect the expertise of people with direct experience of poverty and give them more control over the research process and more influence over how findings are used. The researchers examine the issues involved when principle turns into practice.

In many of the rural development projects implemented in the past, there was a large gap between plan and implementation. The integrated rural development concept to fill this gap with the participation of the rural population which, hitherto, has been the mere object of projects. The success of integrated rural development programmes depends on the degree to which a population can be motivated. This again depends on how much their interests, their felt needs are taken into account, and to what extent they are involved in the planning and decision-making process.

Thus, the question of motivation leads to the problem of decentralization of planning, i.e. to a discussion which has been going on for years under the slogan of "development from below". In principle, centralized planning, bottom-up planning, involves all groups in the process, this being the prerequisite for the mobilization of local resources. It guarantees that the felt needs of the population, and not those of the planners, are taken care of, and the population considers the plans as their own. This altogether increases the efficiency to a crucial point because rural development does not seem to be possible as long as the rural population considers it to be the governments and not their own task. This is why the concept of integrated rural development attaches so much importance to decentralization and participation.

However, there are some problems and limitations. Local planning may easily come into conflict with national planning because the target-setters, their evaluation of the situation, and their priorities may differ. Lack of information on the overall situation, as well as limited competence at the local level, are difficult to deny. (In view of the ignorance of national planners regarding local circumstances, this shortcoming ntay be compensated for by similar lacks on the other side).

However, local planning is no guarantee for planning in the best interest of the local population. It is not unusual that local participation in reality means participation of the rural upper class, and minorities are easily neglected. Likewise, the disparities among regions can easily grow because the better regions and those in which typical leader personalities are encountered are often preferred to the others. Decentralized planning means a reallocation of power and influence, and is bound to meet with the antagonism of groups with vested interests. There is probably no clear answer as to "bottom-up" or "up.down" planning, but different subjects require different procedures. For instance, target planning, like the planning of agricultural production, is a field for "top-down" planning. Here, the initiative is at the top and, with incentives, planners will induce farmers to implement their concepts. However, resource development planning and planning of people infrastructure are typical fields for "bottom-up" planning, and the task of the national planning agency is merely to coordinate, and to outline the limitations produced by available resources.

This indicates that the? whole question of "up-down" versus "bottom-up" planning is void. Of importance is an optimal mix of central and regional planning activities with a participation of the population in keeping-/with the functions. This is not easy to implement, last but not least, the difference between planning and implementation as far as administration and the persons involved are concerned plays a great role.

Even local participation often results in some people doing the planning and some the work, and this division reflects the local stratification. Although the difficulties are great, the solution of the problem of local participation and motivation is a key to the success or failure of any integrated rural development programme.

- Reasons for using participatory approaches range from recognizing the particular expertise of people with experience of poverty in putting forward their own realities - and their right to do so - to increasing the effectiveness of research and deepening understanding of poverty and policy impact.
- Basic building blocks to make participatory approaches work include: time to allow people to go at their own pace; adequate financial and other support; and opportunities for personal exchange.
- Key factors in getting the most from participation are: clarity about aims, rather than allowing limits of resources to dictate the extent and quality of participation; and involving people in poverty in making sense of the information produced, by using their 'insider expertise'.
- And adequate funding should be provided to organizations working with people living in poverty.

Promotion of People Participation

Given the importance more and more placed on beneficiary participation, no wonder firstly that the number of participatory projects are increasing; they are supported by I/NGOs, UN agencies, various progressive governments and furthermore to a great extent civil society organizations. Secondly, that conventional projects, though easier to design and to manage, are regarded increasingly as out-dated and after all less feasible, cost-effective and prone to be successful.

The positive aspects of both conventional and participatory projects should be more and more merged. For example, the economic feasibility, marketing, etc. and technical research, technology transfer, etc. requirements for the development of certain sub-sectors e.g. irrigation, crop production, livestock, extension, credit must be fully taken into account also in participatory approaches. Top-planning e.g. by a national body or a district development committee and grassroot (bottom-up) planning (e.g. by groups or federations which come out with small-scale production plans) must be matched, for example by a workable coordination committee. Indeed feasible forms of vertical integration of development efforts are indispensable on the need for a receiving-cum-delivery system. We can conclude that the common essential elements of people participation in the specific objectives are: to help identify, plan and implement employment - and income-generating and other group activities for small farmers, tenants, fishermen and/or laborers; to assist the beneficiaries to organize themselves into self-run groups and organizations in such ways that firstly they have access to programmes of training, credit, inputs, marketing and processing as well as education, health and sanitation and, secondly, they can more and more satisfy their economic and people needs and become eventually self-reliant; to assist line departments and other agencies including banks and I/NGOs to increase their effectiveness to better serve the rural weak, to develop innovative farm and also off-farm income-raising activities, and to encourage self-development efforts; to develop a strategy for expanding the successful features of the project as well as promote the rural development activities in the country.

References

Aryal, Bojendra, (2003)."Approaches and Methods of Rural Development" *Sociology of Rural Development.* Dikchayanta Pulication, Kritipur.

Bista, Kumar, (2000)."An Alternative strategy". Rural Dvelopment in Nepal, Udya Books, KTM.

Manzuri, Ghazala and Vijayendra Rao. (2004). *Community-Based and -Driven. Development: A Critical Review.* World Bank Policy Research Working Paper 3209.

Peter Oakley. (1988). *The Monitoring and Evaluation of Participation in Rural Development,* by FAO, Rome.

Singh, Katar. (1999). "Rural Development Policies and Strategies". *Rural Development Principles, Policies and Management.* Sage Publication, India.

World Bank. (2004). *World Development Report 2004: Making Services Working for Poor People.* Oxford University Press.

2

Participatory Rural Development and Poverty Alleviation

The term 'participation' has recently come to play a central role in the discourse of rural development practitioners and policy makers. At the same time, people's interpretations of the term – and criticisms of other people's interpretations – have multiplied, and the intentions and results of much participation in practice have been questioned or even denounced. In other words, participation has become a hotly contested term, in a debate with deep implications for the ways in which community, society, citizenship, the rights of the poor and rural development itself are conceived, and for the policies that are formulated about and around some of these concepts and the social realities to which they refer.

It examines Asian experience and provides brief overviews of past interpretations and practices and of current debates. Its main purposes are to identify some of the main challenges facing the use of participatory approaches to rural development and poverty alleviation in Asia, and to propose a number of topics for discussion. It also includes a short discussion of a particular family of methods, broadly associated with rapid and participatory rural appraisal (RRA/PRA), which has acquired considerable prominence in recent years.

Background to People's Participation

A form of participation can be traced back at least to colonial times:

> In Eastern Nigeria in the late 1940s and early 1950s British colonial officials pursued a policy with many similarities to […] participatory development […] The chief propagandist of this policy was E.R. Chadwick, the Senior District Officer i/c Community Development. He wrote frequently about how self-help development could transform the capacity of Nigerians (as individuals and communities) to identify their own needs and strengthen their abilities to improve their own conditions. He was puritanical in his refusal to 'deliver' development since this undermined the very transformation that the policy sought to achieve.

This surprisingly modern view already contains many of the central themes that are still present in current approaches: self-help, the community as well as the individual, transformation and capacity building and, at least by implication, a limited form of empowerment. Not much of significance was added by the community development approach that originated in India after 1950 and spread to other developing countries in the 1960s, with its underlying modernization ideology and its practical combination of adult education, institution building, social welfare (especially education and health) and development projects. Only in the 1970s were the other main themes of modern participatory approaches added: increasing the awareness of the poor and oppressed of asymmetric power relations and of their own situation, creating or reinforcing networks of solidarity, gradually building up their confidence in their own knowledge and abilities, and consequently also a sense of entitlement.

People's participation as a concept was formulated – or rediscovered – in the 1970s, in response to the growing awareness that the various approaches then employed for rural development, such as community development, integrated rural development or basic needs did not often lead to significant rural development and especially poverty reduction, largely, as was then thought, because there was little involvement in development projects of those undergoing 'development', and particularly the poor.

An important milestone in people's participation in rural development was the World Conference on Agrarian Reform and Rural Development, which declared participation by rural people in the institutions that govern their lives 'a basic human right':

> If rural development was to realize its potential, the Conference said, disadvantaged rural people had to be organized and actively involved in designing policies and programmes and in controlling social and economic institutions. WCARRD saw a close link between participation and voluntary,

> autonomous and democratic organizations representing the poor. It called on development agencies to work in close cooperation with organizations of intended beneficiaries, and proposed that assistance be channelled through small farmer and peasant groups.

After WCARRD, and throughout the 1980s and 90s, participation in rural development – as well as in development at large – gradually became more established among governments, donors and international organizations, to such an extent indeed that, as Stirrat put it, 'it is now difficult to find a rurally based development project which does not in one way or another claim to adopt a participatory approach involving bottom-up planning, acknowledging the importance of indigenous knowledge, and claiming to empower local people'.

Inevitably, at the same time as participation became a 'good thing', there was also a trend towards greater diversity in the interpretations of what it really means and in the forms of its application in practice, as the various actors involved – ranging from consultants and academics to developing country governments, NGOs, bilateral donors and international organizations – chose from the different approaches, principles, methods or simply emphases available, to fit their own missions or interests. Participation thus became what some describe as a 'new orthodoxy of development', but one lacking an ideology.

Definitions of Participation

The diversity mentioned above may best be illustrated by a brief analysis of some of the many definitions of participation that have been proposed. The FAO Informal Working Group on Participatory Approaches and Methods (IWG) transcribes some useful definitions in a web site dedicated to participatory project formulation. First, two definitions from the 1970s:

> With regard to rural development ... participation includes people's involvement in decision-making processes, in implementing programmes, their sharing in the benefits of development programmes and their involvement in efforts to evaluate such programmes.
>
> (Cohen and Uphof, 1977).

> articipation is concerned with . . . the organised efforts to increase control over resources and regulative institutions in given social situations on the part of groups and movements of those hitherto excluded from such control.
>
> (Pearse and Stifel, 1979)

Cohen and Uphof were among the first to stress the importance of participation in the various stages of the project cycle, particularly decision making and evaluation, rather than simply sharing in the benefits of projects. Pearse and Stifel complement this by stressing control and, by implication, also issues of power. Power and empowerment are brought in explicitly in the following characterization:

> Participation can be seen as a process of empowerment of the deprived and the excluded. This view is based on the recognition of differences in political and economic power among different social groups and classes. Participation in this sense necessitates the creation of organisations of the poor which are democratic, independent and self-reliant.
>
> (Ghai, 1990).

Two other definitions are associated with international agencies:

> Participatory development stands for partnership which is built upon the basis of dialogue among the various actors, during which the agenda is jointly set, and local views and indigenous knowledge are deliberately sought and respected. This implies negotiation rather than the dominance of an externally set project agenda. Thus people become actors instead of being beneficiaries.
>
> (OECD, 1994)

> Participation is a process through which stakeholders influence and share control over development initiatives and the decisions and resources which affect them.
>
> (World Bank, 1994)

OECD definition adds useful elements by stressing dialogue and negotiation between the 'developers' and the 'developed', as well as the fact that through participation people become actors in their own development rather than just passive beneficiaries. Along similar lines, the World Bank definition broadens participation from just the poor to other 'stakeholders', a term that has become almost widespread 'participation' itself. Together, the definitions above clearly illustrate the diversity mentioned in the preceding section. IWG combines several of the elements in the five definitions above and gives its own definition of participation in development as

> ... a process of equitable and active involvement of all stakeholders in the formulation of development policies and strategies and in the analysis, planning and implementation, monitoring and evaluation of development activities. To allow for a more equitable development process, disadvantaged stakeholders need to be empowered to increase their level of knowledge,

influence and control over their own livelihoods, including development initiatives affecting them.

Degrees of Participation

An influential participation typology has to do with degrees or levels of participation. Writing in North America, Arnstein defines participation as

> … the redistribution of power that enables the have-not citizens, presently excluded from the political and economic processes, to be deliberately included in the future […] It is the strategy by which they can induce significant social reform which enables them to share in the benefits of the affluent society.

She puts forward a model that consists of a ladder with eight rungs, as illustrated in Figure 1 below. Arnstein stresses that the ladder is a simplification and that the eight rungs are an imperfect representation of what is really a continuum, where a clear distinction between levels is not always possible. Still, she claims, it helps to illustrate the fact that there are different degrees of citizen participation

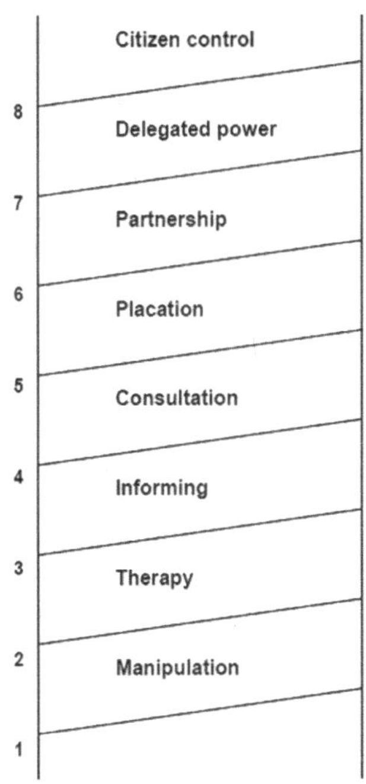

Figure 1: The Ladder of Participation

This model is not neutral: as pointed out by Hayward et al., 'reading the ladder from bottom to top, it suggests a hierarchical view that promotes full participation as the goal to be achieved. This value-laden view deligitimises non- and/or peripheral participation'.

Efficiency and Empowerment Views of Participation

Both Arnstein's ladder and the typology in Table 1 carry the implicit assumption that different positions correspond to different degrees of one and the same thing (i.e. participation) and that therefore it would be possible to move gradually from one level to another.

Table 1. A Participation Typology

Type of Participation	*Some Components and Characteristics*
Passive Participation	People are told what is going to happen or has already happened. Top down, information shared belongs only to external professionals.
Participation in information giving	People answer questions posed by extractive researchers, using surveys etc. People not able to influence the research.
Participation by consultation	People are consulted and external agents listen to their views. Usually externally defined problems and solutions. People not really involved in decision making. Participation as consultation.
Participation by material incentives	Provision of resources, e.g. labor. Little incentive to participate after the incentives end, for example much farm research, some community forestry.
Functional Participation	Groups are formed to meet predetermined objectives. Usually done after major project decisions are made, therefore initially dependent on outsiders but may become self dependent and enabling. Participation as organization.
Interactive Participation	Joint analysis to joint actions. Possible use of new local institutions or strengthening existing ones. Enabling and empowering so people have a stake in maintaining structures or practices.
Self-Mobilisation	Already empowered, take decisions independently of external institutions. May or may not challenge existing inequitable distributions of wealth and power. Participation as empowering.

Source: Pimbert and Pretty, 1994.

However, much of the theorizing of participation is based on a distinction that for some people implies a rejection of this assumption. This is the distinction between the *efficiency argument* and the *equity and empowerment argument*. The former envisages the use of participation instrumentally, to achieve better project outcomes or greater sustainability in rural development terms, for instance by mobilizing beneficiaries' contributions through their involvement in implementation, or by increasing project acceptance, local ownership and sustainability.

The latter regards participation as a process that empowers the poor and strengthens their capacity to take independent collective action in order to improve their own situation (and can, in some cases, even lead to changes in the distribution of power, as successful collective action and the associated increase in awareness and self-confidence lead the poor to claim a larger share of power and resources in the rural community). Its advocates dismiss instrumental uses of participation as inadequate, since they rarely if ever lead to the effective empowerment of the majority, particularly the poor and oppressed. Against this, some people argue that some beneficiary involvement is usually better than none, and that instrumental forms of participation may, over time, lead to more comprehensive and more empowering participation, particularly if care is taken to protect rural development projects from elite capture. Social scientists caution that institutions do not usually work like that, and that processes of empowerment can stop or move backwards as much as they can move forwards.

Scope and Applications of Participation

In the project cycle, the diagnosis of situations and problems, leading to project identification and formulation, is a field where the current trend is towards the use of various participatory approaches. As van Heck puts it,

> Participatory research is to be included in any participatory project as it is indispensable firstly for the collection and analysis of the necessary information on the action areas and the disadvantaged people and secondly for project expansion and replication.

Other stages of the project cycle where participation is used include project planning and design decisions, project implementation, monitoring and evaluation.

In addition to these forms of participation at the *micro* level of projects, participatory approaches are also used at other levels. For instance, participatory poverty assessments (PPAs) are designed to influence policy at the *macro* level, particularly in relation to development and poverty reduction strategies. Exercises of this kind have acquired a new importance with the introduction of poverty reduction strategy papers by the Bretton Woods Institutions in 1999 and the virtual imposition of the obligation to formulate them, supposedly with the active participation of the poor, upon a considerable number of developing countries.

Between the micro and the macro level, a number of exercises in participation at an intermediate or *meso* level have also been carried out. These include participatory budgeting in local governments and various forms of territory-based rural development, among which the LEADER programmes of the European Union are notable for their support for decentralized development and participation of the local communities.

Special Case of Participatory Rural Appraisal

Because of the role that it has played in spreading ideas of participation in rural development and in recent debates on participation, participatory rural appraisal (PRA) deserves a special mention here.

PRA has been described as

> ... a family of approaches, methods and behaviours that enable people to express and analyse the realities of their lives and conditions, to plan themselves what actions to take, and to monitor and evaluate the results. Its methods have evolved from Rapid Rural Appraisal (RRA). The difference is that PRA emphasizes processes that empower local people, whereas RRA is mainly seen as a means for outsiders to gather information. The key elements of PRA are the methods used, and – most importantly – the behaviour and attitudes of those who facilitate it.
>
> (Chambers and Blackburn, 1996: 1).

Poverty and the powerlessness of the poor are central concerns of PRA. PRA uses a wide range of methods developed by practitioners specifically to help local people, rural and urban – many of whom are not literate – express and share information, and also has several methods in common with RRA. Many of these methods are visual, and they include participatory mapping and modelling, transect walks, flow diagrams, seasonal calendars and matrix scoring, institutional diagramming and analytical diagramming, all undertaken by local people. Triangulation, i.e. the use of several methods, types of information, investigators and disciplines for purposes of cross-checking and progressive learning and approximation, is also a key principle of both RRA and PRA.

An influential finding of PRA is, in the terms of one of its most proponents, that 'villagers have a greater capacity to map, model, quantify and estimate, rank, score and diagram than outsiders have generally supposed them capable of'.

The success of PRA depends critically on facilitators maintaining very high standards of perszonal and professional behaviour:

> … as convenors and catalysts, but without dominating the process. Many find this difficult. They must take time, show respect, be open and self-critical and learn not to interrupt […] In PRA, facilitators act as a catalyst, but it is up to local people to decide what to do with the information and analysis they generate. […] there must be a commitment on the part of the facilitating organization to do its best to support, if requested to do so, the actions that local people have decided on.
>
> (Chambers and Blackburn, 1996: 2).

The use of PRA has helped involve communities in the various decisions concerning their own development, including appraisal, planning, implementation, monitoring and evaluation. The 'developers' have also benefited from the interactions of PRA, in the sense that development practitioners have become more open to and respectful of local knowledge and more receptive to local priorities for research, action and policy. This has also helped development and research-oriented organizations move away from top-down, standardized procedures and towards a more open culture of learning.

In the early 1990s, as donor agencies and international NGOs caught on to its potential, the practice of PRA spread very fast to many countries and organizations, initially in the NGO sector but increasingly also in government departments, aid agencies and universities. This was the high point of neoliberalism, and 'PRA's potential to deliver "locally owned" and "community-based" solutions led to meteoric uptake – in speed and scale'.

Participatory Three-dimensional Modelling

Participatory three-dimensional modelling (P3-DM) is an innovative PRA technique conceived to support collaborative processes and help resolve conflicts of interest related mainly to land and resource use and tenure. It starts with the production of an accurate relief map of a particular territory, upon which community knowledge composed from the mental maps of the local participants is superimposed. Because the base map is accurate, it becomes possible to combine local knowledge with additional geo-referenced information obtained from field surveys, Global Positioning Systems' readings, and secondary sources.

As often happens in similar cases, scaling up created problems. Abuse and bad practice became common, which prompted a soul-searching on the part of a number of people close to the core of the PRA 'community of practice'. It seems interesting to mention the concerns expressed at that time, published in *PLA Notes 22,* in 1995:

- the assumption that using PRA methods and/or approach in itself brings about positive change;
- lack of conceptual clarity, transparency and accountability;
- emphasis on information extraction with the rhetoric of political correctness;
- unchallenged assumptions of community harmony;
- lack of in-depth analysis which obscures awareness of political realities within communities;
- one-off training, with no follow-up by trainers or institutions;
- poor integration of PRA into project planning and implementation;
- lack of clarity about reasons for using PRA;
- agendas driven from outside the community, not from within; and
- co-option of the acronym, making it a label without substance.

What this list shows is that it is easy to use PRA badly. Aware of this problem, the PRA 'community of practice' dedicates considerable time and energy to critical analysis of its own practices and to the search for quality, as is evidenced by the themes of the various issues of *Participatory Learning and Action.*

Modest initial arguments that RRA, with its emphasis on 'appropriate imprecision' and 'optimal ignorance', was basically 'organized common sense' and was preferable to conventional research methods for certain kinds of action-oriented research, gradually gave way to claims that PRA is actually superior to conventional methods in the production of valid and reliable knowledge. This has generated considerable disagreement and controversy, some of which will be mentioned below.

In recent years, participatory methods have increasingly been used in national poverty assessments, initially for enabling the poor to express and analyse their priorities and realities. Participatory Poverty Assessments (PPAs) are promoted for instance by the World Bank, with the stated aim of helping the perspectives and priorities of the poor influence development cooperation and national policies, particularly in relation to poverty reduction strategies. Norton *et al.* speak of second generation PPAs, as the early focus on 'generating textual representations of realities of the poor, to contribute to policy recommendations', gave way to a concern with 'creating new relationships within the policy process – bridging public policy, civil society, people in poor communities, donor agencies'.

Another PRA-related development towards the end of the 1990s was the new emphasis on participatory monitoring and evaluation (PM&E). As Guijt and Gaventa state, the idea is to place the perspectives of local people, and particularly the poor, at the centre of M&E exercises:

> [PM&E] ... involves local people, development agencies, and policy makers deciding together how progress should be measured, and results acted upon. It can reveal valuable lessons and improve accountability. [...] By broadening involvement in identifying and analysing change, a clearer picture can be gained of what is really happening on the ground. It allows people to celebrate successes, and learn from failures. For those involved, it can also be a very empowering process, since it puts them in charge, helps develop skills, and shows that their views count.

The same authors then go on to identify four principles at the core of PM&E:

(i) *participation*, to include those most directly affected;

(ii) *negotiation,* to reach agreement about what, how and when to monitor, what the data actually means and what will be done with the findings of the monitoring;

(iii) *learning*, for improvement and corrective action; and

(iv) *flexibility*, to adjust to the various changes in the conditions under which the M&E exercise is carried out.

Cornwall and Guijt (2004: 165) portray the 'taking off' of PM&E as a process similar to that of PRA:

> Everyone had to do it, all projects needed a PM&E system or component, it was a conditionality of loan agreements – and yes, the World Bank too, took hold of this phenomenon. [...] Here the slogan shifted from that of PRA – 'whose reality counts' (Chambers, 1997) to that of PM&E – 'who counts reality' (Estrella and Gaventa, 1998). Just as with PRA, there was and is a huge diversity of understanding what PM&E is, and what it contributes. The wave of critical thinking about PM&E has, however, yet to hit the development discourse.

Thus PRA, together with the approaches it influenced, has been influential in contributing to bring participation in many forms into the mainstream of development practice.

Ideologies of Participation

A simple perusal of the concepts and/or definitions discussed in the preceding sections is sufficient to bring to the fore the important fact that they are influenced by, or aligned with, different ideological positions. In line with Bastian and Bastian may distinguish three very different ideological positions at the root of various proposals on participation in development:

- A position close to the mainstream – i.e. liberal or neo-liberal – discourse on development, such as that of the World Bank or the Development Advisory Committee of the OECD, where participation is proposed as a central element of a coherent model for sustainable development, which is however conceived 'within a framework of a market economy and a dependence on the private sector as the engine of growth'. The main argument in favour of participation from this perspective is that it is necessary for the relevance and sustainability of development efforts.
- A view of participation as 'a part of a "third way" of development, neither market-oriented capitalism nor state-centric socialism', a view supported by 'donor countries with a strong social democratic tradition', as proposed for instance in the publication entitled *Another Development,* published by the Dag Hammarskjöld Foundation of Sweden. In this view 'people' were given a central position, both as sources of needs that define the priorities of development and as actors of their own development.
- A set of more or less radical perspectives, characterized by an awareness of the asymmetric distribution of power in society and its consequences for poverty, and seeking in participation a new means of helping bring about social transformation by empowering the poor and ultimately changing the distribution of power. Empowerment of the poor and social transformation are clearly the main reason for participation in this perspective.

The fact that people and organizations with such diverse ideologies can all agree that participation is 'a good thing', to such an extent that it has become part of the development mainstream, clearly indicates that the term is used to designate very different practical realities, which inevitably causes some confusion.

Poverty, Rural Development and Participation in Asia

In the early years of the new millennium, and despite remarkable progress in its reduction, poverty remains one of the main challenges facing Asia and the Pacific, which is still home to two-thirds of the world's poor. While some Asian countries experience spectacular growth, certain others, or certain regions within the growing countries, remain poor, and millions of their citizens are afflicted by disease, hunger, malnutrition, unemployment, illiteracy, discrimination, lack of adequate shelter and other manifestations of poverty.

Poverty also remains a predominantly rural phenomenon: it is estimated that 70 per cent of all poor in the region, or approximately 475 million, live and work in rural areas. In some countries, such as Thailand, Cambodia or Viet Nam, more than 90 per cent of all poor people live in rural areas. Rural development, leading to rural poverty reduction, thus appears as a key priority for the region. And that means *participatory* rural development.

The use of the word 'themes' serves here to signal that will not systematically follow any of the accepted typologies of participation. Instead, each of the themes is chosen for its intrinsic interest, without trying to define them in a completely consistent way and without worrying about the possibility that they may overlap to some extent, or that certain other areas or themes may not be as well treated as they deserve.

Community Planning, Project Identification and Formulation

This includes all efforts to involve the local population in defining their own problems, diagnosing the situations that give rise to such problems, setting priorities for their resolution, and identifying and formulating project interventions that may help solve some of those problems. An important distinction here is between cases where organizations or projects come into an area with certain interventions in mind and involve the local population in decisions that do not change this broad design, and those where, in line with the principles of PRA mentioned above, local people are called upon to determine even the kind of intervention that is needed. The former case tends to be found more often, because organizations, even in the non-governmental sector, are constrained by their mandate and mission or by conditions placed upon the use of funds at their disposal.

Even with PRA/PLA approaches, however, despite the supposed subordination of the facilitators to the local people, these kinds of organizational constraints sometimes make themselves felt. This was the case for instance in a study in the Punjab, Pakistan (Ahmad, Tabassum and Gill, 2003), where the purpose was to identify the main problems faced by rural women who engaged into income generating activities such as poultry rearing and sewing. Because the study was carried out in the context of a FAO project, it was possible for the project to do more in support of poultry rearing than in support of sewing, in relation to which the authors simply state that '... the solutions to the problems identified do not come under the purview of the project activities'.

Peters analyzes a rural development project in the uplands of Vietnam, and traces some of its shortcomings to the project having forgotten four lessons from past rural development experiences: 'beware of "participatory" rural appraisal, start small and go slowly, introduce limited technologies, and help farmers adapt the technologies'. This forgetfulness he sees as a consequence of participation lip-service, big and fast donor-driven development, the availability of unlimited inappropriate technologies, and institutions that are not adapted to their putative functions.

Old-style Participation: Fisherwomen's Activities in Bangladesh

The Bay of Bengal Programme (BoBP) assisted a pilot project that used a participatory approach to improve the standard of living of marine fisher-folk. The project started out with a socio-economic survey of two fishing communities, 40 miles apart. Women from the communities were helped to organize themselves into small groups; income-generating activities were identified and implemented. Education-cum-action programmes on health, sanitation and nutrition were also launched. In the process, women were encouraged to discover and develop their own leadership abilities and to fortify themselves in their effort to better their condition. Net-making was started first as an income-generating activity. Other activities followed, such as the raising of chickens, ducks and goats. Loans were distributed for these as well as for the regular activities of fish drying and marketing. Members of the project received training on preventive health care, basic nutrition and on supplementary and weaning food.

Two women field workers based in Chittagong travelled frequently to the villages to guide project activities. They organized several groups of 5 to 6 members each. Each group had a coordinator selected from the members, called a link worker, usually a young person with the time and inclination to organize project activities. In three years, 178 fisherwomen were organized into 13 groups with nine link workers. Apart from the link workers, voluntary leaders also emerged who took on responsibilities like teaching primary health care, for which they received a token wage. When a few link workers left the project, voluntary leaders took their place. The link workers and voluntary leaders became a valuable human resource in the villages.

Integrated Rural Development in Philippines

The Philippines has a long tradition of integrated rural development (IRD) projects. In recent years, some of these projects have had a participatory dimension added to them. This is the case, in particular, of the Cordillera Highlands Agricultural Resource Management (CHARM) Project, implemented from 1996 to 2003 (Estrella, 2002). This project had the usual components of rural infrastructure development, agricultural support services and reforestation. In addition to this, development priorities and sub-projects addressing local needs were identified with the direct involvement of residents of poor communities and the participation of elected officials, NGOs and local government agencies. Subprojects identified by the communities then went through a collaborative screening and selection process involving the stakeholders—including government agencies — at municipal and provincial levels. Despite some imperfections (low participation of women and the poorer households), the consequences of participation included strong commitment to the process, increased ownership by citizens and officials and a strengthening of the collaboration between government agencies and NGOs.

Research and Extension, Innovation, Knowledge

Part of second theme borders with the first: there is a difference in degree but not in quality between cases where local people participate in diagnosis or planning and those where they play an active role in research. This is partly a consequence of a shift in perspectives concerning the complex question of indigenous knowledge and its status. After the implicit assumptions concerning the superiority of scientific knowledge that prevailed during the XIXth and most of the XXth centuries, the spread of postmodernism towards the end of the latter century ushered in extreme relativist positions according to which all knowledge (and belief) systems are basically equivalent so that there is no sense in even asking questions concerning the superiority of one over another. Together with other, less felicitous, consequences, this had the advantage of restoring respectability to indigenous – or folk, or vernacular, or, in agricultural contexts, farmer – knowledge, and to open up the possibility of serious research on this important subject, which tended to reveal situations far more complex, nuanced and dynamic than had been assumed before. Another was a substantial increase in the recognition and acceptance of the role that farmers can play in agricultural research, development and extension, particularly from the late 1980s onwards.

Agricultural research was for a long time seen as the exclusive domain of scientists, with extension as the (one-way) delivery of the scientists' findings to farmers, whose own role was seen to be in implementation, basically limited to adopting the technological innovations handed down to them. This kind of agricultural research and extension was criticized for, among other things,

(i) the relative isolation of agricultural research stations, leading to research which is not always relevant to farmers' needs and circumstances;

(ii) excessive focus on yield, which is only one among several variables farmers consider when making choices (others include risk, food security and dietary preferences);

(iii) a top-down approach to extension, disregarding farmers' knowledge and experience; and

(iv) ignorance of or disregard for the socio-economic constraints facing farmers. This, critics claimed, often led to poor research, based on wrong assumptions and failing to solve real problems.

Crop-based pig production in Vietnam

Sweet potato-pig production is an important and widely practiced system that generates income, utilizes unmarketable crops, and provides manure for soil fertility maintenance. It is also usually characterized by low growth rates and low economic efficiency. The project in Vietnam used situation analysis, participatory technology development (PTD), and scaling up to improve sweet potato-pig production and to disseminate the technologies developed. Situation analysis included a series of pig production assessments, as well as pig supply-market chain identification, in several provinces. PTD involved a limited number of farmers participating in sweet potato varietal selection, sweet potato root and vine silage processing, seasonal feeding combination, and pig feeding with balanced crop-feed diet and silage. The main improvements included improved growth, higher feeding efficiency, increased year-round local feedstuff, and considerable labour reduction. A farmer-to-farmer training model was designed for scaling up the adoption and impact. Farmer trainers from seven communes in seven provinces received training in these technologies. In turn, they undertook the responsibility of training other farmers on sweet potato selection, processing, and feeding. An impact study showed that both participating and non-participating farmers took up the technologies, although the former had higher rates of adoption, generated more income and saved more labour from adoption of the technologies. The project has since broadened to a pig-cropfeed system perspective, based on farmers' needs. It has included other crop feeds such as cassava and peanut stems in the research portfolio. New technologies based on on-going PTD will continuously be incorporated into the future training curriculum.

In farmer participatory approaches the relation between research, extension and implementation, and the relations between the actors involved, are very different:

> … the research and development realm (…) consists of co-creative processes to identify needs and opportunities, generate new information and innovations, consolidate them with existing farming practice, and then translate them into learning objectives and activities for enhanced farmer performance. …[Extension and implementation] contains the phases during which efforts are made – either in a formal or a non-formal setting – to share innovations with larger groups of farmers, who then test, evaluate, and internalize (or reject) them in their farming practices, finally leading to impact. (van de Fliert and Braun, 2002: 28)

Examples of participatory approaches to research and extension include for instance applications to setting priorities for the development of a research agenda for water management in a village in Khon Kaen Province, Thailand, to sustainable agriculture development in uplands of West Sumatra, Indonesia, to the development of forage technology with smallholders, or the application of participatory technology development to improving crop-based pig production systems in Vietnam. There is also a great deal of participatory research applied not just to agriculture, but to natural resource management as well. Ashby uses the term 'research *for* development' to characterize an approach which she describes as emphasizing 'the iterative, adaptive nature of innovation in complex ecosystems, which is achieved through systematic enquiry combined with learning based in action".

Natural Resource Management

Within the broad field of rural development, natural resource management development is a main area of application of participatory approaches. In general terms, the purpose of these interventions is to improve the living conditions of local people, particularly the poor, by helping them manage the natural resources available to them or under their control with greater effectiveness, sustainability and equity. For Pimbert, writing from a PRA/PLA perspective, the importance of participatory approaches to natural resource management lies in that:

> Eliciting and making visible diverse *local* realities, priorities, categories and indicators through participatory learning is still very much needed today to challenge top down, 'one size fits all' science, policy and practice in natural resource management. However, claims that one tradition of knowledge and practice (local, vernacular systems *versus* external, science-based systems) is always better than the other may ultimately restrict possibilities. Instead, a key challenge for participatory learning and action lies in creating *safe* spaces where plural traditions of knowledge can be purposefully combined for the local adaptive management of natural resources and their equitable use.

Wasteland Development Project, Almer District, Rajasthan

For over two decades, the Pissagan block in Ajmer district, Rajasthan, faced problems of soil erosion due to flow of rainwater from the Aaravali Ranges. The rainwater in its course deposited stones and pebbles on the land, which had become unfit for cultivation. The soil lost moisture and the water table level fell. This had a negative effect on the lives of the people. As the land was not fit for cultivation the villagers earned their living as daily wageworkers in Ajmer or nearby towns, and most of them lived in poverty. They had to walk up to 4 - 5 kilometres to fetch water, fodder for cattle and fuel wood. The Wasteland Development Project started in Ajmer in 1995. Its main objectives were: (i) soil and moisture conservation measures; (ii) raising the water table level; (iii) providing fodder and fuel wood, and (iv) improving the socio- economic conditions of the villagers. This was to be achieved by means of construction of check dams and guard trenches to slow down and divert the water, water harvesting structures, tree planting, aforestation and horticulture. Meeting the objectives would not have been possible without people's participation. A sense of ownership was essential to ensure long run sustainability. Users committees, including villagers, farmers and project staff were formed. Membership varied from village to village. The office bearers of the users committees are elected and are changed on non –performance. Users committees were entrusted with the following responsibilities: (i) Implementation of the project (ii) Management of the project (iii) Protecting the construction activities and (iv) Distribution of fodder and fuel wood and wages to labourers.

Community participation was key to the success of the project. It ensured all through the implementation of the project that the people's enthusiasm and interest would not wane away after the initial euphoria. Most importantly, the project staff were from the beginning distant spectators, only providing the technical inputs but leaving design, execution and management to the users committees. This micro-level planning provided people with an opportunity to learn how to manage the scheme and gave them the confidence that they can now do things without government support. In the seven years it lasted, the project has changed the whole block of Pissagan. Today, Pissagan is a model for soil conservation measures. The lost flora and fauna are returning and even the villagers are reaping benefits. This project has raised hopes that wasteland can be made fertile and bring prosperity to the area. It has checked soil erosion and has helped retain soil moisture. Also, fodder and fuel wood are plentiful. In fact with each year production has grown and so has distribution

Participatory approaches to natural resource management have been implemented in connection with a considerable variety of natural resources, including forests and woodlands, coastal resources, water and watersheds, fisheries in flood-prone ecosystems, soil and water conservation and conservation of nature reserves, to mention only some examples.

Participatory approaches are naturally complemented, in some of these cases, by the use of a *sustainable livelihoods framework*, which considers that a livelihood comprises the capabilities, assets (including both material and social resources) and activities required for a means of living. Because it takes into account not only agricultural but other assets and activities as well, the livelihoods approach is particularly suited to natural resource management, where very often the resources being dealt with are not of a strictly agricultural nature. Reddy *et al.*, for example, analyse the impact of India's programme of watershed development on the livelihoods of rural communities, by looking at its impact on the five types of capital assets and strategies required for the means of living. They also analyse the vulnerability and stability of those capital assets as well as the participation in the programme. They conclude that, even in difficult environmental conditions where the watershed cannot bring direct irrigation benefits on a large scale, watershed development, if supported with other programmes, has potential for sustaining rural livelihoods.

Another interesting intersection between participatory and rural livelihoods approaches was a PPA carried out in Mongolia, which has 'shed new light on what might be an appropriate approach in public policy and investment to foster secure and sustainable livelihoods both within and outside the extensive livestock sector'.

Governance and Decentralization

Governance plays an important role in determining the conditions under which participation can take place and, through its mechanisms, processes and institutions, it critically affects the possibility of participation as well as its likely success. Good governance makes it possible for citizens, individually or in groups, to articulate their interests, exercise their legal rights and negotiate their differences. Within the broad area of governance, decentralization, which brings decision-making closer to the local level, is potentially important to participation, since it may, if it is done well, lead to more responsive government and new opportunities for citizens to participate. The qualification is important, since there is also the danger that decentralization may provide little space for the poor to participate in local decision-making, may be misused by powerful sections of the community and end up fostering clientelism and strengthening local elites. One of the ways to 'do it well' is by strengthening participation at the same time as the decentralization is carried out.

A number of studies examine the linkages between governance (and decentralization) and participation. Agrawall and Gupta carry out a statistical analysis of who participates in environmental decentralization programmes in protected areas in Nepal's Terai. They find that the likelihood of participation in community-level user groups is greater for those who are economically and socially better-off and who have greater access to government offices and officials related to decentralization policies. Their analysis support the argument that for decentralization policies to be successful in dealing with equity issues, it is important to build institutional mechanisms that encourage poorer and more marginal households to access government officials, improve access to educational opportunities, and create incentives to promote more interactions between less powerful rural residents. He finds that, largely bercause of a lack of administrative and financial resources, panchayats have at best become the implementing arms of state governments rather than institutions of self-government.

The Kecamatan Development Project

The Kecamatan Development Program (KDP) is a Government of Indonesia program aimed at alleviating poverty in rural communities, strengthening local government and improving local governance. KDP provides block grants of 350 million to one billion rupiah (USD 40,000 to USD 114,000) directly to subdistricts (kecamatan) and villages for small-scale infrastructure, social and economic activities. KDP began in 1998 at a time of tremendous political upheaval and financial crisis, which reversed years of progress in poverty reduction and plunged millions of rural people below the poverty line. KDP has a very flexible structure, which gives power to communities by entrusting them with planning and decision-making responsibilities and placing funds directly in their hands. By pushing decision-making down to the lowest levels, KDP aims to allow villagers to participate in decision-making. The program in essence seeks to empower the rural poor and encourage more democratic and participatory forms of local governance by delivering its resources via inclusive, transparent and accountable decision-making mechanisms designed on the basis of extensive prior social research in Indonesia. All KDP activities aim at allowing villagers to make their own choices about the kinds of projects that they need and want. 'Community participation' is regarded as an important element in KDP, as is evident from the process of planning, decision making, and implementation. However, implementation is not perfect. Frequent problems include low participation by the poor in the planning process and elite capture of the participatory processes. The replication of KDP has been exceedingly fast, and its scaling up has also gone substantially beyond the programme itself. Particularly interesting is the extension of the KDP principle of direct transfers to support participatory

In addition to this, and despite important steps to include marginalized communities in the power structure of local government institutions, 'it cannot be said that panchayats have been able to take effective measures for removing the economic and social deprivation of the marginalized people'. Mathew concludes that there are grounds for cautious optimism and that local government institutions need various kinds of support from higher tiers of government to succeed, such as legislation, constructive directions, monitoring, training and resource transfers.

Examining the same experience, Gaiha and Kulkarni come to broadly similar conclusions. They emphasize the informational and administrative advantages of community involvement in the design and implementation of anti-poverty and related programmes, mention the danger of 'elite capture' of the panchayats and conclude that only in a few cases has the system benefited the poor. They see collective action by the poor as key to the success of poverty alleviation, although the prospects for this are limited, given that they are divided by caste and religion. They conclude that the panchayat system's potential for poverty alleviation is hard to dispute.

Finally, a reference must be made to the Kecamatan Development Program, started in Indonesia in pilot form in 1997, and implemented from 1998 onwards one of the world's largest participatory development programmes implemented in Indonesia. This World Bank-funded programme is described by the Bank as 'an effort to address long-term structural poverty through targeted, decentralized block grants [and] at another level [...] an effort to increase community prioritization and management of government-funded local development projects'.

Other Themes

Practicalities preclude the possibility of elaborating further on these themes, or discussing some other interesting themes, such as for instance self-help groups and collective action by the poor, or the supposed – and often rather unsatisfactory – participation of the poor in poverty reduction strategy papers or, along a completely different dimension, the challenges of participatory rural development in the particular social and political environment of China. What needs to be stressed is that, despite differences in approach, all the examples discussed represent a clear and strong illustration of the statement that participation has become part of the mainstream of development. At the same time, and *because* of the differences in approach, they also clearly illustrate the ambiguities in the use of that term.

Much of the more interesting criticism of participation, and particularly the so-called tyranny critique, started precisely with criticisms of participation (especially PRA) as the 'new orthodoxy', which the critics felt had lost track of its original objectives as a consequence of co-optation into the mainstream. A brief overview of some aspects of this critique may help clarify ideas about participation and – since nothing is more practical than good theory – throw additional light upon some of the difficulties that it faces in practice.

Tyranny and Other Criticisms

Participation and especially PRA have been subjected to frequent critical analysis from inside their own 'communities of practice'. For PRA, the results of this analysis have appeared from time to time in *Participatory Learning and Action* or its predecessors. 'Self-critical epistemological awareness' is for Robert Chambers an essential aspect of participatory ideology and practice. For this reason Cooke and Kothari, who organized and then edited the proceedings of a conference on *Participation: The New Tyranny?,* place it at 'the border between the orthodoxy and more critical positions'. Although recognizing that this boundary is blurred, their aim with the conference was to move beyond criticism that might legitimize the participatory project, to more fundamental critiques.

Knowledge Claims of Participatory Approaches

The first set of criticisms targets the knowledge claims of participatory approaches and, more specifically, PRA. Chambers makes considerable claims of validity and reliability for the knowledge about the world through PRA. Campbell expresses reservations about these claims, on methodological grounds. He argues that 'though RRA and PRA were intended to provide roughly accurate information, the tendency has been to use them as a stand-alone set of techniques to undertake research' and that failure by participatory researchers to engage with issues of validity and reliability as defined in the qualitative research tradition will result eclectic and unfocused work, of limited practical, theoretical and policy value. Campbell makes the case for the integration of PRA with 'qualitative and quantitative methods that produce greater insight and more in-depth understanding than is possible from casual observation or from forms of inquiry that depend upon highly structured ways of interacting with respondents'.

Mosse raises doubts about the nature and validity of the information, such as statements of community needs and priorities, generated by PRA and other participatory methods. He sees it as problematic because it is produced in a social context strongly influenced by power, authority and gender inequality. In particular, he sees the *public* nature of PRA as causing the production of local knowledge to be subjected to the effects of 'officializing strategies' and 'muting'. On the basis of his own experience, Mosse also stresses that information or knowledge generated in PRAs is the outcome of a complex game shaped by the concerns of 'outsiders' and their interaction with 'insider' community members, where each group repeatedly tries to anticipate the other's wishes and intentions. This leads him to question the assumption that 'learning and "local knowledge" defines or redefines the relationship between local communities and development institutions [...] Rather than project plans being shaped by "indigenous knowledge", it is farmers who acquire and learn to manipulate new forms of "planning knowledge". In this way local knowledge becomes compatible with bureaucratic planning'.

Furthermore, Mosse makes the crucial point that there are important insights about a local social reality that are necessarily external and analytical, rather than participatory, and are not, and probably cannot be, generated in group discussions by villagers: 'Like other analytical models, and like the knowledge gained from the critical reflection on project activities, they represent... an external viewpoint'.

Along a slightly different line, Stirrat criticizes the practice of positing two separate and opposed forms of knowledge (as in local or indigenous knowledge *vs.* scientific knowledge) as misconstruing the nature of forms of knowledge, which in this age of globalization do not exist in isolation but in terms of a global field of mutual interrelationships.

Finally, from another perspective, Kothari also throws doubt on the claims of participatory methodologies of acquiring more appropriate and relevant local knowledge and of including and empowering those previously marginalized. She stresses the importance of examining how power relations run through a particular social body and are expressed in a variety of ways. She concludes that

> By constructing dichotomies of power and oppositional social groupings, participatory approaches simplify highly complicated social relations. Thus participatory techniques can conceal inequalities and in certain circumstances reify them. What counts as "local knowledge" is often the effect of specific kinds of techniques of power, of regulation and of normalization.

Illusions of 'Community'

A second line of criticism of participatory approaches focuses on what Cleaver describes as 'myths of community': 'The "community" in participatory approaches to development is often seen as a "natural" social entity characterized by solidaristic relations. It is assumed that these can be represented and channelled in simple organizational forms.' This perspective is criticized on a Pottier and Orone make a similar point when they say that 'The major obstacle is that workshops, no matter how participatory they may be, are still public activities during which certain aspects of everyday social life must remain hidden from the outside world. [...] Public discussion does not move beyond the ground rules, the safe discourse, the official model. It is therefore no more than a first step in learning about actual practices.' number of counts. First, the image of the community – or the village – as a natural entity, with clearly defined limits and membership, appears simplistic in the light of available evidence of the shifting, overlapping and subjective nature of 'communities', and of the permeability of their boundaries. As Stirrat points out, villages are physical groupings of houses where people interact, but the social processes of which these people are a part have a much wider physical range, so that to idealise villages as significant social entities is to participate in the reification – indeed the invention – of an imaginary form of rural life. Cleaver (*loc.cit.*) concurs: 'a concentration on boundaries highlights the needs in development for clear administrative arrangements, more to do with the delivery of goods than a reflection of any social arrangement'.

Secondly, participatory approaches stress – and rely upon – community consensus and solidarity; they tend to pay insufficient attention to social differentiation and conflict, negotiation, inclusion and exclusion, with all that this implies. Harmony and cooperation are the exception rather than the rule in rural societies, where division and conflict are much more common.

Stirrat argues that descriptions of rural society that emphasize 'village', 'community', 'local people', consensus and harmony can be characterized as a 'new Orientalism' that, just as the old, is crucially connected with power and domination: 'Put crudely, the Neo-Orientalist view of rural society is part of the continuing relationship of power and control, in which the rural population in all its forms is depicted as in need of protection and 'mobilization', through the actions of outsiders. Yet this relationship of dominance is presented as its opposite'.

In the third place, there is 'the myth that communities are capable of anything, that all that is required is sufficient mobilization (through institutions) and the latent capacities of communities will be unleashed in the interest of development. The evidence does little to support such claims'.

Even when collective action takes place, the critical units for decision making and action are often above or below the community level.

Logic or Bureaucratic Organizations

Mosse gives a concrete example of the conflict between ideals of participation, striving to independent capacities, local autonomy and eventual project withdrawal, and 'the core rationale of the same project from the organization's point of view, based on its network of patronage and the delivery of an expanding range of programmes, increasingly through village volunteers who operated as the lower orders of the project delivery mechanism. […] Why would the organization want to rid itself of its best customers, and villagers take leave of a serviceable patron?' 'Empowerment' may then become a means to managerial effectiveness, and this may in turn require a form of subjection of those that are supposed to be empowered.

Similarly, as Stirrat points out, NGOs working in rural development may talk of empowerment but in practice they are often accountable not to their members or those they work with, but to their donors, and it is the donors' criteria that they have to satisfy in order to continue being funded. This may lead to the adoption of very similar views to the donor's and create shared interests that work against too close a questioning of the structure.

Other Criticisms

Both in the 'tyranny' book and elsewhere, participatory approaches to rural development are criticized along other lines, largely complementary to those mentioned above. Much of that criticism may best be summed up by saying that participatory approaches fail to take into account what Cleaver calls the *recursive relationship between structure and agency.*

Consequently, they ignore the considerable progress made by the social sciences in trying to understand the complex and diverse interactions between individuals and social structure; posit simplistic models of individual action, alternating between 'rational choice' and 'social being'; fail to analyse social structure and the linkages between individuals and the structures and institutions of the social world they inhabit; are naive about the complexities of power, power relations, how power is embedded into social and cultural practices and how empowerment may occur; and their practice tends towards treating participation as a technical method of project work, lays excessive emphasis on the local level and on the organization of collective action, and depoliticizes what should be an explicitly political process. As Stirrat argues rather bad-temperedly, most participatory discourse is bad in theory, limited in methods, and epistemologically weak.

This is strong criticism, which needs to be taken seriously by theorists and practitioners alike. Taking it seriously means, among other things, that the easy way out, which is to dismiss all such criticism as referring to instances of bad practice, must be avoided no matter how strong the temptation. For that way lies participation – or PRA – as a closed system, and the impossibility of learning and changing.

From Tyranny to Transformation

Hickey and Mohan edited a book with this title, aimed at evaluating the state of participatory approaches in the aftermath of the 'tyranny' critique. They mention evidence suggesting that participation has actually deepened and extended its role in development, with new approaches emerging in theory, policy and practice and, most importantly, people in developing countries continually devising new and innovative strategies for expressing their agency in development arenas. The book tries to explore the extent to which the new approaches respond to the critique and can re-establish participation as a 'legitimate and genuinely transformative approach to development'. An underlying theme is that 'politics matter' in international development, and that the way towards a more transformative approach to development is through understanding how participation relates to existing power structures and political systems.

Hickey and Mohan advocate a radical political project based on the promotion of citizenship as a way of overcoming the 'tyranny' of local, project based approaches to participation and establishing a link between participation at the project level and governance and political action at the state level. It is in the context of such a multi-level political project that the agency of the poor, expressed in active citizenship aimed at local governance reform, as possible and meaningful: 'Relocating 'participation' within citizenship situates it in a broader range of sociopolitical practices, or expressions of agency, through which people extend their status and rights as members of particular political communities, thereby increasing their control over socioeconomic resources'.

Cornwall, looking for new entry points to understand the dynamics of power and difference, explores the concept of spaces for participation, where 'citizens gain meaningful opportunities to exercise voice and hold to account those who invite them to participate'. She sees these spaces less as concrete locales than sites that both constitute and express power relations, and that condition the subjects' presence, action and discourse, their competence and performance. She argues that 'by illuminating the dynamics of power, voice and agency, thinking spatially can help towards building strategies for more genuinely transformative social action'. Gaventa defines a variety of different spaces from a participation point of view, ranging from *closed spaces* in which 'decisions are made by a set of actors behind closed doors, without any pretence of broadening the boundaries for inclusion', to *claimed/created spaces*, 'which are claimed by less powerful actors from or against the power-holders, or created more autonomously by them'. Between these two, *invited spaces* are those 'into which people (as users, as citizens, as beneficiaries) are invited to participate by various kinds of authorities, be they government, supra-national agencies or non-governmental organizations'. Cornwall sees invited spaces as an important way in which development intervention may support transformative participation.

Gaventa links participation and citizenship, and explores the transformative possibilities of citizen engagement with local governance, and the conditions under which such engagement can lead to both a strengthening of democracy and pro-poor development outcomes.

Although recognizing that the citizenship approach of Hickey and Mohan, also elaborated by Gaventa, has potential particularly through the possibility of multi-level approaches to participation, Cleaver returns to the recursive relation between agency and structure when she cautions that agency cannot be exercised in a vacuum. The forms that citizenship can take are shaped by the minutiae of social life and relationships, which may prove slower and more difficult to transform than public spaces and institutions of the state. The short-term costs to the poor of fully assuming their citizenship and their rights and confronting the unequal and oppressive relations on which they depend may be too high when compared with the costs of simply allowing those relations to continue. Cleaver identifies three key factors that 'both enable and *constrain* the exercise of agency and therefore shape citizenship: moral understandings of action and the unconscious motivation of many acts, the complexity of both individual and collective identities and the (often unequal) interdependence involved in the exercise of rights and livelihood interests', and concludes that recognizing those constraints, and 'the limits of the makeability of social life', is crucial to achieving something in development.

Relevance of the Debate

Both the criticisms of participation and the potential for transformation that recent approaches have identified are extremely relevant and utterly practical. It is an ever-present temptation for practitioners to gloss over the problematic nature of much of the knowledge generated with participatory methods, to be lulled by the illusions associated with the concept of community and the assumptions that accompany it, to assume that the constraints of social structure can be easily overcome by proper participation, or to ignore the clash between organizational constraints and objectives and the desires and interests of the local poor. The same may be said of the transformative potential of participation.

Challenges of Participatory Rural Development:

The question then is whether can have a 'good enough participation', what that would look like and what it would require. Perhaps the main criterion would be that the interventions associated with it should do no harm, and preferably some good, in terms of the main objective of poverty alleviation, while at the same time contributing towards creating at least some of the conditions that enable participation, agency and the full exercise of citizenship by the poor to take place. If such interventions remove some of the constraints of everyday life, by increasing the productivity of agricultural labour or bringing clean water closer to where people live, alleviating the burden of disease caused by malnutrition and lack of hygiene, decreasing vulnerability to natural disasters or to the vagaries of climate and rainfall, or making people less dependent on relations of patronage for daily subsistence, they are a step in the right direction. If this is done for instance through the permanent and expanding presence of an organization that offers 'better technology and more affordable inputs rather than autonomy and independence', it may not fit in with the fashion for empowerment and farmer-managed development, but may still represent significant progress.

Multidimensional Rural Poverty and Sustainable Livelihoods Approach

The complexity and multi-dimensionality of poverty in general, and rural poverty in particular, are generally accepted nowadays. A recent ESCAP document calls for

> … a deeper knowledge and understanding of the emerging dynamics and local processes that cause and maintain rural poverty. The rural poor face multiple deprivations from lack of assets, isolation, alienation, dependence, powerlessness, vulnerability and lack of freedom of choice. Disparities also exist within rural areas: in particular, disparities between ruling rural elites and small farmers or landless households; and disparities among farmers over access and rights to fertile lands. In this context, a distinction between the different but closely related dimensions of poverty is important : (a) a lack of income and productive assets; (b) a lack of access to essential economic and social services; and (c) a lack of power, participation and respect. These different dimensions of poverty reinforce each other, keeping the poor trapped in poverty.

Lack of awareness of this multi-dimensionality, or a reluctance to confront it, may explain much the failure of past rural development strategies in reducing rural poverty. The implication is clear: new, sharper, multi-targeted rural development strategies are called for, taking this complexity and multi-dimensionality fully into account and going beyond the old approaches that were based solely on the growth of agricultural productivity and focused almost exclusively on the small farmer.

An approach to rural poverty and rural development that appears capable to encompass this complexity and multi-dimensionality is the so-called sustainable livelihoods approach. As Ellis and Biggs emphasize, this approach '… embodies no prior requirement for the poor rural individual or family to be a "small farmer". The livelihoods approach takes an open-ended view of the combination of assets and activities that turn out to constitute a viable livelihood strategy for the rural family'. The same authors add that empirical research indicates that farming amounts on average to only about 40-60% of the livelihood 'package' put together by rural households in South Asia and sub-Saharan Africa, and conclude:

> van Roosmalen and Guimarães made a similar point 25 years ago, when they stated that in Southwest Bangladesh farmer's strategies often involve investing agricultural surpluses in activities such as educating their children, setting up small businesses (if possible in neighboring urban areas), buying land in different locations, lending money and generally diversifying their economic activities. As Bendavid

also noted, even large farmers only

> If a new paradigm of rural development is to emerge, it will be one in which agriculture takes its place along with a host of other actual and potential rural and non-rural activities that are important to the construction of viable

> rural livelihoods, without undue preference being given to farming as the unique solution to rural poverty. It is in this sense that the cross-sectoral and multi-occupational diversity of rural livelihoods may need to become the cornerstone of rural development policy if efforts to reduce rural poverty are to be effective in the future.

Such paradigm will probably combine participatory approaches with rural livelihoods, given their compatibility and potential for mutual reinforcement.

Contextual Factors and the Role of the State

The success or failure of participatory rural development interventions depends as much on the conditions surrounding the particular intervention as on the quality of the work done at the local level. Among the conditions most frequently mentioned are economic growth, a favourable political and administrative environment characterized by administrative decentralization and more generally good governance at the macro level, and the presence of cultural traits or ideologies that favour participation, self-reliance and collective action by the poor.

It must, however, be kept in mind that:

(i) as experience has repeatedly shown, there is no automatic cause and effect relationship between economic growth and poverty reduction;

(ii) decentralization and good governance work primarily by removing constraints and barriers; and

(iii) even when culture and ideology favour collective action by the poor, there are limits to what they can do, as their agency is constrained as much as it is enabled by structure.

Although the poor can be resourceful and imaginative, they are unlikely to be able to escape poverty by themselves. This means that neo-liberal solutions to the problem of poverty are unlikely to work: the problem will just not go away without deliberate and proactive government policies, backed by appropriate resource allocation. This does not imply a return to the government-led, top-down interventions of old, which did not work either: rather, the state must work with the poor, creating the conditions for their participation and supporting it with resource transfers, stimulating pro-poor growth and working to reduce inequality and promote social justice.

Policies specifically aimed at participatory rural development include legislation for rural people's organizations, including full freedom of

Economic growth and poverty reduction in Vietnam

Vietnam has important lessons in participation, rural development and poverty alleviation. In the recent past, the share of people living in poverty fell from 58% in 1992 to 37% in 1998 and 29% in 2002; rural poverty fell from 45.5% in 1998 to 35.6% in 2002. The International Fund for Agricultural Development (IFAD) and the World Bank supported rural development projects in Vietnam that take a participatory, bottom-up approach:

> 'The most important first generation project, the Participatory Resources Management Project (PRMP), was designed in 1993. [...] The project sought to [ensure] equitable access to all development planning with the full participation of communities in the province of Tuyen Quang, one of the poorest in the country. The project introduced new approaches to poverty reduction, including decentralization and promotion of provincial autonomy, to promote food security, build management capacity at the community level, and introduce participatory, demand-driven approaches in institutions providing rural support services. Second generation initiatives [...] have built on the success of the PRMP and scaled up decentralization and community-driven development in Vietnam's poorest areas. These projects have done a good job of targeting poor people, and decentralization and participation have empowered rural people to identify, plan, implement, and evaluate interventions, giving them a greater stake in development efforts'.

Factors explaining the country's success in reducing rural poverty include the existence of an environment conducive to rural development, with a national policy focus on poverty reduction and a policy of economic reforms that has delivered remarkable growth for a considerable period of time. Without this favourable economic and policy environment, the story might have been very different.

association; reorientation of the delivery system, in particular the extension services, towards the needs of the rural poor; full integration of women in development; decentralization of decision-making, planning and resource allocation; rural poor-oriented research, extension, input supply, credit and marketing, supported by the necessary financial resources and aimed at enhancing income-generating activities, both agricultural and non-agricultural; and just fiscal and pricing systems. Participatory rural development projects must involve government institutions, such as line departments or local governments, banks, training and research institutions, women and youth councils; they must also continue to involve civil society organizations at all levels.

Government institutions need to become more open to the advantages of using local knowledge for improved productivity in farming, water conservation and natural resource management, and of associating local communities and small farmers to their research. Equally needed is research on sustainable and labour-intensive agricultural production systems, rural off-farm employment and enterprise development.

Pilots, Innovations and Scaling Up

Many of the most innovative rural development projects start small. This makes it possible to experiment with new approaches (e.g. to participation) or technologies, while keeping costs and risks within acceptable limits. Such projects are thus, for all practical purposes, pilot projects. This means that, if they are successful, they will at some point need to be scaled up. Scaling up has its own problems that need to be resolved before successful projects – or parts of projects – can yield significant benefits. These problems are not trivial, and if they are not resolved, the initial promise may lead to disappointing results.

On the basis of a number of case studies of scaling up of technical or institutional innovations, Biggs points out in relation to poverty reduction and social inclusion that effective innovation in the policy and institutional arenas is generally location and time specific, and *has* to be, because the significance of institutional innovations can only be understood with reference to time, place, culture and political context. In the cases studied,

> …major and significant institutional innovations were coming up all the time from within the local context. Informal, unplanned R&D was always taking place […] In addition, and significantly, in 'scaling up' processes, it was the local institutional innovations that were the critical elements that gave rise to the way the technology or institutional model was scaled up and to the pattern of outcomes as regards who benefited from the process. Consequently, for those concerned with being effective in poverty reduction and social inclusion, the most important research starts at the so-called 'scaling up' stage. Scaling up is not a minor 'development' job to be done at the end of an R&D pipeline [...] Institutional innovation in the local context is not in any way similar to the 'adaptation' to local circumstances of outside technical innovations.

Biggs then goes on to argue for the importance of 'learning from the positive'; policy and development personnel should constantly be on the look out for the positive changes that are always taking place wherever poverty and social exclusion exist, and monitor, learn from, support and promote these changes.

Scaling up can be interpreted in two separate and complementary ways:

(i) as replication on a large scale, from a small to a large project (a variant of which is from a small to many coordinated small scale projects in different places); and

(ii) as 'mainstreaming into policy making'. Each of these meanings implies different challenges.

Large-scale replication of a small participatory rural development project requires that many facilitators or extension agents pay the same amount of concentrated attention to their work and their clients as did the initial pilot team. They have the advantage of being able to learn from other people's mistakes; on the other hand, what was for the initial participants a process of learning by doing, with a significant research component, is now something to be taught and learnt, then applied. There is less incentive to perform well, and it is easier to fall into routinized, mechanical approaches. To deal with these challenges, at the very least motivation, indoctrination and institution building (including the provision of suitable incentives) are needed before the replication starts, close monitoring and control at the beginning of implementation, and spot checks throughout.

As to scaling up in the sense of mainstreaming into policy making, its success is a function of the capacity of institutions and organizations to learn, and of the existence of enabling environments that provide the conditions, stimuli and incentives for institutions and individuals to act in desirable ways. Focusing on the scaling up of participatory watershed management in India, Kolavalli and Kerr maintain that, given the limited availability of NGOs, a realistic strategy must be to improve the capabilities and incentives of government agencies to work more like NGOs. They argue that institutionalizing participatory approaches in government bureaucracies may include

(i) creating an enabling environment where the necessary conditions and appropriate incentives exist, plus

(ii) strengthening upward accountability and

(iii) introducing downward accountability.

Joshi and Moore argue that the outcomes of public programmes to tackle poverty in developing countries are more likely to be decided in the implementation than the decision-making phases of policy making, and conclude that it is vital to try to 'plug the gaps' at this stage.

Searching for ways in which this might be done through a 'self-correcting' mechanism that creates an enabling environment for the poor, they focus on the extent to which anti-poverty programmes succeed in mobilizing their own beneficiaries. They argue that the likelihood of collective action by the poor to defend their rights in the context of anti-poverty interventions depends on the *predictability* of those interventions from the point of view of the poor, or of the social activists and political entrepreneurs needed to galvanize them into collective action. This in turn has three components: *credibility* of the officials implementing the anti-poverty programmes; *stability of the programmes* over time, in content, form, procedural requirements, etc.; and *formal entitlement,* which includes but is not limited to legal rights to benefits of the programme. Such predictability, argue these authors, encourages and supports collective action in favour of the anti-poverty programme.

Importance of Territory

From the local to the territorial it is a small step, but one that adds a rich layer of meaning to the discussion. The territorial dimension can contribute significantly to participatory rural development, by providing it with a spatial and social context within which participation may become easier and more meaningful. In recent years, the concepts of *territory* and of *territorial competitiveness* have acquired considerable importance as a result of economic and social changes within countries, in the context of accelerating globalization. The word 'territory' designates a rural region, which will normally include one or more small or intermediate urban centres together with their rural hinterland. Because of its scale and of the closeness of the interactions that take place within it, the territory is increasingly seen as a privileged space for participation in rural development.

The concept of territorial competitiveness starts from the usual definition of the term competitive and adds to the concept a number of normative elements that broaden its meaning and enrich it as a policy objective. Interpreted in this broader way, "a territory becomes competitive if it is able to face up to market competition whilst at the same time ensuring environmental, social and cultural sustainability, based on the dual approach of networking and inter-territorial relationships".

In order to strive for territorial competitiveness, the actors in the territory engage into negotiation leading to the formulation of a collective *territorial project:* a vision of the future of the territory in which territorial competitiveness is assured and therefore the territory fulfils its potential. This depends on local actors and institutions acquiring four types of skills: the skills to take joint action, to assess their environment, to create links between sectors by ensuring that maximum added value is retained, and to liaise with other areas and the rest of the world. These skills link to the so-called "four dimensions" of territorial competitiveness, present in each area in different combinations: social, environmental and economic competitiveness, plus positioning in the global context. These processes are seen as forming part of a long-term approach that is at the core of each area's development strategy. The presence of divergent or even opposed interests implies that negotiation, usually managed negotiation, is explicitly present and plays a key role in the definition of the territorial project, itself a process of social learning. The presence of an urban centre (or more), and its linkages with the rural areas, is a crucial part of each territory's identity, a focus of negotiation and participation processes and of local institutional innovation, and a key factor of success in achieving territorial competitiveness.

In order to move from an analysis of the situation to the identification and design of a territorial project, to charting out a path for the territory's future, it is necessary to carry out an analysis of what is known as *territorial capital,* defined as

> *...all of the elements available to the area, both tangible and intangible, which in some respects constitute assets and in others constraints.*
>
> The concept of "territorial capital" is not static but dynamic. It corresponds to the analytical description of how those seeking the room to take action see the area. It is therefore related to the territorial project concept and to the bid for territorial competitiveness. Each area endeavours to find its place by focusing on access to markets, its image, its potential to attract people and businesses, its ability to renew its governance, etc.

At its heart, the idea of territorial competitiveness is a very simple one: the actors in a territory join forces to analyse their situation, agree on *what is their difference* and then decide how best to enhance its value. The similarity with concepts such as Thailand's 'one tambon, one product', or Vietnam's handicraft villages, is obvious although, as seen above, territorial competitiveness may be realised in more ways than just through the sale of a particular product or combination of products from the territory.

Processes of territory based rural development do not overcome the constraints of structure over agency; furthermore, they make sense only where basic conditions for negotiation are present; but when such conditions *are* present, they complement and give new strength and meaning to participation, by integrating it into a jointly agreed project at the local level.

It seems reasonable, in the light of these discussions, to conclude that the use of participation in rural development will continue, and that this may not be bad. If use them well, the criticisms need not be a source of discouragement; but by reminding of the need to *take nothing for granted,* they should help practitioners resist smugness and strive for better ways of achieving its ideals. In this, the idea of a *good enough participation* seems to hold some promise, because good enough may both be worth doing and, because it is not ideal, be worth improving. This is important for practitioners, who need to feel that what they do makes sense, but need at least as much to avoid self-satisfaction.

Other challenges facing participatory rural development include a fuller incorporation of the sustainable rural livelihoods paradigm; finding a stronger and more proactive role for the state without falling back on old practices that did not work in the past and would not work in the future; combining pilot interventions where new ideas can be tested with facing up to the challenges of scaling up and the nontrivial research that that entails; and, given the right conditions, taking advantage of the potential of territory-based participatory and negotiated rural development. The future of rural development, in Asia as elsewhere, seems inseparable from participation, and that may not be bad, since despite all the criticism, participation, like life, seems better than the alternative.

References

Agrawal, A. and K. Gupta (2005) 'Decentralization and Participation: The Governance of Common Pool Resources in Nepal's Terai'. *World Development,* Vol. 33, No. 7, pp. 1101–1114.

Cooke, B. and U. Kothari, eds. (2001) *Participation: The New Tyranny?* London: Zed Books.

Ellis, F. (2000) *Rural Livelihoods and Diversity in Developing Countries.* Oxford: Oxford University Press.

ESCAP (2007) *Persistent and Emerging Issues in Rural Poverty Reduction.* Bangkok: ESCAP

Francis, P. (2001) 'Participatory Development at the World Bank: The Primacy of Process'. Chapter 5 in Cooke and Kothari, 2001, pp. 72-87.

Heck, B, van (2003) *Participatory Development: Guidelines on Beneficiary Participation in Agricultural and Rural Development.* Second edition. Rome: FAO.

3

Local Communities and Integrated Rural Development

Despite the massive rural-urban migration, nearly two-thirds of people in the Asia-Pacific region live in rural areas and rural development has been a pivotal mechanism in the overall economic strategy of most of the countries. Many countries in the region have adopted a variety of programs and projects to alleviate poverty and to uplift the general well-being of the rural people. Even the more "urbanized" economies of Eastern and Southeastern Asia have adopted strategies to accelerate social and economic development in rural areas, to make rural areas attractive, both in economic and social dimensions, and to reduce urban migration. Such strategies included restructuring and modernizing agriculture, promotion of agro-industries and creating special economic zones in rural areas, enhancing community facilities and fiscal incentives. The developing countries on the other hand, have adopted policy measures and implemented special programs and projects aimed at poverty alleviation, employment generation and improving general well-being of rural masses.

The realization of effective rural development requires complementary efforts, for example:

a) developing and strengthening local institutional capacities;

b) improving rural infrastructure and related services;

c) a supportive policy framework (e.g., policies to promote financial intermediaries in the rural areas);

d) developing agriculture as well as rural industries and other off-farm activities;

e) provide education, skill training, health and other essential services; and

f) most importantly, measures to ensure socio-economic and environmental sustainability of such efforts.

In addition, development programs and projects should be responsive to the needs of the poor and promote their active participation. Therefore, an *integrated program* would be more effective.

Local Communities and Institutions

A wide range of institutions and organizations could be included under "local communities and institutions". These would range from government institutions on extreme, to people's organizations (focusing on collective action) on the other. Uphoff identified nested levels of decision-making and action, ranging from the individual level up to the international level.

> "At the lower end, there are three levels of decision-making and action that do qualify as 'local' in the sense that people within them know each other, or have a chance to know each other. 'Local' refers to relationships where some *common interest* exists and is understood, and people are willing and able to engage in *collective action.* Above local levels, they can participate as citizens, but within local arenas they have a bond of membership. The *community* or *village* level has a very visible manifestation: a set of dwellings, and associated residents, clustered together or at least designated by common agreement to 'belong' to a particular village. The *group* level is generally smaller than the community level, because most groups are subsets of persons within communities. Capabilities for *local-level development* are crucial for advancing people's productivity and well being".

Common understanding on the concept of IRD and clarity on responsibilities and roles of different stakeholders is vital. The role of the government in community development is changing and therefore, it would be important to clarify and identify the specific roles of the government vis-à-vis the local communities. Obviously, effective IRD, which cuts across multiple sectors, is a multidisciplinary affair and it is *difficult to separate* the roles of different stakeholders. This will be followed by brief accounts on the specific roles of: a) government with special emphasis on that of local government; b) local communities; c) NGOs; and d) OPS.

Evolution of Rural Development Approaches

In the past, international donors and governments in the developing countries followed a "sectoral approach" in their development efforts. However, there were shortcomings in this approach and it has been established that sectoral investments alone would not adequate for rural development. While this approach has the potential for improving the provision of public services, it is clear this usually promotes deconcentration of sectoral line Ministries and Departments and prevents effective decentralization. Also, it does not address cross-sectoral issues. Hence, it has been realized that, in order to achieve the expected benefits of the decentralization efforts, sectoral investments/ programs need to be linked with decentralized integrated development efforts.

In the 1960s, the international donors and recipient governments started "Integrated Rural Development Projects (IRDPs)" and "Area Development Projects (ADPs)", mainly with the aim of alleviating rural poverty. These projects followed a multi-sectoral and "regional" approach and included such components as: agricultural development, education, road infrastructure, health services, etc. Despite the fact that these were focused on specific regions, more often than not, the IRDPs adopted a "centrally-planned" local development approach and involved expensive external advisory inputs. It has been often argued that IRD projects have been adversely affected by top-down approaches to development planning and has become "supply-driven" in many countries. Policies, development strategies and even programs and projects designed at the top by government authorities, sometimes with donor assistance, did not necessarily take into account the demands and the capacity of local populations. Consequently, such efforts did not address the specific problems of different communities and social groups.

There was very little flexibility during downstream implementation and a "learning process" was not visible. In certain countries, special implementing authorities have been established, while in other cases, the government agencies were responsible for implementation. Also, this top-down style had contributed to the "dependency" of local communities on direct external assistance, especially from central government, through donor-funded projects. For example, most of the investment and inputs for rural infrastructure development in the past few decades came mainly through direct government support or from special projects such as IRDPs, usually supported by bilateral and international donors and development agencies. Another major dilemma in the public provision of these services has been the tendency to put inadequate emphasis on user maintenance and cost recovery.

In the late 1980s, there was a debate on the IRD project approach. For example, a World Bank-sponsored study identified the major gaps/problems associated with IRD projects including the following:

i. Difficulties encountered in linking and integrating with government institutions;
ii. Top-down and inflexible/rigid approach;
iii. Solutions are not matched with regional realities;
iv. Lack of participation of the local communities; and
v. Weak concepts.

Out of these, the inadequate involvement of local communities could be considered as the most critical issue. With this experience, some donors diverted the attention towards sectoral programs while few others focused on poverty-specific programs and regional development. One of the most striking features of this latter category of projects is to focus on specific areas.

Recent developments in the decentralization processes have provided opportunities for a new approach towards IRD. A new concept has emerged; namely, "Regional Rural Development" with emphasis on spatial dimension of development. For example, in Sri Lanka, IRD projects are "being replaced" by the "Regional Economic Advancement Programs" (REAP), which are focusing on employment and income generation in the regional economy through strengthening the local service system for micro, small and medium enterprises, including agriculture.

Shared Roles and Responsibilities in Rural Development

In many countries, now there is a tendency to decentralize authority and responsibility for rural development. Decentralization strengthens democracy and civic responsibility, and enhances the potential for community-level interventions. In addition, governance closer to communities will be more accountable to the downstream and the communities will have better opportunities to participate in the design, implementation, and monitoring of development efforts.

Development of community consciousness is important for community development. And, it is important to respect the "felt needs" of respective local communities. These are the needs as perceived and felt by the community and could be different from those "needs" which have been identified by "outsiders". People should be consulted and informed of different choices. Effective decentralization could lead to an institutional transformation, which is more conducive to such a regional approach. Particularly, the local government institutions and local community organizations could establish a collaborative partnership in undertaking the responsibility for developing a local "vision" and strategy; and designing/ planning, allocating resources, implementing and monitoring/evaluating of development activities that would better cater the local needs. They would "jointly" become the driving force towards development, develop a "sense of shared ownership" and become "managers" of their development initiatives.

In the past, rural development had been adversely affected by top-down approaches to development and has become "supply-driven" in many countries. Policies, development strategies and even programs and projects designed at the top by government authorities, sometimes with donor assistance had failed to adequately take account the demands and the capacity of local populations. On the contrary, decentralization advocates a "demand-driven" strategy and has the merit of considering the specific demands and potential of each locality. Decentralization can take place in different ways with different degrees of intensity. It could cater effectively to public needs by bringing planning and decision-making closer to people, provide opportunities for beneficiary participation and community management of its own development and help reduce inequity and instability. After decentralization, as the individual's access to the required services and supplies cannot be assured through bureaucratic modes, the evolution of new forms of organized service delivery is imperative. Community organizations and the private sector should assume this responsibility in a business mode.

Recently, the APO organized a seminar on "Effective Decentralization for Community Development". The seminar examined the systems of governance in participating countries.

The seminar concluded that in most countries, there is already some institutional framework in place within which effective community development can be promoted. Hence, it is a matter of adding appropriate roles, procedures and powers to existing structures, and of modifying present relationships to become more productive and participatory. The comparison of systems of governance, from the center to lowest level revealed that the systems of governance among countries are diversified but there are some common elements. At the same time, it seems that the smallest administrative units in some countries, such as Village Development Committee (VDC) in Nepal and *Tambon* Administration Organization (TAO) in Thailand, are too large for development initiatives by local people to be effective. The most appropriate level for decentralization for effective community development is one where it is possible for people to have face-to-face interaction, leading to collective action and self-help. Depending on the pattern of settlement and size of communities, this may be a single village or a set of hamlets – often called the ward level, e.g., in India and Nepal – or a set of villages – often called the locality level, e.g., the *tambon* in Thailand. These basic units may become more effective if they are subdivided into smaller groups for collaborative work at the lowest level.

The success of decentralization depends on many factors such as: stage of development; quality of governance at different levels; effective devolution of responsibility and authority to local levels; transformation of public institutions and change in attitude; availability of resources including financial, human, physical and natural; quality of the information available to decentralized units; strength of local organizations and local governments; participation of local people and adherence to local priorities; preparation of decentralized units – local governments, communities and others – to market realities and competition; accountability and transparency; efficient management of financial and other resources; effective M&E system; vertical and horizontal integration, especially the efficient management of interactions among different actors – community organizations, local governments, private sector and the central government; and effective mechanisms for managing conflicts.

There are constraints associated with decentralization and local governments and communities have to manage them efficiently. For example, it may take time to resolve many of the constraints prevailed prior to decentralization. Such problems may include resource constraints, lack of accountability and transparency, political conflicts, and inadequacies in support services. Another problem confronted with decentralization is the economies of scale. Especially in small countries, this may act as a constraint in resource utilization, including human resources. If they are distributed thinly, as demanded by a typical process of decentralization, this could affect efficiency. Scale economies in agriculture, industry, trade and other services could also affect production. Regionalization could be a solution and regional centers for planning and managing development as well as regional specialization in production and trade, etc. could be attempted. These are shared responsibilities and the local governments and communities should collaborate in such ventures.

It is also clear that the roles and responsibilities "assigned" or "allowed" to different actors; namely, the central government, local governments, communities and the OPS, would depend on the type of decentralization and the effectiveness of such instruments such as the policy framework and legal system, institutional framework, fiscal system and resources, etc. To elaborate further, roles and responsibilities of different actors under decentralization would depend on issues such as: to what extent the decentralized units are assigned with the authority of policy formulation and the access and management of financial and other resources?; to what extent the geographical boundaries and resource limits are assigned and the economies of scale are affected?; and what are the institutional arrangements, organizational strengths, coordinating mechanisms available at different levels and within and across different units? This implies that *local capacity building* becomes a crucial part of this new approach.

Role of Local Government

Past approaches of central governments as "providers", "owners" and "managers of rural development" have resulted in the nurturing and perpetuating of a dependency syndrome, which effectively prevented the rural community being developed as valuable human resource. In other words, this process has had negative effects in developing human capital stocks. And, the direct state involvement in community development has been on the decline in the recent past. There is however, a need for continued central government involvement in the rural sector, but it should be different from the approaches and strategies adopted in the past. As the individual villager's access to the required services and supplies cannot be assured through bureaucratic modes, the evolution of new forms of organized service delivery is imperative. And, the government, especially the central government, should perform a facilitating role.

In the past the respective governments have intensively involved in protecting, preserving and developing the local communities and incurred heavy expenditure as direct assistance in the form of the creation and management of economic and social infrastructure, technical assistance, for example in the form of extension, etc. In doing so, the governments, with the influence and assistance of the donor community, have adopted different concepts and approaches of socio-economic development in different names and at different times.

This process has had negative effects in developing human capital stocks. At the same time this process has negatively influenced the social capital investment and its outputs such as collective action. However, with the governments finding it increasingly difficult to maintain even the minimum levels of support to the rural communities, mainly because of budgetary constraints and with increased evidence of success in experiments involving beneficiaries in managing rural development, there has been a growing tendency for respective governments and the donor community to adopt participatory or shared management processes, mainly as a strategy to reduce heavy expenditure on rural development in general and on rural infrastructure, in particular.

Relative inefficiencies in the government bureaucracies in delivering support services to the rural sector have also motivated the respective governments to look for participatory and joint or collaborative processes. Therefore, governmental support in facilitating a process of more intensified and strengthened organizational activities on the part of the local people, needs special emphasis. In addition, the policy imperatives of governments on "privatization" need to be implemented in a manner that would promote the interest of the large rural segment of the population. With the creation of a competitive environment to ensure quality and fair cost, these policies will have to be implemented to benefit the ordinary villagers than to strengthen the intermediaries.

An important function of the government would be the formulation and implementation of policies to facilitate the effective functioning of the new roles assumed by the other actors. This includes preparation and adoption of legislature and other regulatory mechanisms; managing fiscal policies; looking after the interests of different groups; ensure the participation of civil society; sustainable utilization of natural resources, etc. Government commitment is a necessary condition for the sustainability of rural organizations. In certain areas, sustainability of organizations is restricted due to inadequate policy support. In certain other areas, different perception on participation by different actors, chiefly the bureaucrats, including policy makers hinder the development and sustainability of organizations.

An efficient and carefully designed legal framework to support the efforts of local organizations is essential, especially in areas where the procedures and structures of the decision-making process of the public service are oriented much more towards control than to innovative and creative work. For instance, it is prudent to provide local organizations with legal rights to participate in decision-making bodies at higher levels. In addition, the state, especially at the take-off or initial stages of this transition, will have to provide technical support and guidance, including research and extension, M&E at macro levels and prediction and forecasting the trends of development. Government at different levels – central, regional and local – should undertake the responsibility of updating the knowledge of local organizations and people on technology, resources, policy environment and potential external links such as markets and trade.

Governmental support in facilitating a process of more intensified and strengthened organizational activities on the part of the people needs special emphasis. Moreover, government commitment is a necessary condition for the sustainability of rural organizations in many countries, especially at the initial stages of social mobilization.

With decentralization, local governments will have to assume greater responsibilities and would become the focal centers for local development. For example, in Korea, local governments are supposed to perform comprehensive functions that affect citizen's welfare and quality of life. These include:

a) administrative matters pertaining to boundaries, internal organization and finance;
b) promotion of local economy;
c) regional development;
d) environmental protection;
e) education, sports, and culture; and
f) fire protection and safety.

In addition, local governments usually responsible for improving the welfare of their residents. This responsibility would include functions such as the following: installation and operation of social welfare facilities; water supply and purification; nurturing of local business; local development projects; establishment and operation of schools, kindergartens and elementary, junior, and senior high schools; and prevention of fire and fire fighting. Also, certain national and provincial affairs are delegated to local governments. These include:

1) vaccination;
2) quarantine stations for contagious diseases;
3) extermination of rats and insects;
4) national tax collections by city/*kun* offices and provincial tax collections by city/*kun* offices;
5) collection of national river utility and occupancy fees;
6) disaster relief work of city/*kun*;
7) maintenance, repair and management of national roads;
8) collection of national road occupancy fees;
9) public health centers and operation of rural guidance institutions; and
10) protection of resident livelihoods.

Local governments have to be effectively linked with the national levels as well as with local communities. They would be expected to undertake certain activities hitherto performed by the central government, such as certain legal and regulatory functions and the provision of services like extension. In addition, especially with increased demand and diversification of economic activities mainly due to the growing emphasis on globalization and associated changes, they would be entrusted with extra responsibilities. These may include guiding local communities, especially at the take-off stage, facilitating the capacity-building of local communities, catalyzing the interactions between the community organizations and the OPS, installation of monitoring mechanisms, etc.

Assuming that they are now adequately empowered with responsibilities and authorities related to the access and management of resources and have decision-making powers devolved through the decentralization process, they should be in a position to promote and institutionalize decentralized planning and ensuring the local financing of community development. Moreover, these local bodies should be transformed as facilitators for integrating the local communities with the OPS and with the national and international levels.

Greater efficiency, transparency and accountability are expected with decentralization or with the shifting of authority from the center to the local level. Local governments are closer to the communities/people and are more knowledgeable about local potential and needs. On the other hand, local people would develop better relationships with their local governments and begin to trust local officials. Hence, accountability and transparency are expected to be improved with decentralization.

There are other advantages in empowering local governments: response to local needs would become much quicker, information for the formulation local programs and projects would be readily available, as the government is closer to the people and especially to community organizations, abusing and corruption would be less, effectiveness in raising as well as utilization of revenues would be high, and the overall efficiency of managing development should be enhanced.

Therefore, it is suggested that decentralization, if planned and implemented in a proper way, could enhance the overall development of a particular country. Thus, conflicts between the center and the periphery would be detrimental and the interactions between the two should be managed efficiently and partnerships should be developed.

Role of Local Communities

For effective IRD, local communities should be organized themselves to undertake planning and managing development and are expected to take over the management of support services. This process takes time and a "blue print" approach or a ready-made model should not be adopted. Instead, it should be treated as an "evolutionary process". In the past, the great potential (social wealth) of people's participation was not generally viewed very seriously. Participation of community people has been limited to giving information (including in many Participatory Rural Appraisal [PRA] exercises), for top-down planning, receiving material incentives and other passive forms. Interactive participation and planned mobilization of social capital were largely missing.

Unlike in huge business firms, in rural communities, where a large number of small-scale "entrepreneurs" making "uncoordinated decisions", there is a need for institutional mechanisms to coordinate the decisions. A rational institutional framework is necessary to involve these "mini decision-making units" through organizational activities and to sustain such processes. Also, many of the rural people in many of these countries do not possess the strength to participate actively in a market economy, strengthening of social capital and collective action should help them benefit from the process of globalization.

To achieve sustainability, the challenge is to facilitate and institutionalize a process through which rural communities themselves would evolve local organizations to satisfy their own local needs. As a prerequisite for accumulation and the effective mobilization of social capital for community development, "improving or upgrading" the human capital is crucial. Developing skills of the individuals in a given society will enhance the quality and quantity of the output of social capital such as the collective action.

Moreover, many other problems may occur due to unplanned and *ad hoc* formation of rural organizations in a "rush". These may include rural elite taking the leadership or organizations, conflicting goals and vague objectives, inadequate or lack of participation by the membership, unacceptable patterns of benefit distribution and malpractice and corruption. Also, in countries with long traditions of dependency on government services, building institutional capacity within communities for achieving self-reliance would be a formidable task.

The intervention methodology requires potential members (of the rural communities) to promote association, interaction and cooperation with each other; develop their perception of problems and needs; and then begin a process of exploring how these needs could be met. In effect, what needs to be done is to make a planned intervention into the community.

Especially with decentralization, local communities are expected to assume greater responsibility for community development. Community organizations/institutions will become the pivotal instruments responsible for managing community development, which include the assessment of community needs/demands as well as the potential – such as the resources available internally and externally – planning and implementing development programs; maintaining information systems; providing goods and services; developing and maintaining rural infrastructure; interacting effectively with local governments and the OPS; developing partnerships and sharing responsibilities; managing conflicts; and monitoring and evaluating community development. Hence, the capacity of community organizations as well as the effective utilization of the wealth of social capital would become important determinants of decentralization.

Effective Utilization of Social Capital

Effective utilization of social capital can be singled out as the most important role of local communities in IRD. Major factors that contributed to "demand" for utilizing social capital in IRD include:

a) declining role of the government;

b) the growing demand for improved and diversified infrastructure in rural areas;

c) relative inefficiencies in the government bureaucracies in rural development, including the delivering of support services to the rural sector; and

d) the experience in efficiency improvements that have been effected through local community participation in development.

Many countries have had traditional systems of "participatory" and collective behavior of rural communities. And, most of such countries are now building on such traditions to accelerate rural development. As rural people in many of these countries do not possess the strength, as individuals, to participate actively in a market economy, strengthening of social capital and collective action should help them benefit from the process of globalization. People's participation in IRD and partnerships between the government, people and the private sector should be viewed in this context.

Community participation and the role of the community, both as organizations/ institutions and individuals in IRD, is not something that can be set once for all in a particular pattern. It is an evolutionary dynamic process and there is a need for institutional mechanisms to coordinate the decisions taken by a large number of individuals. To achieve sustainability, the challenge is to facilitate and institutionalize a process through which rural communities themselves would evolve local organizations to satisfy their own local needs. As a prerequisite for effective mobilization of social capital for IRD, "improving or upgrading" the human capital is crucial. Developing skills of the individuals in a given society will enhance the quality and quantity of the output of social capital such as the collective action.

Social capital is an asset that can produce streams of benefits that can be measured, such as income. Mutually Beneficial Collective Action (MBCA) is the most common benefit or outcome of social capital. It should be stressed that, here include only the MBCA or collective action that generates benefits to the society as a whole and not only to the individual. Collective action aimed at purely self-centered purposes and at the expense of others is excluded. Hence social capital is different from other types of capital; namely, physical, natural resources and human capital and is expected to produce goods that are more public than private.

In general, either structural or cognitive forms of social capital can be identified. Roles, rules, procedures, and precedents as well as social networks that establish patterns of social interaction can be included under the category of structural form of social capital while the cognitive form is characterized by norms, values attitudes and beliefs. The latter category of social capital creates a supporting environment that motivates beneficiaries in MBCA. The structural form provides mechanisms for collective action and facilitates the process. For example, established roles for cooperation will facilitate decision-making, resource mobilization, communication, and conflict resolution.

For example, developing specific skills of the individuals in a given society will enhance the quality and quantity of the output of social capital such as the collective action. Investment in education, skill development, nutrition, etc. would strengthen the stock of human capital. Usually, there is a growing concern about the need for improving human capital. However, investing social capital in IRD is a novel approach.

The four basic functions of structural social capital that could facilitate and support MBCA would be:

- if people are to work together predictably, fruitfully, efficiently, they need to have roles – supplemented by rules, procedures and precedents – for *making decisions*.
- to *mobilize resources* and manage these, there need to be some designated roles for this, supported by rules, procedures and precedents.
- there should also be roles, rules, procedures and precedents for *communicating* efficiently and effectively, and for *coordinating* activities that are decided upon.

- finally, whenever *conflicts* arise or are incipient, there should be roles, rules, procedures (processes), and precedents for resolving these, so that disputes do not impede collective action and are, if possible, prevented.

These may be accomplished through *formal* or through *informal* roles. Therefore, societies are not limited to just formal social structures. Informal structures – roles with associated rules, procedures and precedents – can also be as effective as formal relationships.

Moreover, the two forms of social capital are interrelated and one may not exist without the other. For clarification, let investigate what happens in catalyzing the development of a farmers' organization. The catalyst/change agent will first try to help people change attitudes and values. More often than not, this will be done on "individual basis". Then she/he promotes favorable interactions among people with the aim of creating organization. The formation of actual organization will come later.

The structural form or the organization (or institutions for that matter) comes as a consequence or as the logical next step. The organization/ institution will produce MBCA – say, for example, cleaning an irrigation canal or undertaking group production or marketing to reduce transaction costs. Now, the profit so generated is also a stream of benefits.

When social capital is used or mobilized, MBCA is generated and MBCA could be used to generate profits. In promoting small farmer companies had argued that if communities could organize and mobilize social capital, the resulting MBCA would increase, not only societal benefits (like reduced conflicts, environmental protection, etc.) but also the individual profits. *The pattern of distribution of benefits and costs is an important factor motivating individuals to organize for collective action.*

If a certain type of collective action reduces the cost to the individual or when the individuals experience more equity in the distribution of profits generated from collective action, then they would be attracted to participate actively in such group action. The common benefit derived from group action should be distributed in a manner acceptable to the individual member. And, the individual member must have the right to enjoy freely her or his share of profit derived from group action.

In addition, if there is a need for "sharing" responsibilities in order to increase individual profits or if there exist "interdependence" of different roles – such as producers, collectors, processors, store or warehouse keepers, managers, etc. – it implies "comparative advantage" for local organizations. Therefore, it would be beneficial if the communities utilize social capital in developing and managing such services. Few selected areas related to IRD, where social capital could effectively be utilized, are explained below.

Social Capital and Rural Infrastructure

More often than not, the rural infrastructure had been recognized as a "public good" and, in general, the establishment, maintenance as well as control and improvement had been considered to be the responsibility of the state. Usually high costs are associated with the establishment of rural infrastructure. However, once the infrastructure is developed, the marginal cost of consumption of that facility by an additional member of the community approaches zero. This would act as a disincentive for an individual or a private firm to produce such public goods. Hence, the collective action has the comparative advantage in handling certain infrastructure. With increased and diversified economic as well as non-economic activities in the rural areas, and because the respective governments increasingly find it difficult to "provide" and maintain rural infrastructure, there is a growing demand for "investing" social capital.

Local governments and communities should find out which rural infrastructure would have the comparative advantage to be handled by them selves. In addition to the benefits generated, the selection of rural infrastructure (to be developed and managed by the rural community) should also be judged on the basis of the capacity of respective communities and local governments. For example, they may take the responsibility for rural roads, especially for farm to market roads and, obviously, the provincial or central authorities would be responsible for the major roads. Similarly, the basic agricultural production would be the responsibility of the individual tiller while the input services, storage, marketing and processing/value addition, etc. and the development and the management of related infrastructure would be the responsibility of the local organization/company.

Social Capital for Diversified Economic Activities

Matured organizations may wish to expand their scope, for instance by expanding their economic activity. Then the organizational structure should be adjusted for efficient handling of these new tasks and roles: it may be diversified and division of management and labor may be necessary to undertake special functions. People's companies or similar institutions may be more appropriate at that stage. They may have better legal power and recognition and are readily accepted by the OPS. This is important for business ventures. For example, companies for agro-based industries could establish legal contracts with OPS companies for forward sale of agricultural products. Moreover, people's companies are independent business organizations that could avoid political and other problems. Such group action would also eliminate the problem of economies of scale and reduce transaction costs as well as the risk of credit agencies.

Social Capital for Input-Output and Financial Markets

One of the most important roles of community organizations and institutions would be to link community with external markets and supply services. In this regard, sustainable financial institutions geared to better serving the needs of medium, small, and micro enterprises including sound and efficient banking systems and capital markets should also be promoted. It would be useful to assist the development of sustainable financial institutions geared to better serving the needs of medium, small, and micro enterprises including sound and efficient banking systems and capital markets.

Especially, the provision of credit directly to the individual users through state-sponsored programs, or donor-driven projects has been a salient feature in rural areas of many developing countries. First, the practice has proved to be unsustainable since it breeds defaulters with the end result of writing off loans by political processes. Second, it does not lead to recognizing the importance of improving user's creditworthiness that could lead to action, improving credit rating of the individual user. Third, it does not recognize the important transactions with community organizations dealing with viable economic ventures in which the individual users are a part. Fourth, it demands certain types of collateral that small-scale users find difficult to produce. Fifth, it involves time-consuming and complex processes of bureaucracy or red tape. Sixth, it incurs heavy administration costs. Because of such costs and high rates of default, the interest rates, if not subsidized, are exorbitantly high. This is true for some existing banking systems as well.

The traditional subsidized credit programs of the government had taken the form of a relief or rescue operation to small farmers. This was a burden on the government budget. These deficiencies do not facilitate the emergence of a production environment that would motivate users to engage in profitable economic ventures, especially in an *open market setting*.

In this context, it is proposed to facilitate the establishment of:

a) *New organizations*, such as community organizations that are structured to deal with community business such as people's companies, where small-scale users could collectively plan their individual economic ventures, and use community action on discipline for credit repayment.

b) *Information systems*: on technologies related to crops of comparative advantage, processing/value-added, markets, transport, legal contracts, banking, etc.

c) *Novel mechanisms* among lending institutions to lower transaction costs, and offer better packages of support with relaxed procedures in supply of credit.

In addition, efficient management of input supplies and out put disposal by community organizations could reduce costs and increase profits of individual members of a particular organization. The benefit or the profit margin of the individual members will significantly influence viability of group action.

Role of Non-governmental Organizations

At the community level, in order to achieve effective and sustainable rural development, the challenge is to facilitate and institutionalize a process through which rural communities themselves would evolve local organizations to satisfy their own local needs. For this, a catalytic process or a "planned intervention" into the community is required. *Such a catalytic effort should be strong enough to generate the internal dynamism of the community and controlled enough not to dominate it.* The intervention methodology requires potential members (of the rural communities) to promote association, interaction and cooperation with each other; develop their perception of problems and needs; and then begin a process of exploring how these needs could be met. In effect, what needs to be done is to make a planned intervention into the community. Carefully selected and well-trained catalysts or change agents could make such interventions. Instead, local organizations are "formed" (and not "evolved" from within the communities) by field officials not to fulfill people's needs, but merely to follow the orders of the superior officials or to satisfy the politicians.

Facilitating the Evolution of Self-correcting Mechanisms

To attain self-reliance, local organizations need to adopt self-correcting mechanisms on a continuous basis. An experienced and committed NGO could help local organizations and institutions to internalize participatory self-assessment procedures to measure and monitor the performance of the organization as well as the development and management processes. In collaboration with the members of other participating organizations, local officials of relevant agencies, resource persons such as technical experts, the NGO could *pave the way for participatory (M&E) and Management Information Systems (MIS) especially at the planning and initial stages of adoption.* Such a planning process and M&E would help the membership to articulate a possible future vision for their organizations.

The Need for Dynamic and Forward-looking NGOs

It should be evident from earlier discussion that, with the diversified and expanded functions expected from the local communities and institutions, the role and functions of the change agency/agent or facilitator/catalyst should also be changed. The added roles of a facilitator/catalyst in such situations would include:

i. *identify and estimate market potential*: e.g., for selected agricultural enterprises and agro-processing, assist in the scheduling of production in a given area, inform the community organization and other technical officers (such as the extension and credit, input supplies) of the availability of markets for enterprises that would match with the agro-climatological and socio-economic conditions of the area and for the selected processed products;

ii. *estimate the production* of these selected enterprises *jointly with the community organization* and then arrange for *forward contracts with identified markets/buyers*. In this way, the facilitator/NGO will link the community organizations with potential markets/private sector firms;

iii. *assist the rural community in monitoring the feasibility of meeting the contractual agreements*: For this, the catalyst/NGO will join the staff of local government and other staff of the community company/organization and assist them to monitor, whether there are any constraints faced by the rural community in the markets, production and processing, etc., which may affect the quantities and quality standards included in the forward contracts or other agreements;

iv. *arrange for expert advice* as well as *other needs* of the organization/company. These will include all aspects of markets, marketing and processing farm products, storage, packing, transport, etc. The objective is to help evolve the required business mode of operation within the organization/company; and

v. *Be accountable* community organizations.

It should be noted, however, that in some cases, due to the relative inefficiency in government agencies or due to the lack of effective community organizations at the grassroots level, funding agencies have tended to load new tasks onto NGOs, whether or not they are suited to such tasks. Looking ahead, and in the context of "reduced role of governments", the NGOs will come under increasing pressure as alternatives, especially to government agencies.

Role of the Private Sector

In open market economies, liberalization not only results in an increased withdrawal of government interventions, but also leaves economic activities open to the market forces. In areas where central government had played an important role, the reforms or the "adjustment and stabilization programs" would induce private sector participation for increased efficiency and to reduce the burden to government. And, with decentralization, government's role as a "service provider" will be diminished. Therefore, this "gap" needs to be bridged by the private sector and community organizations. In addition, as discussed earlier, a variety of new activities, including production of goods and services, would be introduced. In the context of national budget constraints, many countries seek private sector involvement. For example, in developing rural infrastructure, certain developing countries already adopting a mode of "rehabilitate, operate, and transfer", with the private sector firms, especially on road construction along high traffic routes. A toll system of fees would be explored along such routes. This system works on the principle that as long as such infrastructure yields significant net benefits to the users, these same users would be willing to pay for the privilege to use them.

Globalization has now become an "unavoidable" process and an organized local community should have the capacity to consider it as an "opportunity" rather than a "threat". It has been argued that the developing countries could benefit from participation in the global economy. Freeing prices and liberalization of trade have the potential for enhanced private sector participation and creating opportunities for new investments and jobs, and promoting more efficient use of resources and higher productivity. In addition, access to external resources and direct foreign investment could be expected with the liberalization of capital flows. Direct investment by foreign investors may also encourage the transfer of technology, managerial expertise, and skills. Under such circumstance, an effective partnership between the OPS (local and international) and organized communities would be *mutually beneficial*. And initially, local governments could facilitate this process. Positive response of communities to globalization and making use of the globalization process creatively to the advantage of local communities would be important. The challenge would be to make rural people active partners in the global economy and improve their living standards.

People's companies or similar institutions may be more appropriate "vehicles" for achieving such an effective partnership with the private sector, and to integrate communities with the external business environment. They may have better legal power and recognition and are readily accepted by the OPS. This is important for business ventures. Sustainable financial institutions geared to better serving the needs of medium, small, and micro enterprises, efficient banking systems and capital markets would be required for effective IRD. And, business organizations *of the community people, such as people's companies*, should have the capacity to deal with such service providers. Group action, which would generate from *social capital* would gain such capacities and also eliminate the problem of *economies of scale* and reduce transaction costs as well as the risk of financing institutions.

Hence, effective partnerships between the community people and the private sector would become crucial. An effective "partnership" may occur when two or more parties have common objectives and would be based on "agreements". Then there will be "collaborative activities among interested groups, based on a mutual recognition of respective strengths and weaknesses". Shared agenda, joint decision-making, deep commitments and mutual benefits would constitute a partnership.

Capacity-building at Local Levels

Building the capacities of institutions at different levels is critical for them to effectively perform their respective roles. At the micro level the capacity of the community should be enhanced, with special emphasis on that of the leaders of the community organizations for them to become the owners and implementers of the development efforts, and to deal effectively with the local government units, NGOs and the OPS. At the same time, local government institutions need to be oriented and their skills and capacity should be strengthened towards community-oriented planning. At the national level, capacities need to be developed and attitudes need to be changed to provide a favorable policy, fiscal and institutional support.

Local Planning and Implementing Units/Centers

It is proposed to establish and strengthen *Local Planning and Implementing Units/Centers*, representing local government institutions and community organizations. Such local planning centers need to be equipped with technical expertise that possess adequate knowledge and experience on development planning procedures, implementing methods and M&E. Such planners should know novel methods of participatory planning – the conventional Rapid Rural Appraisals (RRAs) and PRAs are time-consuming and less effective.

More often than not PRA/RRA are being used merely as "knowledge generation activities", especially for outsiders. Instead, participatory appraisals should be considered as a first step of an *action program* and aimed at developing a package of *interventions*. For example, in rural resources planning, interventions may be related to *technology, organization/ institutions, resources and policy*. More specifically it should focus on a process of participatory appraisal of the current levels of management of (internal and external) resources, participatory design of a *future vision* and *goals* of reconciling environmental concerns and production goals, and the development of collaborative action plans to achieve such goals. Also, the accuracy of PRA can be improved if its use is integrated with other techniques such as: advanced mapping and incorporating more of external (in addition to indigenous) inputs, statistical sampling, direct measurement, and the use of objectively verifiable indicators and rigorous analytical tools.

Decentralized planning units should maintain an integrated and accessible information systems, especially on the resources available to the community and for M&E. Similarly, the training and skill development needs of local organizations and institutions that are engaged in new tasks are of different types and are of continuous in nature. Changing technology and the expansion of activities of the local organizations with their maturity will call for new kinds of training and skill development. Also, the matured organizations will enter into transactions and business with outsiders such as the OPS. Therefore, the sustainability of the organizations will depend, among other things, on the knowledge and skills of their managers and those who are entrusted with specific functions. For example, training on financial management, acquiring skills in managing different types infrastructure, etc., are essential, especially for a multifunctional organization. A healthy and rigorous financial management system should be an integral component of an organization undertaking financial transactions. Organizations will have to develop their own financial plans, maintain proper records on financial transactions, assess their own financial activities (self-assessment) and establish and maintain an effective system of internal control.

Communication Technology in Capacity Building

Utilization of communication technologies in rural development in developing countries is gaining momentum at present. In this regard, the Village Pay Phone initiative of the Grameen Bank, which is aimed at reducing poverty through the economic empowerment of women in rural Bangladesh, provides an excellent example. The Grameen Group provides credit to village women to purchase cellular phones. The phone owners could then rent out the phones to other members of the community for a fee and also provide messaging and incoming call services. The Grameen goal is to serve 500,000 subscribers in six years. Already there is evidence of:

a) increased savings, investment and incomes;

b) improved farm productivity and small farmer profits, for example through the enhanced access to market/price information and to better markets;

c) improved investment on children's education; and

d) better access to public services.

However, there are challenges: cell phone technology is relatively expensive (compared to land phones) but it has been "difficult" to integrate with the national landline telecommunication system. Such obstacles need to be removed.

When the pace and scale of flow of information across the globe is considered, it is clear that there exist a tremendous potential for human resources development. For example, if the access to Internet is enhanced, many people in the developing world, who are excluded from such gains in human development at present, could benefit from that technology. And, the marginal cost of connecting individuals and groups for exchanging ideas and experience as well as providing opportunities for knowledge and skill development through the Internet is negligible. As the Internet communication plays a crucial role in the globalization process, this option should not be overlooked.

To assist in the identification of potential opportunities, the information must encompass a wider range. Information on resources, production technologies, and infrastructure as well as on value-added production and marketing, etc., becomes important when attempting to discover new economic potentials.

The objectives of the information systems are manifold. First, the information on new and sustainable technologies, relevant to the activities undertaken by the local communities, should flow down from appropriate sources to the local organizations. Such technology should be affordable by the respective communities and viable. Second, information on opportunities available for local users such as banking and credit facilities, market and processing, etc. should be made available to the local organization. Third, the flow of information on policy, legal and regulatory aspects and information on relevant government or private sector collaboration/assistance and on the work of other relevant user groups/local organizations is of significant importance for pronounced growth and sustainability of local organizations involved in IRD.

A continuous flow of information is required to enrich the implementation process facilitating interaction, debate and resolution. The prudent use of information technology (IT) in the generation, process and analysis of information needed is crucial to support the planning, implementation and evaluation of IRD. For this, the local communities and institutions may use a MIS and a rigorous self-M&E activity through a participatory procedure.

Similarly, the training and skill development needs of organizations that are engaged in new tasks are of different types and are of continuous in nature. Changing technology and the expansion of activities of the local organizations with their maturity will call for new kinds of training and skill development. For example, training on financial management, acquiring skills in managing different types infrastructure, etc., are essential, especially for a multifunctional organization.

Coordination Mechanisms

There is a need for effective coordination mechanisms at different levels as well as cutting across different hierarchical levels to ensure effective rural development. And, it is important to coordinate, not only the activities within communities, or the decisions taken and activities performed by the large number of people at the community level, but also the activities between communities and other "actors" of the rural development process, such as the local governments and, "outsiders" like the service providers at different levels, and the activities between those "outsiders". For example, coordination between different national, provincial or local government agencies dealing with development is important in mobilizing scarce resources to achieve maximum efficiency and impact. One of the most critical problems of rural development in many countries is the existence of several government agencies/departments, which often duplicate, instead of coordinating activities. Moreover, it has become even more important to establish adequate coordination among donors, development agencies, NGOs, etc., at all levels.

Monitoring and Evaluation

The degree to which the local communities have control over local resources and the degree, to which they manage their development, could be regarded as good indicators for measuring the success of participatory IRD or the success of "community-driven" development. At the same time it is important to effectively link the decentralized local units, community organizations and their activities, especially the economic ventures/business, with outer environment, including international markets.

Similarly, one could examine the degree to which local people recognize their rights and responsibilities and to what extent other actors respect those rights. In both these aspects, community organizations could play a dominant role. Organizations could ensure the equitable participation by community members.

To attain self-reliance, local communities and institutions need to adopt monitoring and self-correcting mechanisms on a continuous basis. They could use participatory self-assessment procedures to measure and monitor the performance of the institutions and organizations as well as the development and management processes. Involvement of the community organizations, local officials of relevant agencies, resource persons such as technical experts and the partners of the OPS, including participating NGOs, at the planning stages, etc. will pave the way for participatory M&E and MIS. Such a planning would help the membership to articulate a possible future vision for their organizations. Database management and assisting the organization in the self-evaluation process should be an essential function and contribution by the facilitators.

Obstacles to the Participation of Local Communities in IRD

Major obstacles to the effective participation of local communities and institutions in IRD include: resource constraints, including financial, human and physical such as rural infrastructure; problems of accountability and lack of transparency; political conflicts; and inadequacies in support services.

Usually the central governments always emphasize the commitment to decentralization and reliance on local authorities. However, certain central governments do very little in practice – there is a "struggle" for control rather than sharing authority; financing is centralized and sufficient funds are not allocated to local governments; in a "donor-driven" development process, the externally-funded projects are handled by the central governments; and thereby restricting the sources of funding for the local governments.

In many developing countries, development is project-driven and the majority of the projects are donor-driven. Most of such projects are managed by the center and therefore, the local governments may lack the expertise and financial resources to effectively manage development and to cope up with the present trends such as the pace of globalization and trade relations. With decentralization, local governments would have the power to raise revenue through different ways, such as tax, cost recovery or user charges and local and international borrowing, etc. However, many local authorities have a poor record of revenue collection and raising funds through other means.

Hence, more often than not, they depend on funds transferred from the central government. This would remain as a constraint for sometime. It is important to transfer the essential services such as financial and human, to the local units, at least at the take-off stage. The private sector, including the NGOs, could also fill certain gaps. At the same time adequate measures should be taken to develop the skills and raise resources (such as tax revenue and service charges for financial needs) at local levels.

Similarly, despite the fact that expertise on local needs and environment are at local levels, the expertise in planning and managing development, which is in short supply, is at national levels. How could local governments maintain a cadre of skilled set of officials, including planning expertise, high-caliber managers, M&E experts, etc?

For this, the local governments have to be competitive with the OPS. If they fail to pay competitive salaries/remuneration packages to their good employees they would lose such people. On the other hand, in many countries, government employees are assured of lifetime employment and there is no adequate incentives or rewards for good work. For example, promotions are given on the basis of seniority or factors other than efficiency.

Another constraint would be the inadequacies in support services, training and the supply of information. Therefore, training and skill development, especially in relation to the goods and services of economic sectors would become crucial. Similarly, the generation of information related to such aspects as technology, macro-economics and policy framework, trade and markets – both domestic and international; as well as the flow of information to local levels, which may not be efficient at present, need to be improved.

The local level too is not homogenous. There are different interest groups with conflicting goals. At the same time, linking local level with the regional level and the national level could be difficult. There could be "center versus periphery" conflicts as well. Politicians in Seoul and bureaucrats in the central government hesitated to decentralize power to local governments. They believed that local diversity was a fiction and that a small country like Korea should be run by the central government with little local administrative discretion" Unless such conflicting interests and rivalries are managed properly, the benefits of decentralization may not be achieved.

Lack of clarity of and the adherence to the responsibilities and accountabilities by different actors also act as a constraint. Such responsibilities and accountabilities may relate to various aspects of development like planning and managing development including fiscal and other resources, transparency, monitoring and evaluation, etc.

Effective IRD, which cuts across multiple sectors, is a multidisciplinary affair and it is *difficult to separate* the roles of different stakeholders. In the past, rural development had been adversely affected by top-down approaches to development and has become "supply-driven" in many countries. On the contrary, recent developments in decentralization advocate a "demand-driven" strategy and have the merit of considering the specific demands and potential of each locality.

The local government institutions and local community organizations could establish a collaborative partnership in undertaking the responsibility for developing a local "vision" and strategy; and designing/planning, allocating resources, implementing and monitoring/ evaluating of development activities that would better cater the local needs. They would "jointly" become the driving force towards development, develop a "sense of shared ownership" and become "managers" of their development initiatives.

An important function of the central government would be the formulation and implementation of policies to facilitate the effective functioning of the new roles assumed by the other actors. With decentralization, local governments will have to assume greater responsibilities and would become the focal centers for local development. Local governments have to be effectively linked with the national levels as well as with local communities. They would be expected to undertake certain activities hitherto performed by the central government, such as certain legal and regulatory functions and the provision of services like extension. In addition, especially with increased demand and diversification of economic activities mainly due to the growing emphasis on globalization and associated changes, they would be entrusted with extra responsibilities. These may include guiding local communities, especially at the take-off stage, facilitating the capacity-building of local communities, catalyzing the interactions between the community organizations and the OPS, installation of monitoring mechanisms, etc.

Usually, NGOs help reduce government domination at local level. It is suggested that the major role of NGOs in IRD should to "*facilitate institutional development/strengthening*" in the communities.

For effective IRD, local communities should be organized themselves to undertake planning and managing development and are expected to take over the management of support services. At the community level, in order to achieve effective and sustainable rural development, the challenge is to facilitate and institutionalize a process through which rural communities themselves would evolve local organizations to satisfy their own local needs. For this, a catalytic process or a "planned intervention" into the community is required. Effective utilization of social capital can be singled out as the most important role of local communities in IRD. As a prerequisite for accumulation and the effective mobilization of social capital for community development, "improving or upgrading" the human capital is crucial. Matured organizations may wish to expand their scope, for instance by expanding their economic activity. Then the organizational structure should be adjusted for efficient handling of these new tasks and roles. One of the most important roles of community organizations and institutions would be to link community with external markets and supply services. People's companies or similar institutions may be more appropriate at that stage. This is important for business ventures.

References

Asian Productivity Organization, (2001). Proceedings of the Seminar on Effective Decentralization for Community Development, 23-31 March 2001, Sri Lanka

IBRD, (1987). *World Bank Experience with Rural Development, 1965-1986*, Washington D.C.

Uphoff, Norman and C. M. Wijayaratna, (2000). "Demonstrated Benefits from Social Capital: The Productivity of Farmer Organizations in Gal Oya, Sri Lanka, 2000", *World Development*, No. 28, Vol. 11, November 2000.

Wijayaratna, C. M., (1985). "Involvement of Farmers in Water Management in Gal Oya, Sri Lanka" in *Participatory Experiences in Irrigation Water Management: Proceedings of the Expert Consultation on Irrigation Water Management* held in Yogyakarta and Bali, Indonesia, 16-22 July 1984, 117-32, FAO.

4

Participatory Natural Resource Management in Rural Areas

The importance of local organizations and institutions in rural development is widely recognized and has become a part of the development policy in many countries. Despite this, the actual integration of these institutions and organizations in development practice has often been ineffective. The author believes that there are two main reasons for this. In some cases the real commitment of governments and government agencies to serious recognition of and support of local organizations has been very limited. The second reason is that understanding of the sociological basis for effective organizations is relatively weak within government agencies.

An underlying aim of the seminar on "The Role of Communities and Institutions in Integrated Rural Development" is to identify some principles that can be applied to support local organizations.

One of the reasons for this focus is that the author wants to suggest that multipurpose (or multifunctional) organizations, which are sometimes associated with "integrated" rural development, are often inappropriate for natural resource management, while they may be appropriate to other aspects of rural development or community development.

Definitions and Concepts

Uphoff distinguishes between organizations and institutions. He uses the term organization to refer to a structure of recognized and accepted roles.

Institution refers to a set of shared norms and behaviors. It is useful to make another distinction, this time between "indigenous" and "sponsored" local organizations.

The basis of the distinction is that the initiative for establishing indigenous (or endogenous) organizations comes from within a community whereas the initiative for setting up sponsored organizations comes from outside the community (usually from government). Within the "sponsored" category it is possible to make a further distinction. Some sponsored local organizations (such as some elected local governments) are set up by external initiative, but are locally controlled. Others are under external control by governments or government agencies.

Discussions of community-based organizations often fail to distinguish between organizations in terms of who initiated them and, even more importantly, who controls them (who makes the decisions). The final distinction is a distinction between indigenous and traditional organizations. Discussions of local organization and local resource management practices tend to use the terms interchangeably. The author prefers to avoid the word "traditional" in most cases, since it implies that something is old and is often assumed to mean that it is unchanging.

The evidence makes it overwhelmingly clear that local organizations and institutions are quite dynamic and respond quickly to change. This is important, because local practices are often dismissed as irrelevant on the basis of assumptions that they are old and unchanging.

Indigenous Forest Management Systems in Nepal: Case Studies

Nepal has become rather well known in the literature on participatory natural resource management for its community forestry program. Under this program use rights to government-owned forest are transferred to communities on a permanent basis subject to an agreement about the way the forest will be managed (including the arrangements for distributing forest products within the community). In the early days of community forestry the transfer of management responsibility was to local government units then called "*panchayats*". Efforts were made to establish new *panchayat*-based community forestry committees to be responsible for community forests. It was assumed that there was something of a local institutional vacuum in terms of forest management and the new organizational arrangements were attempts to fill that vacuum. However, research in the late 1980s showed that there were many local forest management systems operating based on indigenous organizations and institutional arrangements. These systems provided lessons for the later development of the community forestry program.

Case 1: Panday Ban

Panday Ban is a patch of about 7 ha of forest on a slope below a road in Kabhre Palanchok district. The users of the forest consist of about 35 households living in two hamlets on the hillside below the forest. The forest is a mixed broadleaf forest, with good regeneration and is generally well protected. The technical practices involved in forest management are very simple and are presented in a number of rules about forest use:

- Leaf litter can be collected at any time except during the monsoon;
- Dry fuel wood, rhododendron flowers, grass and small bushes can be collected at any time; and
- Cutting of green wood or green leaves is completely forbidden.

The rules are very conservative and quite modest changes (such as pruning and removal of selected trees) would enable increased harvest of forest products without damage to forest regeneration.

In 1990, the social arrangements involved all members of the user group (the residents of the two hamlets) who watched the forest for infringements. Previously there was a system of rotating responsibility for watching the forest. The bamboo was circulated to people in turn and, according, to the order in which the names appeared, a household member spent a day guarding the forest from transgressors. No committee was involved either in 1990 or in the past.

Case 2: Mahankal Ban

Mahankal Ban consists of about 14 ha of mixed broadleaf forest, located in Sindhu Palchok district to the east of the Kathmandu valley. There are some abandoned agricultural terraces inside the forest area. According to local accounts, protection was commenced in 1963 because the forest was in poor condition. Under protection the forest regenerated and was in a healthy condition by the late 1980s.

A number of villages surround the forest, which is on a slope. Of these villages, the main (primary) users come from Archale village, which is located below the forest. People from two other villages have secondary rights, as do some people who live seasonally in *goths* (temporary shelters, usually associated with livestock grazing). The use rights are as follows:

i. Primary users are allowed to collect grass and dry wood from the ground (they are not allowed to cut green timber or even dry branches still attached to trees). They are able to collect the fruit of the *Katus* trees when it appears (every two years). This represents a considerable source of income.

ii. Secondary users living in *goths* have the same rights as primary users during their period of residence. When living in their normal residences they are not allowed to collect firewood.

iii. Other secondary users are also entitled to collect grass and *Katus* fruit, but are never allowed to collect firewood.

iv. Grazing is free, but the number of livestock is small because fodder species are notreadily available.

These use rights reflect strong emphasis on protection. The permitted uses minimize interference with shrub and tree growth, thus encouraging regeneration. Although the rules are quite clear in prohibiting harvesting of live wood, in fact some pruning of branches for fuel does occur. It seems that the illicit pruning is tolerated as a source of fuel wood for poorer families. Interestingly, pruning is done very carefully so as not to unduly damage tree growth, suggesting that the "ethic of *sadupayog* (wise use)" is widely accepted, even when necessity forces people to cut wood for fuel.

The social arrangements for forest management at Mahankal Ban have gone through a number of stages. In the first stage (from the beginning of the protection system in the early 1960s), there was no formal organizational structure: there were no forest watchers and there was no committee. Later a committee was established and at one time a forest watcher was employed with money collected from households in the user group. Later, the watcher was paid with money from the project. Although the committee ceased to function, the management system continued.

It appears that formal organization really was not particularly important to the functioning of the system. Several prominent high caste men had been prime movers behind the establishment of the system and these men continued to be rather dominant. They were sometimes criticized by other villagers for preventing the imposition of less restrictive rules about forest use. The relatively high degree of adherence to the rules seems to have been the result of a combination of a relatively high degree of consensus about the need for forest protection, combined with a reluctance to upset embedded social relationships. Tolerance of limited and necessary cheating no doubt contributed.

Indigenous forest management systems in Nepal are highly varied in terms of organizational arrangements and institutional forms. These two case studies represent only a small portion of the variety, which exists. Within the context of this variation, it is possible to make some generalizations:

- The indigenous systems were built around a group of people with mutually recognized (and unofficial) rights to use resources. These user groups amounted to a "communities of interest" with reference to a particular area of forest. The user groups were not based on formal political-administrative (*panchayat*) boundaries. In fact a major problem with the original practice of implementing community forestry through the *panchayats* was that they represented the wrong people for common property forest management because they ignored use rights.
- Organizational aspects are highly variable and, in fact, sometimes no organizational features (in the sense of Uphoff's "recognized structure of roles") exist at all. Interestingly, within the same local system, organizational features may be present at some times and not at others.
- While organizational features seem to be very much optional, all effective indigenous systems have institutional features.

The relationship between organizational features and institutional features in indigenous Nepali forest management systems can be illustrated in terms of a "house" model. In this model, agreed rules, shared values and shared behaviors can be seen as an institutional base (the walls of the house). This base must always be present(there must always be agreed rules and shared behaviors, or nothing will happen in terms of collective action). The roof of the house represents an "organizational superstructure" made up of roles such as committee member, chairperson, or forest watcher. This superstructure can be different in shape in different cases and may sometimes be missing.

In indigenous systems the walls are essential. The roof cannot be built without the walls and is not always necessary. To take the analogy further, in the case of sponsored systems emphasis is often placed on building the roof, but not much effort is put into building the walls needed to support the roof.

Indisputably, it is often true that Forest Departments setting up community level forest management arrangements concentrate on forming committees (usually according to standardized rules about membership and procedures) rather than spending time working with communities to build consensus about what (if anything) needs to be done and how it should be done. This does not only apply to Nepal, and it does not only apply to forest management. It is frequently true of many efforts by government agencies to establish community organizations.

In the case of community forestry in Nepal before indigenous systems were studied, the absence of visible organizational features (the roof of the house) usually lead to forest officials failing to notice the less obvious, but more important, institutional base. The result was the incorrect assumption that there was a local "institutional vacuum". This tendency of government agencies to ignore existing "indigenous" arrangements and to concentrate on establishing new organizations is fairly common in government organization building activities.

The tendency of government agencies to build new organizations is associated with another tendency – the tendency to establish these along the lines of standard form or structure. This usually involves specified rules about executive positions, membership and constitutional rules of procedure. Standardization like this can lead to distorting effects:

- Requirements for representation by local officials (elected or appointed) may place power in the hands of people who previously had no interest in a resource and who were not part of the mutually recognized community of resource users.
- Existing arrangements for intra-community conflict resolution may be lost in new constitution al arrangements.

It is understandable that government agencies dealing with large numbers of communities would want to deal with somewhat similar organizations in order to simplify such things as record keeping, financial allocations and so on. Nevertheless, administrative convenience often occurs at the cost of effective organizations. The more the organization is designed externally and the more decisions are made externally, the more likely it is that "felt-needs" will not be met.

One further point that can be made from the Nepal experience is that there are strong tendencies within local communities, which encourage people to follow rules established through locally managed and transparent processes. In rural communities, people live within complex patterns of reciprocal social relationships. There are kinship ties, marriage ties and patron-client relationships; some people depend on others to work for them, others are dependent on others to earn income. Such *embedded* social relationships make people interdependent, and thus provide incentives to cooperate with others. It is just this type of interdependence that many common property theorists forget when trying to understand the basis of common property management.

There is nothing about any of this that idealizes communities. Conflict and inequality are quite normal in communities. Sometimes these conflicts are so great that cooperation becomes impossible. But often, even in the context of hierarchical social relationships, cooperation occurs.

Form Follows Function

The key reason for the variation in organizational arrangements in natural resource management systems in Nepal (and indigenous local organizations of all kinds in Nepal and elsewhere) can be summed up in the phrase "form follows function" (which translates to structure depends on function).

What this means is that people will set up organizational and institutional arrangements that they think will meet their objectives. In fact, arrangements, which do not work or involve too many transaction costs will either disappear or be modified. This is why people who want to manage a small patch of forest surrounded by a fairly coherent group of users (as in Panday Ban) do not need much in the way of formal roles. Everyone contributes just by keeping their eyes open for people breaking rules. Where the group of users is more diverse (and the resource is more difficult to observe) other arrangements such as paid watchers might be advisable. If experience shows that most people follow the rules, this may become unnecessary.

Where achieving objectives is more complex (such as in an irrigation management system several kilometers long and involving several otherwise largely unrelated villages), more complex organizational arrangements may be appropriate.

From this point of view, a problem with the standardized organizational models associated with bureaucracies is that they impose one form to fit different functions, imposing unnecessary transaction costs in some cases and failing to meet situation specific needs in others.

Multifunctionality and Common Property Management

It is a premise of IRD that different types of development activities should be integrated rather than implemented by different sectoral departments. This has sometimes been extended to the idea that community organizations concerned with development ought to be multifunctional. At first sight this seems quite reasonable and this sort of idea is common. However, the author's experience and analysis suggest that multi-functionality is often inappropriate for natural resource management, particularly where common property resources are involved.

In the case of common property management the main reason is that effective management must focus on the needs to recognize all mutually recognized users (those who have an interest in seeing the resource maintained and whose behavior will most directly affect the resource). In addition to involving all the users, effective common property organizations will generally exclude people who don't have a recognized interest in the resource. For a multifunctional organization to manage more than one common property resource, the recognized user group would need to coincide. This usually does not happen.

For example, the users of irrigation systems in mountainous areas tend not to be the same as the users for forests in the same area. Irrigation systems follow a long line and the users are those along the line who take water from it and are responsible for managing it. In mountain areas irrigation canals tend to follow rivers and cross through a number of micro-watersheds. Forests tend to be on ridges or valleys and the users tend to come from villages surrounding them. Only a small number of users for a particular forest would be users of a particular irrigation system and the users of the irrigation system would include users from a number of different forests. Many of the forest users would have no interest in managing the canal and canal users would have interests in only one or two forests. The transaction costs of a system big enough to cover all the forests and the canal would be very high.

There are cases, however, where different conditions make a multifunctional system appropriate. For example, in Hawaii the traditional resource management system involved integrated management of whole watersheds. This was possible (perhaps even necessary) because of the specific physical shape of Hawaiian island landscapes. The islands in Hawaii are effectively the tops of tall mountains growing out of the sea. The tops of the mountains are tall and the slopes steep. Watersheds (*ahupua'a*) tend to be quite distinct. In traditional Polynesian society, each *ahupua'a* was occupied by a particular clan ruled by a chief. The resources of the watershed (including forests, grazing areas, farming land, irrigation systems and fishing areas inside the reef) were managed as a whole by the chief on behalf of the clan members. This was possible because the social and resource boundaries (for all resources) fell within a clearly defined and manageable territory. Multfunctional management was, therefore, possible. Again, organizational form (the hierarchical clan structure) follows function.

Voluntary Natural Resource Management Organizations

The discussion will now turn to another aspect of natural resource management, which has quite different organizational implications. It was argued earlier that effective organizations for the management of common property resources should represent all right holders and be accepted by them and that they should not represent people who are not right holders.

There is another type of community-level natural resource management organization, which is voluntary. Voluntary associations for farmers interested in improving management of various on-farm activities (i.e., on private land) are quite common. An example would be voluntary interest groups for poultry raising. Such a group might have joint meetings with extensionists to learn improved techniques, or purchase equipment or medicines to be shared among members. Another example might be a dairy cooperative, which functions to provide improved market access. In these cases, non-membership of some farmers does not usually pose a problem for members, whereas non-cooperation in a common property system would.

Participation and Decision-making

"Participation" is very much an overused and misused term. It has many different meanings and distinctions between these meanings are rarely made clearly. Arnstein identified a number of different types of process, which have all been lumped together as participation. She presented these in the form of a ladder in which token types of participation were placed at the bottom and forms of participation involving genuine "citizen power" were placed at the top. The principle of ranking is essentially the extent to which participants have real powers over decision-making.

This is a very useful model. It is proposed that the crucial reason why local people often fail to "participate" in sponsored local organizations is that they do not feel that these organizations meet their needs, because the real decision-making power is located outside the organization. In other words, organizational objectives are set by others (such as government, or government agencies).

Perhaps one of the most important factors in effective local organizations (indigenous or sponsored) is whether participants have a genuine input in setting objectives and making decisions about matters that affect their lives.

General Community Development Organizations

It is appropriate at this point to make a few remarks about general community organizations (those not concerned specifically with natural resource management).

Much of what has been said above is relevant to local organizations concerned with development in fields besides natural resource management. The importance of developing a sound institutional base (agreed vision, rules, practices) applies to all effective organizations.

Many local organizations in rural development are of the voluntary or interest group type. Organizations supporting schools, health clinics or other resources, and micro-credit organizations are of this type. Such organizations are generally concerned with a single function. The other type of local organization is the type of organization that performs the function of integrating efforts. This is often the function of local government.

Regarding multifunctional local organizations (the type that perform the integrating and coordinating functions), the following propositions are in order:

- They need to have genuine decision-making authority (and not just be implementing decisions made "from above").

- They need to represent a local constituency and be answerable downwards rather than upwards.
- They should not be responsible for everything, especially where other groups can perform particular tasks more effectively.

A potential problem with IRD is that the emphasis on integration can easily turn into an emphasis on centralized planning, which works against effective local level decision-making and which has demonstrably not worked well in rural development or natural resource management in the past. This presents a real dilemma for governments and perhaps the only way out of the dilemma is for governments is to think in terms of setting up platforms in which various local organizations and stakeholders can negotiate solutions to local development and resource management issues.

Rather than setting specific objectives for local level development and resource management, governments (supported by NGOs and other organizations) can play essential roles such as providing technical support, assisting with capacity development and providing mediation and facilitation between competing interests.

The lessons are:

- organizations and institutions for common property resource management need to involve all mutually recognized users.
- where effective local institutional and organizational arrangements exist, these should be recognized, supported and strengthened rather than replaced.
- establishing sponsored organizations on the basis of standard structures should be avoided.
- effective local organizations are often concerned with a single function. While interests may sometimes expand to involve other activities, it is not advisable to impose multiple functions.
- where new organizations are being established, processes for developing institutional arrangements (vision, agreed rules/norms and practices) are more important than organizational structure and should come first.
- effective local organizations need to have the capacity (and right) to make meaningful decisions about objectives and implementation rather than having these imposed from above (the capacity to make

meaningful decisions does not preclude making these decisions in collaboration with others, but it does require meaningful negotiations, without predetermined outcomes, in such cases).

- where new organizations are being established, processes for developing institutional arrangements (vision, agreed rules/norms and practices) are more important than organizational structure and efforts at "community organization" should place priority on the dialogue and negotiations needed to establish these.

References

Fisher, R. J., Hukum Bahadur Singh, Deepak Raj Pandey and Helmut Lang, (1990). *The* Management of Forest Resources in Sindhu Palchok and Kabhre Palanchok Districts *of Nepal*, Mountain Populations and Employment Discussion Paper Series 8, ICIMOD, Kathmandu.

Messerschmidt, Donald A., (1984). *Using Human Resources in Natural Resource Management Innovations in Himalayan Development*, Working Paper WSM I/1, ICIMOD, Kathmandu.

Nepal Australia Forestry Project, (1990). *Gaunle Ko Ban Byavastha: Indigenous Forest Management in Nepal*, film produced by Worldview International Foundation, Nepal for NAFP.

Uphoff, Norman, (1986). *Local Institutional Development: An Analytical Sourcebook with Cases*, Kumarian Press, West Hartford, CT.

5

People's Self-Organizing Actions for Rural Development

A significant body of literature has already argued the importance of people's organizations for rural development. However, organizing rural people has not always been an easy task. Many organizations malfunction and then dissolve within a short period. The respective governments and other development agents, then, have to focus their attention on the formed organizations, or resume creating new organizations. This is not to say that rural people have been unorganized. Rather, they formed traditional organizations, such as labor exchange groups and mutual financing associations, for their economic survival. Such traditional types of organizations, however, cannot cope with the changes brought on by economic development.

Now, the scale of each villager's economic activity is growing, and economic transaction among farmers and traders happens more frequently. Competition for economic survival becomes more and more serious. Under these circumstances, people form new types of rural organizations in order to secure more resources than those secured through traditional organizations or individualistic methods, such as market transactions. People become more conscious about calculating the cost and benefit in their participation to the organization. Then they closely watch on the management of organizations. Now the managerial capability that benefits the organization, as well as the formalized management system that realizes fair resource distribution among the members, is indispensable. With this in mind, it is no easy task for the governmental and non-governmental development agencies to form and sustain rural organizations.

We focus on the endogenous and sustainable system of people's self-organizing because it reduces the administrative cost associated with starting organizations and creates more effective organizations. The endogenous mechanism is necessary because it induces people's spontaneous efforts to organize themselves. The sustainable mechanism here means not only that organizations have staying power but also there is a built in mechanism, for managing and adapting to the environmental change, even to the extent disbanding and starting from scratch. The endogenous and sustainable system for self-organizing implies that local people are able to mobilize resources both inside and outside their locality and combine them to meet their needs.

However, even before rural people are organized into development organizations, they have already been members of other types of local organizations. For example, they may belong to neighborhood organizations, consanguineous groups, and village communities. At the same time, they belong to a local administrative organization. These organizations are not narrow in scope, but rather serve as a social instrument for maintaining peace and order among local people, as well as facilitating the people's efforts for making their organizations.

Importance of Communal Organizations

Communal organizations are important for making development organizations because of the following reasons:

- Communal organizations can be organizers of development organizations. The endogenous process of organizing does not start without an endogenous organizer. Even though an outsider initiates the project, there needs to be a group of people to contact for the initial organizing process. Communal organizations, if necessary, scrap and remodel development organizations.
- Communal organizations may have institutions that guide local people's behaviors for collective action. Development organizations bring economic benefit for the members only after they successfully cooperate with each other. They must have, in advance, tools to control each other's conducts. Such a social system may enhance the stability of development organizations.

There are two types of communal organizations. One is endogenously formed organizations or groups, in other words, social organizations. The other is exogenously formed organizations, such as local administrative bodies. Both of them have institutions of guiding the members' behaviors. While those of the former are informal and traditional, the latter has formal system backed by the state's authority. It is not new to stress the importance of social background in making rural organizations. Most researchers, however, place more importance on the endogenous communal organizations. This is reasonable to some extent because development organizations formed by local administrative bodies have often failed to show good performance. However, the government cannot contact local people without local administrative bodies. The governmental effort for rural development should not be undervalued since it provides more resources for a wider area than other development agencies like NGOs.

Based on the above conceptualization, it intends to discuss the following issues:

- The features of communal organizations in each locality determine the adequate form and the feasible method for forming development organizations. This does not mean the communal organization is only the determinant factor.
- The features of social organizations and local administrative bodies determine the uniqueness of communal organizations in each locality. This does not mean only the individual features of each organization but also the combination of the two organizations.

The following discussion will use micro-finance organizations (MFOs) as the example of development organizations.

Micro-finance Organizations as Development Organizations

In Thailand, the dominant form of MFO is the savings group. This is an MFO that pools the members' funds and makes loans to some of the members (*pool-and-distribution type*). This organization, which invariably has a considerable number of members, 80 on average, relies on the collective consent of members for controlling each other's conducts (*cooperative type*). The leaders of the village community, especially in the case of the northeast region, organize and manage this organization. The role of outside agencies is limited to bringing ideas of organization and information about management methodology.

In the Philippines, especially its Central and Southern Luzon areas, NGOs tend to apply Grameen Bank replicas for their rural finance program. In this form of MFO, the fund is provided by the outside development agencies (*receiver type*). Local people are asked to form small groups, generally around five members. This implies that every member has very close mutual relationships, which serves as social pressure for securing loan repayment to the fund provider (*peer group type*). Outside agents play crucial roles not only in providing loan but also in organizing people and supervising each group.

In Indonesia, especially in Central and East Java, NGOs tend to promote "self-help groups" (SHG) with around 20-30 members, and provide funds for loans to the group (*receiver type*). Since its membership is larger than the Grameen group, it relies on collective consent beyond personal relationships to regulate the members' behavior (*cooperative type*). NGOs do not believe that local administrative bodies can be the organizer of these types of MFOs. However, at the same time, the administrative village (*desa*) shows their capability by managing a bank called *Bank Desa* (BD) for many decades. The fund for loan is owned by the organization itself (*internal common resource type*). The villagers access the fund as customers rather than as organization members. Therefore, the organization relies on formal authority backed by regulations rather than on mutual consent for cooperation for controlling people's behaviors (*bank type*).

Comparison of Micro-finance Organizations

Why does such a contrast happen? The following discussion illustrates the structure of communal organizations that defines the uniqueness of each MFO.

Thailand

In rural Thailand, the savings group is the dominant form of MFO. The governmental agencies, as well as the NGOs, usually expect village leaders to organize villagers by themselves. It is not typical that outside agencies provide funds for this MFO; rather, they offer only ideas and some technical instructions on how to have better management.

1. Local Administrative System in Rural Areas

Administrative levels down to the district are part of the central government administration.

		Major Institution for Controlling Members' Behavior			Name of Each Type
		Law and/or State's Authority	Collective Consent	Dyadic Social Relationship	
Main Source of Funds	Organization	Bank Desa (Indonesia)			Internal Common Resource Type
	Each Member		Savings Group (Thailand)		Pool and Distribution Type
	Outside Agencies		SHG (Indonesia)	Grameen Group (Philippines)	Receiver Type
	Name of Each Type	Bank Type	Cooperative Type	Peer Group Type	

Figure 1. Comparison of Micro-finance Organizations

As the basic unit of village autonomy under the local administrative system, a *muban* exhibits two major characteristics. One is that priority is given to demarcating *mubans* by the geographical conglomeration of their residents. Since introducing the *muban* as the local administrative unit in early 20th century, the government has designated spontaneously unified settlements of people into a *muban* as much as possible. The size of a *muban* is based on the range over which people can maintain their acquaintanceship. Another major characteristic is that village headmen have traditionally been selected from villagers by the villagers themselves. Thus village headmen elections reflect the social relationships of the villagers themselves. Administrative villages in Thailand have thus been formed for the most part by taking into consideration the unity and social relationships of the village residents themselves.

In contrast to *mubans, tambons* had little function of self-governance until 1994. One *tambon* consists of more than 1,000 households and 6,000 people on average, making it difficult for the residents to have face-to-face relationships over the village boundaries. Also, *tambons* did not have any regular budget for administration. Since there are *mubans* as official units of local administration under each *tambon*, the governmental projects are mostly implemented by the *mubans*. As a result, the *tambon* used to be just a "pipeline" through which the resources from the government went to each *muban*. However, since 1994, many *tambons* have been converted to *Tambon* Administrative Organizations (TAOs) that have their own budget, assembly and regular staffs. This reform was crucial because it has created a new communal structure for organizing local people in development projects.

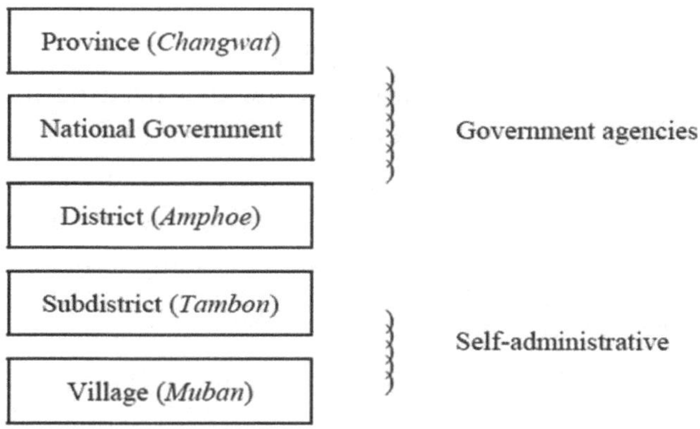

Figure 2. Local Administrative Hierarchy in Thailand (Rural)

2. Structure and Functions of Village Community

The feature of an endogenous village community in Northeastern Thailand can be illustrated as follows. Nearly every village settlement, generally a clustered shape, has its own shrine of a guardian spirit for protecting the entire settlement from the evil spirits that were believed to inhabit the surrounding forest. In order to protect the entire village, the villagers must accept their common responsibility as residents and define who should enjoy the collective protection. Through such traditional beliefs and rituals, people have created a sense of "we-feeling" at this indigenous village level. Furthermore, the indigenous village becomes the unit for a number of collective activities. The most popular ones are those related to Buddhist temples in the village. In order to construct and maintain temple facilities and to have festivals, villagers organize themselves to gather and manage resources (materials, money and labor) at certain intervals. Villagers sometimes organize collective activities around utilizing common natural resources such as swamps as well. Through such common resource management, villagers have been expanding their capability to engage in collective actions.

As mentioned already, the administrative village has generally been formed in indigenous village in Northeastern Thailand. This means that the villagers commonly have two institutions for organizing themselves: the administrative village and the indigenous village. As the members of an indigenous village, people have "we-feeling" and have accumulated the experiences of collective activities through temple affairs. On the other hand, they do have formal institutions for collective decision-making, such as village meetings and village development committee. Then, the villagers utilize the institution of administrative village even for organizing activities concerned to indigenous unit, such as temple activities. On the contrary, the administrative unit can mobilize the sense of unity at the indigenous unit.

3. Micro-finance Organizations in Rural Thailand

Historically speaking, the first MFO in Thailand was a credit cooperative promoted by the government in the early 20th century. It was a small organization with less than 20 members, which relied on the funds from the government (receiver type). It failed to show sustainability and efficiency, and thus was replaced by large-scale agricultural cooperatives that were semi-governmental institutions rather than people's organizations. Later, the Bank of Agriculture and Agricultural Cooperatives (BAAC), a government bank for rural finance, started to provide loans directly to individual farmers. However, its loans were confined to agricultural purposes. Because of the complicated procedure of application, many farmers were, and are still today, reluctant to borrow such a small amount of money from BAAC. These limitations of BAAC have allowed informal sources such as moneylenders who require a high rate of interest to be active in the financial market of rural Thailand.

4. Formation of Savings Group

The above-mentioned condition in the rural financial market provides the economic opportunity for creating savings groups (*klum omsap*). The idea of this MFO has been implemented in rural Thailand since the mid-1970s. In this organization, the members deposit their savings together on a regular basis, usually once a month. Members declares the amount of monthly savings they will contribute at their entry and are then obliged to keep this promise (compulsory savings). Then the gathered deposit is lent to the members. The loan rate is, in most cases, 2 percent per month. The profit is shared by the members according to the amount of savings. It requires guarantors instead of collateral, but the loan amount often exceeds the deposit amount of borrower and his/her guarantors. The members are limited to those living in the same locality, mostly in the same village, for the convenience of savings and availability of mutual control. The leaders of the savings group operate all the management.

5. Why are Savings Groups Dominant?

Organizational characteristics of savings groups in rural Thailand can be summarized as follows:

First, as members are mostly poor villagers, the amount of deposit given by each member is consequently very small. Therefore, it is necessary to have a considerable number of members in order to secure economic scale. The average membership of savings groups is more than 80, which is significantly larger than that of credit cooperatives.

Secondly, the organizers are the village leaders. Even though the idea of savings groups is brought by outside agencies in most cases, this organization cannot be established without the villagers' motivation and consensus formation. After the group is founded, the local leaders become the managers of the group. They take responsibility for every aspect of operation, such as receiving deposits, accounting, lending, collecting debt, and distributing profit. The outside agencies can assist, but just to provide advice for better management.

Thirdly, membership is usually limited to the residents of an administrative village (*muban*), especially in the northeastern region. As explained before, people have a sense of unity at the administrative village level because it usually coincides with the indigenous village. It is natural that the people accept the project as their village's project and start recruiting members from within the same village. Another aspect of the *muban* is its formal institution for collective decision-making. It is quite appropriate for the outside agencies, including NGOs, to regard the administrative village as the platform for organizing people.

Table 1. Number and Size of Savings Groups by Region in Thailand (only the group under supervision of Community Development Department, March 1997)

Region	*Number of Groups*	*Percentage to the Total Number of Villages*	*Members per Group (persons)*
Lower North	824	15.9	69
Central	1,035	16.6	78
East	665	15.5	70
West	542	11.9	115
Lower Northeast	3,136	21.6	63
Upper Northeast	2,747	25.1	80
Upper North	940	16.1	108
Upper South	673	17.4	119
Lower South	615	15.8	165
Whole Kingdom	11,177	18.9	85

Source: Community Development Department, Thailand, 1997, pp.5-8.

6. Reformation of Communal Organization for Further Development

Such a structure of communal organization, however, can be an obstacle to the development of savings groups. When a savings group tries to enlarge the sphere of members beyond the village boundary, it has to face the lack of social unity among members. This lack of cohesion may make the organization vulnerable. The issue of size and stability is a central dilemma of savings group. This limitation is rooted in the fact that the *tambon* was not a unit that worked as a communal organization for making development organizations.

However, after the reformation of the *tambon*'s organizational structure in 1994, it now has the assembly of people's representatives, staffs for professional administration, and a budget for supporting development. At the same time, the *muban* still keeps its function of mobilizing people's collective actions. This new setting of local administrative system allows the new *tambon* organization to work as a body for making federations of savings groups at the village level. This new set of communal organizations may break the size-and-stability dilemma of development organizations in rural Thailand.

The Philippines

NGOs in the Philippines tend to apply a "receiver" and "peer group" type MFO for their micro-finance projects. They usually organize local people directly rather than persuade village leaders to do so. This phenomenon stands in clear contrast to the Thai case.

1. Barangay as an Administrative Village

The *barangay* is the local administrative body that directly governs rural people.

The *barangay* as a social unit existed even before the colonial period under Spain. Most of them were small kinship gatherings with 15-100 households in the Luzon inland area. During the colonial regime of Spain, people who sparsely populated rural area were gathered into a *pueblo*, the terminal unit of local administration with about 500 households of residents. A quarter of those residents was called the *barrio* and regarded as the town subdivision of the *pueblo*. Each *barrio* had a *barrio* lieutenant who was assigned by the provincial governor. Later, those who had been forced to live in a *pueblo* gradually moved away from the township and formed a kind of "breakaway *barangay*". The priest of church in the *pueblo* did not neglect these people in the new settlements and started to visit them regularly.

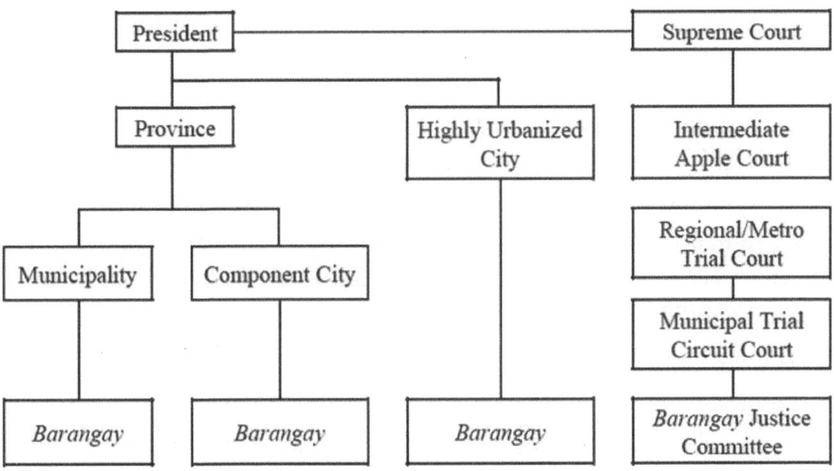

Figure 3. Local Administration Ladder of the Philippines

Later, a small chapel was built in the settlements. In this way, the *barrio* became an administrative unit in the rural area. Now, the *pueblo* is called municipality, while the *barrio* has been renamed *barangay*.

This system was in effect for the post-independent period. However, the role of the *barangay* has been changing in the following three ways: firstly, the government has been increasing resources allocated to the *barangay*, since it is considered the body for implementing rural development policy. Secondly, the *barangay* receives more authorities to govern its residents. Each *barangay* has its council for making decisions on its own matters. The residents directly elected the councilmen and the village headman, or *Barangay* Captain. By *Barrio* Charter enacted in 1960, the *barrio* became a legal body and gained the authority to collect taxes by itself. President Marcos promoted the *barangay*'s authority and utilized it for his own political purposes.

Thirdly, the procedure of administration has been highly formalized. *Barangay* council enacted the *barangay* ordinances to control or coordinate the residents' conducts. *Barangay* justice was formed to exercise jurisdiction to some extent. The method for implementing such authority is also regulated by law. For example, the law specifies that the *barangay* ordinance should be discussed in three readings of the *barangay* council, and outlines what should be done in each reading. There are several thick manuals on the procedure of the *barangay* administration published for the village leaders.

2. Structure of Social Organizations

The average population size of a *barangay* in Central Luzon and Southern Tagalog region was around 2,000 persons, or 320 households, in 1995. This is more than twice the size of a *muban* in Thailand. A *barangay* tends to keep its boundary regardless of population increase once it is established. From 1980 to 1996, the number of *barangays* increased only 5 percent. Consequently, it is not rare to find thousands of households in a *barangay* in Central and Southern Luzon. In the large *barangays*, the social relationship among the residents has become loose.

Each *barangay* has chapels. People recognize them as belonging to the village. People also organize a fiesta, an annual festival for worshiping the patron saint of the village. However, the chapel does not have its priest living in the village, and villagers' contribution to the chapel is largely limited to once a year, the time of fiesta. Even though there is a patron saint that is assumed to protect the entire village, there is no ritual that connects the existence of the patron saint to the fate of the entire village. The sense of protection by the patron saint is weak among villagers nowadays.

The *barangay* has few communal resources. Its popular assets are *barangay* halls, healthcare centers, daycare centers, and basketball courts. These do not require many maintenance activities collectively organized by villagers. A sense of communal holding of these assets is weak, too.

In this way, the sense of collectivity among the villagers of a *barangay* is weaker than that of a northeastern Thai village. This does not mean that a cooperative spirit is lacking in Filipino villagers, but that it appears in different manner. Valsan and Hayami and Kikuchi find cooperative actions between dyadicly related people and within small groups. Abueva describes such Philippine communities as "individualistic and unorganized" and "their primary attachments and loyalties are to their nuclear family, their kins and neighbors". Jocano writes "outside of the family, the neighborhood is the only larger social unit which provides the venue for local affairs". Jocano analyzes further that "neighborhood" in the villagers' sense does not necessarily mean a geographical sphere but rather closeness in terms of human relationship. With such close human relationships between two people, cooperative actions are smoothly organized in rural Philippines.

3. Micro-finance Organizations in Rural Philippines

The Government of the Philippines has always promoted some form of cooperative in the rural area. The first serious attempt was to create Farmers Cooperative Marketing Associations, large cooperatives that had an average of 582 members in 1957. There was no mutual control working among the members and there were serious financial problems – four-fifths of cooperatives were operating at a loss and two-thirds had arrears in 1959.

The second attempt was establishing *Samahang Nayon* (SN) during Marcos' regime. SN was formed at the *barangay* level with the membership no more than 200 persons. The funds were gathered from its members. These "pool-and-distribution type" MFOs, however, could not become self-reliant cooperatives in most cases. The failure of these cooperatives does not mean that there was no economic need for micro-finance activities. Rather, moneylenders are still active in the rural Philippines. After the liberalization of the financial market in the late 1980s, credit cooperatives and Grameen Bank replicas are popular forms of MFOs in rural Philippines.

Grameen Bank is a micro-finance program that originated in Bangladesh in order to provide small loans to the local poor without requiring collateral or charging high-rate interest. People are instructed to create a five-member group that takes joint responsibility for the repayment of the loan provided by the outside fund source. The dominance of Grameen-type organizations in the Philippines stands in good contrast to the other two countries.

4. Micro-finance Organizations under NGOs Projects

As for the situation of NGOs' MFOs, the Philippine Coalition for Microfinance Standards (PCMS) has surveyed 223 organizations among all 300 NGOs running micro-finance activities in 1997. The survey showed that most of the NGOs let people organize small groups of less than 10 members. It is infeasible for such a small organization to rely on their own funds for lending activities. Among the 36 active NGOs surveyed in detail by PCMS, 18 NGOs used group-lending methods, and 13 of them applied a Grameen Bank-like system. This data indicates that most of the people's organizations supported by NGOs in the Philippines are receiver and peer group types, especially Grameen bank replicas.

Table 2. Distribution of group Size of the Micro-finance Programs of the NGOs

Size of the Group	*Number*	*Rural-based Groups*
1- 9	38	23
10-24	24	19
25-49	15	12
Over 50	3	3
Total	***80***	***57***

Source: Survey questionnaire for the inventory of the NGOs in savings and credit.

Similar to the Grameen Bank in Bangladesh, those NGOs let local people form a group of around five members. The NGOs provide training to enhance norms of members before lending. Then, the NGOs provide loans to one of the members under the condition that the group takes responsibility of repayment. The borrower pays back the principle with its interest according to the weekly repayment plan. The NGO worker comes up every week to collect the repayment and closely monitor the performance of each group. The mutual control among small groups of people, together with the close supervision of an outside agency (NGO), is crucial for the success of this MFO.

5. Why is Grameen-type Dominant?

The Grameen Bank model, the popular type of NGO-supporting MFO, was introduced into the Philippines after unsuccessful attempts by other types of MFOs. For example, CARD (Center for Agricultural and Rural Development), before it was one of the initiators of the Grameen-type system, formed an association of about 45 landless workers in each target *barangay* and provided loans to the association. However, CARD faced delinquency problems eight months after implementing the project, because the group size was too big for the leaders to control members' conduct.

Then, it applied a Grameen system. It is successful in the Philippines because, according to CARD, the group size is small enough for people to control each other.

Such experiences have important implications. It suggests that a small group of five members can utilize social relationships to foster mutual control among members. In the Grameen system, local people choose their neighbors with whom they have close relationships as the members of the same group. As mentioned before, cooperative actions in Philippine rural society are possible along dyadic relationships rather than in a collectively organized group. Therefore, if the group size is as small as five or so, all the members may be interwoven by dyadic cordial relationships. In other words, NGOs understand how to utilize these close social relationships among rural people in order to create a successful MFO.

When NGOs try to organize people, they tend to bypass the *barangay*. Initially, they send their workers to the *barangay* captain and ask him/her to call a meeting about their project. The NGO explains their project to the attendants and persuades people to form a group. When the NGO identifies those who intend to join the program, they investigate whether each applicant satisfies the conditions of program. After the training course, the NGO formally admits the membership and lets them submit applications for loans. The NGO provides loans only after the application is approved. In this process, the role of the *barangay* captain is simply to call a village meeting; thus, the NGO, not the *barangay* captain, is the organizer of local people.

The *barangay* cannot be utilized for organizing people for the following reasons: Firstly, since many *barangays* in central and southern Luzon area are big as 400 households or more, the social relationships among the villagers are becoming loose. Secondly, local people have not formed any sense of unity at the village level. The *barangay* as a local administrative body was historically formed by the rulers' needs rather than local people's necessity for self-governance. It lacks an endogenous institution that fosters a sense of unity at the village level.

Indonesia

Indonesian NGOs tend to promote small membership, around 20-30, for their micro-finance projects. They do not expect local administrative bodies to be the organizer, but instead rely on social organizations as the platform of MFOs. However, the administrative village (*desa*) shows that it is capable of managing the village bank that is not seen in the other two countries. This contradictory phenomenon represents the uniqueness of the Indonesian case.

1. Desa and Village-level Local Administration

The *desa* and the units under *desa* are local units administered by a representative of local people, while the other administrative bodies are the agencies of national and regional government. Since the candidates for *desa* chief are screened by local government before the election by the local people, those who are unfavorable for the government cannot be the chiefs. The chief of *dusun* is nominated by the *desa* chief and designated by district chief. However, it is impossible to neglect local people's view for appointing a *dusun* chief, since his/her duties are closely related to the daily life of local people. The chief of lower units under *dusun*, *Rukun Tetangga* (RT, neighborhood group) and *Rukun Warga* (RT, communal group; RW is a collection of several RTs), are decided through the consultation between the residents. Therefore, even though the *desa* is regarded as the local government in rural areas, the government maintains the system of intervention about the assignment of *desa* chief, who has strong authority about the assignment of leaders in the lower units for administration.

Each *desa* has its own budget. In the provinces of Java, it secures 70 percent of its total revenue from internal sources, which comes mostly from communal land and various kinds of fees (Kano, 1987). Besides land, *desas* have healthcare centers, a *desa* hall and the other resources. In this way, *desa* is not just an agent of central government but also an autonomous body with its own resources. The administrative units under the *desa* have no such autonomous budget or assets except a communal cemetery. Although officially the *desa* has no judicial authority, it is not uncommon for villagers to unofficially sanction those who violate the peace and order of the locality.

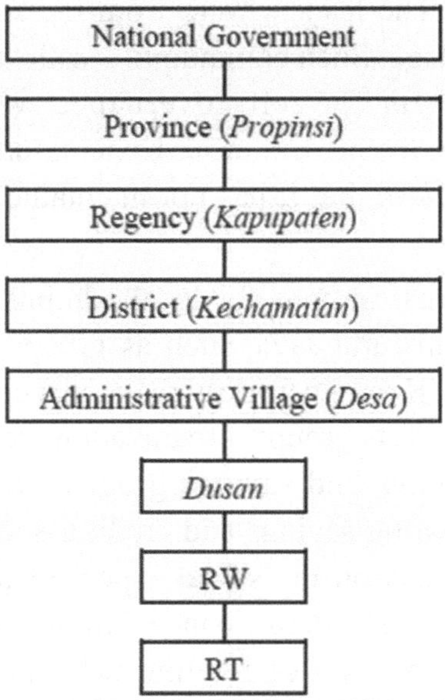

Figure 4. Structure of Local Administration in Rural Indonesia

In the administrative units under the *desa,* some collective activities called "*gotong royong*" are organized among the residents. It is commonly practiced for night-watch rotation (*ronda*) and infrastructure maintenance by the chief of the *dusun* or RT. If there is a dispute related to the land, the *desa* chief will be the arbitrator. The *dusun* chief usually deals with other disputes.

2. Endogenous Social Organizations in Rural Java

According to Kishi, there used to be an indigenous unit of settlement, called "*desa*" in the colonial Java. This was a community that worshiped a village spirit and had communal lands. However, during late 19th century and early 20th century, the Dutch consolidated these *desas* into new and larger *desas* as administrative villages. A 1906 law transferred the communal properties of the indigenous villages transferred to the new administrative villages. Therefore, the present *desa* is not originated in indigenous community. Kano has compared the historical records of Central Java in 1846 with his field survey results of 1987, and found that the villages with less than 100 households in 1846 have become five times larger in 1987. Kano also shows that all of the land in two villages surveyed in a Central Java land title survey in 1860s was communal land. At the same time, the villages in earlier years had a shrine for worshiping the village ancestor, village festivals, and a sense of unity as a village. The leaders were from the kinsmen of early settlers who governed the village. Such communities with "we-feeling", communal resources and a system for self-governance were integrated into an administrative village, the present *desa*. Kano assumes that the *dusun* used to be the indigenous *desa*, but it has not maintained the social unity as its population increased.

Besides these organizations for local administration, there are many social organizations in rural Java, such as groups for literacy education, groups for reading the Koran, cemetery maintenance organizations, singers' groups, dance clubs, sports groups, organizations related to mosques, *zakat* (donation) organizations, and savings groups. Nearly every village has *arisan*s (a kind of rotating savings and credit associations. People in rural Java put much emphasis on the social aspect of *arisan*. *Simpan-pinjam*, another type of traditional micro-finance activity also has social function since its deposits are spent for celebrating Lebaran, the end of Ramadan.

3. Micro-finance Organizations in Rural Indonesia

The government of Indonesia established many cooperatives under the Cooperative Act of 1958. However, in 1967, three-fourths of them were dissolved under Suharto's New Order and village unit cooperative was newly introduced. KUD, in spite of its name, does not stand at the *desa* level, but at the *kechamatan* (district). Therefore, this cooperative does not rely on any communal organizations from the beginning. KUD took a strategic role in the *Bimas* program for promoting the green revolution, but the rate of arrears was around 50 percent in 1983.

Currently, people in rural Indonesia cannot access soft loans if they do not have collateral, generally land ownership. As Mizuno argues in detail, most of the land in rural Java is left without a land title. Informal moneylenders do not require collateral, but charge a high rate of interest, sometimes 25 percent a month. This may be one reason that people have formed traditional mutual loan and savings groups such as *arisan* and *simpan-pinjam*. However, as mentioned already, these organizations do not seek continuous fund accumulation. In case of *arisan*, the members cannot calculate when he or she will get the loan, because they decide a loan receiver by drawing lots. Consequently, there is still an economic opportunity for MFOs that support economic development of local people.

4. Small Group Formation by NGOs

NGOs in Indonesia place importance on forming small groups of local people as MFOs. One group has around 20-30 members, which, in most cases, is larger than the Grameen-type groups in the Philippines and smaller than the savings group in Thailand. For example, Bina Swadaya, one of the largest rural development NGOs in Indonesia, has been encouraging local people to form SHGs for micro-finance since 1988. In this project, Bina Swadaya borrows money from commercial banks and re-lends it to SHGs. According to Bina Swadaya, there are many social organizations, including *arisan* and *simpan-pinjam*, indigenously formed by local people. Bina Swadaya assesses these social groups and then "short-lists" them as the beneficiaries of its loan program. Bina Swadaya tends to choose the groups with membership of 15-25 people. Since most *arisans* have 10-30 members, Bina Swadaya seems to follow the size that people indigenously regard as adequate.

Bina Desa, another active rural development NGO, also encouraged villagers to form SHGs of 20-25 members and provided some funds to the group for financing activities. Bina Desa contacted informal leaders of localities, not the *desa* administration, to organize local people. These leaders talked about the economic problems of villagers on the occasion of *Majelis taklim* (a meeting for religious activities of Islam) and persuaded villagers to form a group for economic activity.

5. Desa Bank

Even though NGOs bypass the *desa* for organizing local people, many *desas* in Central and East Java have been managing a bank-type MFO called Bank Desa for a long time. It was established in 1908 with initial capital from *lumbung desa* (*desa*'s rice bank) or BRI (Bank Rakyat Indonesia), a government bank focusing on rural finance.

Up to the present, the *desa* has been the unit of BD. The *desa* chief is the first commissioner and he/she assigns two other commissioners from the villagers. BD has a professional accountant called JTU (*juru tata usaha*). The salary of commissions and JTU are calculated from the loan outstanding of BD and paid from the profit of BD. BRI's local branch recruits JTU.

Loan disbursement and collection of BD are carried out as follows: Once a week, BD opens its office. The JTU visits the *desa* and works for loan disbursement and debt collection with the commissioners. The interest rate was 3-4 percent per month with a repayment period of 3-4 months.

There is no need for customers to prepare collateral or guarantors. Every villager of the *desa* can be the applicant of the loan at the BD. The commissioners know the customers well, so that the procedure for lending is very simple, which attracts local people. Therefore, this is a "bank type" organization and local people are customers rather than the members of organization even though the beneficiaries are limited to the residents of that village.

According to BRI's statistics, more than 60 percent of the loan is repaid without delay. If including the amount of "still possible to repay", more than 70 percent is expected to be collected. It is considerably higher than the repayment rate of KUD loans in the *Bimas* program.

6. Communal Organizations behind the Two Contrastive MFOs

Why is the BD successful? As previously mentioned, BD can collect more than 70 percent of the loan. This is possible because the commissioners, especially the *desa* chief, have motivation and authority to secure repayment. Since the fund of BD is a common property of *desa*, its chief has more incentive to collect the money compared with the money from the outside. Moreover, 20 percent of BD's profit is sent to *desa*'s general budget. At the same time, the *desa* chief has authority backed by the state.

The JTU also plays a crucial role for the sustainability of BD. JTUs have high educational background and receive training for professional accounting skills at BRI. JTU is not hired by *desa*, which makes its position independent from the *desa* chief. This prevents collusion between a JTU and the *desa* chief related to accounting.

On the contrary, SHGs rely on social organizations, including *arisan* and *simpan-pinjam*. They are organizations with collective consent and clear membership, and mostly consist of 20-30 members. Moreover, there are many informal leaders in rural Java, such as religious leaders of Islam. The richness of social organizations in rural Java is illustrated by the fact that Bina Swadaya had to "shortlist" indigenous groups to form SHG.

However, the *desa* administration fails to mobilize such capability of local people. Rather, its capability is shown in managing a bank-type organization and controlling its villagers' conduct as the customers. Its subunits like *dusun* and RT also lack institutions to facilitate people's self-organizing actions. That is why NGOs do not intend to utilize formal local administrative systems, but informal social organizations. It seems that there is a mismatch between endogenous and exogenous systems for organizing local people in rural Java.

Policy Implications for Making Rural Organizations

This summarized empirical study has the following policy implications for installing an endogenous and sustainable system of people's self-organizing.

Even if the savings group is successfully operated in Thailand, this organization should not be introduced into an area like the rural Philippines that has no locality-based community. Additionally, Grameen type organizations are not the efficient model in areas like Java and Northeast Thailand where the larger size of collectively bound group is easily formed. As for the method of organizing, the administrative village plays a key role in Northeast Thailand, while informal social groups and social relationships should be focused as the initiator of organizing in the other two areas. There is a suitable form of MFO according to the structure of communal organization in each locality.

Therefore, it is indispensable to know what kind of functions each organization has and how they are combined with each other.

The following three factors are required for communal organizations that may work as a facilitator of creating development organizations.

- First is a sense of unity among local people. In other words, have to know in which sphere or group of people with whom they feel most comfortable to get together. Axelrod has also proved, by using game theory, that if a certain group of people shares a sense of affiliation, they develop cooperation.
- The second factor is the institution of collective decision-making, or the institution for manifesting each one's needs and coordinate them as a common target. Without such institutions, the organizational process may not proceed smoothly.
- The third element is the institution of enforcement. People cannot feel sure about the rewards of organization, unless there is a system for policing deviations of members.

Lastly, if can find no adequate communal organization, should consider the reformation of the local administrative system. For example, the reformation of subdistrict level administration (*tambon*) in Thailand has provided wider opportunities to change *tambon* to a communal organization for expanding savings groups beyond the boundary of *muban* without sacrificing its stability. The mismatch of formal and informal local organizations in rural Java suggests a need for reformation of the local administrative system. At any rate, the designers of local administrative system should take account whether the design installs a mechanism of facilitating endogenous and sustainable efforts of local residents for development.

References

Abueva, Jose V., (1969). "Local Government, Community Development, and Political Stability", in J. V. Abueva and Raul P. de Guzman (eds.) *Foundations and Dynamics of Filipino Government and Politics*, pp.468-475, Bookmark, Manila

Shigetomi, Shinichi, (1998). *Cooperation and Community in Rural Thailand: An Organizational Analysis of Participatory Rural Development*, Institute of Developing Economies, Tokyo

Soemardjan, Selo and Kenon Breaseale, (1993). *Cultural Change in Rural Indonesia: Impact of Village Development*, Sebelas Maret University Press, Surakarta

Valsan, E. H., (1970). *Community Development Programs and Rural Local Development: Comparative Case Studies of India and the Philippines*, Praeger Publications, New York.

6

Participatory Rural Development in Bangladesh

Bangladesh is bounded by India on the west, the north, and the northeast and Myanmar on the southeast and the Bay of Bengal on the south. The area of the country is 56,977 miles or 1,47,570 km. Except the hilly regions in the northeast and the southeast, some areas of highlands in the north and northwestern part, the country consists of low, flat and fertile land. A network of rivers of which the Padma, the Jamuna, the Teesta, the Brahmaputra, the Surma, the Meghna, and the Karnaphuli are important, and their tributaries numbering about 230 with a total length of about 24,140 km covering the country flow down to the Bay of Bengal. Heavy silts deposited by rivers during the rainy season are thus continuously enriching the alluvial soil.

Administrative Structure

The territory constituting Bangladesh was under the Muslim rule for over five and a half centuries from 1201 to 1757 A.D. Subsequently, it was under the subjugation of the British after the defeat of the last sovereign ruler, Nawab Sirajuddowla in 1757. The British ruled over the entire Indian subcontinent including this territory for nearly 190 years from 1757 to 1947. During that period Bangladesh was a part of the British Indian province of Bengal and Assam. With the termination of British Role in August 1947 the subcontinent divided into India and Pakistan. Bangladesh was then a part of Pakistan. It appeared on the world map as an independent and sovereign state on 16 December 1971 following the victory at the War of Liberation from 25 March to 16 December 1971.

A parliamentary system of government headed by Prime Minister is responsible to run the country. The Prime Minister is assisted by a council of ministers. A minister heads each ministry. A civil servant designated as secretary who is a permanent secretary of the government assists the minister. Under each ministry, there are subordinate bodies like director, etc. which are responsible for the execution of the government policies.

For administrative purpose, the country is divided into six divisions; Divisional Commissioner who belongs to the civil service and who acts for the Central Government heads each division. There are other divisional officers under various line ministries who are to implement the plan and programs of the respective ministries.

There are 64 districts under the six divisions. To administer all development activities of the district, the Deputy Commissioner acts as the coordinator of all departments functioning in a particular district. He also exercises the authority of the Central Government. There are other district level officers also in the district of the line ministries who are responsible for implementing plans and programs of the respective ministries.

The district is again divided into a number of *Upazillas* and *Thanas*. At present there are 496 *upazillas* and *thanas* of which 36 are in metropolitan cities and 4,451 union *parishads*, which are all in the rural areas. Under control of district administration, *Upazilla Nirbahi* officer who also belongs to the civil service heads *upazilla* level administration. Other officers of the line ministries are posted in the *thana* level to implement plans and programs of the respective ministries.

For convenience to form local level government institutions, each *thana* is subdivided into a number of unions and then again into villages. Local government bodies in cities and urban areas are called City Corporation Municipality or *Pourashava*, respectively. Of late, there are four city corporations and 127 municipalities in the country. The local government institutions like *zilla parishad, upazilla parishad*, union *parishad*, municipalities and the city corporations are run by the public representatives elected direct election and these local institutions are autonomous.

This hierarchical arrangement is illustrated in Figure 1 below:

Ministry

↓

Divisions

↓

Districts

↓

Upazilla Union

↓

Parishad

Figure 1. Hierarchy of Government Institutions

Rural Development in Bangladesh

Community development means an improvement in the quality of life of the country people. It includes the process of development of both economic and social sectors. In Bangladesh more than 77 percent people live in the rural areas. Most of the rural people are poor and living below the poverty line. For example, if the level of nutritional intake is taken as the indicator, 69 percent of the population falls below the line. So rural development has become the focal point for all development efforts in Bangladesh.

The rural area of Bangladesh has villages as its lower unit. The village inhabitants include rural farmers, fishermen, weavers, blacksmiths, artisans, traders, laborers, etc. Therefore, in order to upgrade the rural lifestyle of such people, programs have been implemented to promote economic growth and social progress, to create employment, to raise income level of the rural poor, etc.

Rural development is a multi-disciplined slow achievement program requiring multi-sectoral intervention. All national organizations, NGOs and other community-based organizations are required to take intra-organizational coordinated activities. The first institutional intervention in rural development was made in 1904 when Cooperative Credit Societies (CCS) were introduced. Subsequently, "union-based multipurpose cooperatives" were introduced in 1954 by the name "Village Agriculture and Industrial Development (V-AID) program. Later on "Commilla Approach Cooperatives" program was introduced in 1961, where the village-based agricultural cooperatives were linked with *upazilla* (subdistrict) central cooperatives. Again to address the landless, women and the poor, "Comprehensive Rural Development Program" was launched to reduce rural poverty through participation of rural poor in production and proper distribution of income and resources.

The importance of providing community participation was underlined in the Fifth Five-Year Plan (1997-2002) both within local government institutions and through local institution building. The objectives of rural development include poverty eradication, creation of employment, income generation, expansion of productive sectors, development of rural institutions like formal cooperatives and informal groups, improvement of basic physical infrastructure in rural areas, facilitate agricultural development and promote participation of women in rural development, etc.

In the development process, participatory local level planning is essential. Bottom-up decision-making process should be emphasized and the coordination between the local level organizations is essential. It is felt that effective peoples participation in decision-making and implementation process is essential for development. So a bottom-up participatory process with emphasis on local level initiative was encouraged under Fifth Five-Year Plan for socio-economic development in Bangladesh.

Rural Development Policies and Programs

Rural development means an improvement in the quality of life of the rural people. It includes the process of development of both economic and social sectors. The economic aspect refers to infrastructure, production, employment and income generation and the social aspect refers to education, health, sanitation, family planning, etc. So, rural development is not confined to one activity, it is a package of economic and social activities with the ultimate object of upgrading the living condition of the rural poor.

The projects sponsored by the government and other agencies have the components mainly with the object of rural development of the country such as infrastructure development, agricultural development, para-agricultural activities, agricultural marketing, non-farm income generation activities, health and nutrition, rural institutions and human resource development.

Poverty being the most pressing problem in the rural areas of Bangladesh, for a rural development plan to be meaningful, it must continue to effectively address the problem of poverty. For this, the Fourth Five-Year

Plan pursued an "employment-led" growth policy. The focus of the policy was to promote greater opportunities for the rural poor for productive employment in both farm and non-farm sectors of the economy. Keeping alleviation of rural poverty as the end in view, the objectives of the plan of the rural development and institutions sector was to:

i. reduce rural poverty by means of increasing gainful employment and income opportunities on a sustained basis through expansion of the productive sectors;
ii. develop rural institutions;
iii. improve technology and skills for productive activities and ensure better access of the rural poor to the means of production;
iv. facilitate agricultural development through institutional support and expansion of irrigation;
v. improve basic physical infrastructure (roads, markets) in the rural areas; and
vi. promote participation of women in rural development.

Small Group Approach

In Bangladesh about 80 percent of the total population live in the rural areas. The rural economy is characterized by low productivity, subsistence agriculture, unemployment and high rate of population growth. From this national point of view, development of agriculture in Bangladesh is of paramount importance. About 85 percent of the total population directly or indirectly depended on agriculture for their livelihood, it accounts for 58-60 percent of the GNP and constitute more than 50 percent labor force. But paradoxically, it is a fact that more than 40 percent of the total work force is unemployed. This situation is due to the outcome of excessive dependence on agriculture, which ultimately creates an inactive atmosphere in other professional groups of the country. Hence diversification of rural economy to ensure optimum utilization of domestic resources and simultaneous improvements in agricultural productivity can invigorate the country's economy for absorbing the vast unemployed labor force of the country. This necessitates creating an atmosphere of spontaneous involvement of the common people with a maximum extent of effective mass participation by all professional groups. This in turn would be possible by mobilizing the resources of the nation through small groups.

Moreover, in Bangladesh, there are wide scopes for the rural women to contribute to rural development by the following field of activities:

> Bamboo, cane, wood works, mat making, paddy pulse making, goat fathering or raising, tailoring, kitchen gardening, sewing and embroidery, bee keeping, poultry and duck raring and other handicrafts, sericulture, pisciculture, weaving, sanitation, health care and family planning.

Also, in the rural areas by forming small occupational group like youth, farmers, porter, smiths, plumber, cobblers, carpenters, weavers, fishermen, small traders, the following activities can be performed for income generation and self-employment:

> Pond fishing, nursery plantation, kitchen gardening, tailoring, wood carpeting, blacksmithing, weaving, cattle, fish and poultry raising, social aforestration, small trading, fruit cultivation, milks cow, bee keeping, umbrella mending, rickshaw van, bull-cart weeding, missionary, and embroidery.

Organizations working for rural development in Bangladesh mostly operate through small groups. Government departments, autonomous bodies, NGOs and cooperatives are involved in small group activities. There are some commonalties in the operation of the groups. There is, however, a marked divergence in the nature of their programs, formation of groups or in organizing the group activities.

Central Planning Process

The Planning Commission of the Planning Ministry regulates all development plans of the government. The Planning Commission is responsible for approving and implementing the development projects. In spite of that, the Parliament is the highest authority for different development project. The National Parliament decides the direction of the total development process.

The implementing authority of the development project submits the project proposal in the form of PCP through respective ministers to the Planning Division. The Planning Division scrutinizes the proposal and places it before pre-ECNEC. The proposal, which has to be considered viable, placed for consideration and approval to the ECNEC. After approval, the proposal comes back to the respective ministry where a "Project Performa" (PP) is prepared. The implementing agency implements the project according to the PP. The PCP directs the location and the beneficiaries of the project. Thus a link has been established between Central Government and the village level.

In the local level planning, the objective of a particular project is determined by the beneficiaries by means of a base-line survey. Usually, local level planning is formulated through participatory methods, implying bottom-up planning. In most cases, bottom-up planning process has been encouraged by the government.

Besides government plans and programs, the number of NGOs are involved in the development process. They are engaged in the activities for socio-economic upliftment of the rural poor. The donors support the NGOs to supplement the government's delivery system to reach the poor and to play a more creative role. Some of these NGOs are very effective in terms of both beneficiary coverage and investment and, they have the ability to reach the poor and address the issues of poverty alleviation. Some of the prominent NGOs are Bangladesh Rural Advancement Committee (BRAC), Proshika, and Association for Social Advancement (ASA).

A number of state-run commercial banks have also been participated in poverty alleviation programs through providing micro-credit to the landless and small farmers. Likewise, Grameen Bank has so far disbursed Tk.72.45 billion to a total number of beneficiaries over two million peoples.

Rural Development Agencies

1. Department of Cooperatives

Department of Cooperatives (DOC) is the pioneer organization working in the rural areas for over a century. Before independence, the DOC was the only organization working on community basis. The DOC implemented *Thana* Irrigation Program (TIP) when there was food deficit in the country. With the formation of agricultural cooperative in this region, mechanized cultivation, adopting high-yielding varieties (HYVs), use of chemical fertilizers, etc. have been introduced to the farmers. Modern fishing equipment was also supplied to the fishermen's programs through DOC. A number of poverty alleviation programs have been implemented and regular training for income-generating activities and management training has been offered to the cooperators.

2. Bangladesh Rural Development Board

Bangladesh Rural Development Board (BRDB) has both cooperative and informal group networks to eradicate poverty as well as rural development all over Bangladesh. It operates micro-credit programs to finance its clientele groups for poverty alleviation. BRDB has been proved as an effective organization in poverty eradication of the country.

3. Local Government Engineering Department

The LGED under the Ministry of Local Government, Rural Development and Cooperatives is implementing rural development infrastructure development projects, particularly construction of rural roads, growth centers, water structures, etc. which help generate employment in the rural areas. During 1998/99 to 1999/2001, 290 million man-days of work had been created. During July-February 1998-99, about 23 million man-days of work had been created in which 22.2 million were in the rural areas.

4. The Rural Maintenance Program

The RMP started since 1983 with food aid from Canada, is playing an important role in alleviation of poverty. The tenure of the phase III has been stipulated for the period 1995-2001. The principal objective of these program is to create employment and income for destitute women (owning land less than 0.5 acres) by engaging them in the maintenance of roads and also helping them in undertaking other income-generating activities from their accumulated savings. RMP is under implementation in 4,100 unions in 435 *thanas* in 61 districts. About 41,000 destitute women are expected to be benefitted in 1998-99.

5. Others

Beside these there are many *prominent NGOs* named BRAC, Grameen Bank, ASA, Proshika, etc. in Bangladesh, which are engaged in rural development activities as local non-formal institutions.

Cooperative Movement in Bangladesh

The cooperative movement started in this country with the enactment of the Cooperative Credit Societies Act 1904. Only the primary cooperatives could be organized under this Act with not less than 10 individual members. The movement was guided by the philosophy and principles to protect the poor peasants from the exploitation of landlords and moneylenders of the society, so that a poverty free socio-economy for the poor people especially of the rural areas can be made. Initially, the movement was launched by introducing agriculture credit cooperatives. But the noble intention of the activities gradually expanded to different sectors, such as fisheries, weavers, transports, milk produce's, handicrafts, housing, banking, insurance, etc. for bringing about an overall upliftment for the persons of limited means as well as for having a balanced socio-economic infrastructure in the country.

Over the decades, though the legal and administrative framework remained same, the cooperative movement witnessed two major trends. Firstly the cooperative network became a three-tier system and the other in two-tier cooperative system. The first type traditional cooperatives are functioning from very beginning of the movement since 1904 under the direct supervision and management control of "Registrar" hierarchy vested to the DOC and the second type, Comilla model cooperatives, popularly known as BRDB cooperatives were functioning since mid 1960s. The new two-tier cooperatives were introduced with the intention of ensuring quick service and supply of credit and input to the members of agricultural cooperatives. Since then the BRDB cooperatives were adopted as the main approach to implement government policies and strategies for rural development. It may be mentioned that BRDB was entrusted with responsibility of supervision of two-tier cooperatives, which run parallel to the three-tier cooperatives of Registrar hierarchy. But the regulatory control of two-tier cooperative however vested to the Registrar.

After the emergence of Bangladesh as an independent state in 1971, fresh ideas were generated and strategies were explored for rural development. Emphasis was laid upon cooperatives with a socialistic framework. The Constitution of Bangladesh has characterized cooperative as one of the most important sectors of economy of the country. In the years after the political change in the mid 1970s a new thrust added to the cooperative movement. Donor agencies became interested to finance cooperative-based rural development programs. For example, the World Bank, Norwegian Agency for International Development (NORAD), ADB, etc., funded largely the cooperative program to make the new two-tier cooperatives fruitful. Cooperatives of Bangladesh have been playing a vital role in introducing the use of modern cultivation, irrigation, use of HYV seeds, application of fertilizers, use of pesticides, etc. In fact bulk of the mechanized irrigation is covered under the cooperative scheme. Also, in other sectors of cooperatives have been playing an important role in the development process, such as transportation, milk production, marketing, fishery, weaving, handicraft, housing, etc.

At present, there are around 1,40,000 primary cooperatives in Bangladesh having 7.5 million individual members covering approximately 450 million people which is about one-third of the total population of the country. Many of the societies are dormant, ineffective and suffer from weak and improper management practice. Cooperatives cannot survive on motivation alone. The prime need at present is to ensure quality of the society rather than quantity. The main task therefore, is to make the societies self-sustaining instead of increasing their number.

There are 1,049 central or secondary level cooperatives and 20 apex or national or national level cooperative organizations in Bangladesh comprising the following cooperative sectors: banking, industry, sugarcane, fishery, milk production, marketing, transportation, housing, women, etc.

There are also two national level cooperative organizations; namely, Bangladesh Jatiya Samabaya Union (BJSU), which is a member of the International Cooperative Alliance (ICA). Cooperative societies of the country are the members of BJSU. BJSU runs its day-today affairs with fund provided by its member societies. It is the voice for its affiliated members in the country. There is no government financial to the BJSU in the forms of grant or aid as in the case of Bangladesh Jatiya Palli Unnanyan Samabaya Federation (BJPUSF), which is sponsored by BRDB.

Cooperative Policy and Legislation

In consideration of the importance of the "Cooperative Sector", the Government of Bangladesh has adopted the National Cooperative Policy in 1989 with the following important objectives and strategies:

a. Increasing contribution of cooperative sector as the second sector of national economy for augmenting GDP under the constitution of the country.

b. Ensuring participation, as creative and productive force of the underprivileged groups of the society particularly the women, the have-nots, different occupational groups and other people of limited means.

c. Increasing the role of the cooperative sector in providing unemployed persons throughout the country especially in the relevant areas.

d. Expanding the role of cooperatives in various sectors of GDP particularly in agriculture, small and cottage industries, trade and commerce, store and marketing, export-oriented industries and trades, etc.

e. Ensuring cooperatives as major instruments in all economic activities in rural and urban areas for poverty alleviation, upgrading lifestyle of common man and removing the disparity that exists in haves and have-nots of different region of the country gradually.

f. Ensuring easy access to education, healthcare and nutrition of the members of cooperative societies and their families through overall upliftment of their economic condition.

g. Ensuring transformation of cooperative activities into a movement through institutional framework.

h. Encouraging the members of the cooperatives to become self-managed and self-reliant, gradually.

i. Ensuring the management of cooperative societies as democratic institution and establishing autonomy in the management.

j. Undertaking supportive measures for the improvement of financial condition of the cooperatives as well as attaining their economic viability.

In Bangladesh, the Cooperative Societies Act 2001 and cooperative societies rules regulate the cooperative societies. The DOC is responsible for administering these cooperative acts, rules and regulations promulgated from time to time.

According to the laws, the cooperative society is a body corporate by the name under which it is registered and is autonomous in function. The management of every cooperative society vests in a managing committee constituted in accordance with laws and bylaws.

To make the ongoing cooperative movement more affective and dynamic, the cooperative policy introduced in 1989 required to be updated. Steps are already being taken for upgrading of the cooperative policy.

Cooperatives and Cooperative Department

Cooperatives are basically an economic movement for the improvement of socio-economic condition of common people. DOC came into existence with the passing of Cooperative Societies Act of 1904. Its administrative ministry is Ministry of Local Government, Rural Development and Cooperatives. All officers and staff of this sector, from department headquarters to *thana* level, have been actively engaged in administration of cooperatives including the formulation of acts and rules, management of disputes, audits, inspection, research, publicity, extension and training activities. The DOC has been working to make the movement more dynamic.

Cooperative is an effective vehicle for socio-economic improvement of the country. People of different occupations such as peasants, the weavers, the fishermen and the laborers are becoming self-reliant through cooperatives. Today cooperative is recognized as an effective vehicle for participatory development in all levels of the country.

Function of the Cooperative Department

The main functions of the DOC are as follows:

- General Administration;
- Administration of cooperative acts/ordinance and rules;
- Organization registration and promotion of professional cooperatives;
- Statistical documentation of cooperatives;
- Audit and inspection of cooperatives;
- Monitoring and evaluation of cooperatives; and
- Overall extension (training and publication; planning and promotion) of cooperatives.

The DOC is headed by the Registrar of Cooperative Societies (RCS) in the rank of Joint Secretary of the Government of the People's Republic of Bangladesh. Additional Registrars, Joint Registrars, Deputy Registrars, Assistant Registrars, and Technical Staffs at the headquarters assist him. In the field level the Divisional Registrar, Deputy Registrars, Assistant Registrar and cooperative officers and skilled employees assist him. In the field of cooperative education and training, the principal (Additional Registrar) of Bangladesh Cooperative Academy (BCA) works under the general administration of RCS. There are nine cooperative zonal institutes (CZIs) in Bangladesh. A lot of cooperatives officers are being trained in these institutions for the upliftment of their own careers and that of the cooperative movement. The Principal (ARCS) of CZIs works under the general administration and supervision of the principal BCA. Although the main objectives of the cooperative movement are to uplift the socio-economic condition of the members of the societies, yet the cooperatives contribute, to a certain degree, to the revenue earnings of the government. In addition, in compliance with the national policy of the country to protect the environment and reducing pollution, the cooperatives with their limited resources participated by planting nearly 10 million trees to minimize environment pollution.

Role of NGOs

Bangladesh Rural Advancement Committee

BRAC established in 1972 primary to carry out relief work is now working on a multidimensional approach, which includes credit, informal education for the children and the adult, primary healthcare and provision of legal advice on women's rights, etc. Nearly 2.2 million families, of which 93 percent women members, in 388 *upazillas* in 61 districts have been advanced loans amounting to Tk.21.72 billion till December 1997 and recovery rate is 98 percent. During this period, the savings generated by the beneficiaries amounted to Tk.1.75 billion.

Grameen Bank

Established in 1983, through an ordinance, Grameen Bank started its operation as early as in 1976 under an experimental project and has expanded its activities through organizing the poor into groups and extending credit to help them generate their own income and capital about 2.28 million members of the groups, 94 percent of whom are women in about 37,937 villages have been provided with credit of about Tk.81.78 billion till December 1997 through its 1,105 branches and savings generated by the beneficiaries has amounted to Tk.6.59 billion. Loan recovery has been Tk.71.33 billion. Besides such employment and income generation activities, Grameen Bank has also undertaken housing schemes for the poor. Up to December 1997, the Bank has distributed house-building credit amounting to Tk.6.24 billion.

Swanirvar Bangladesh

Established in 1975, the organization has been carrying out its programs of credit disbursement, population control and healthcare through formation of village committees and has covered 11,050 villages in 164 *thanas*. Up to December 1997, an amount of Tk.1,734.7 million has been disbursed to 0.78 million loan recipients of whom 0.54 million are women (70 percent). During this period, savings generated by the beneficiaries has amounted to Tk.213.4 million. Out of the total loans of Tk.1,734.7 million disbursed, Tk.1,535.1 million has been advanced to income-generating projects (purchase of rickshaw and cow, petty trade, rearing poultry, vegetables cultivation, cane products, etc), Tk.150 million for family planning and child care program, Tk.31.6 million for rural development, and Tk.14 million for rearing poultry and livestock.

Proshika

Established in 1976, this organization operates in multidimensional activities. These include provision of credit, development of fishery and livestock, development of silk, irrigation programs, health and nutrition, sinking of tube-wells and distribution, environment-friendly agriculture, social forestry and housing programs. During 1990/91-1996/97, credit amounting to Tk.3,960 million was disbursed to about 1.0 million members (40 percent women) from 156 *upazillas* of 48 districts. The credit recovery rate is 92 percent.

Comprehensive Village Development Program

Comprehensive Village Development Program (CVDP) is a modest effort of experimentation that would pursue increasing production, employment, income, social development and equitable distribution of benefits based on local level planning within a common and single institution for all villagers. This institution will develop common facilities and services (physical and social) as well as economic activities for the villagers. Under the CVDP concept, a multipurpose single village institution as a forum or platform is being used by all development agencies, irrespective of the type (whether they are government organizations, or NGOs). This helps gradually to reduce duplication, wastage and inefficiency in the rural development sector and in turn contribute to the development of a sustainable process to build self-managed village institutions.

Objectives of CVDP as a Sample Village Development Plan

i. To develop common village facilities and make available at the village level various social and economic services relating to literacy and education, population control and family planning, minimum healthcare and nutrition, income generation activities and others;

ii. To increase production in both farm and non-farm sector, productive employment and household income, utilizing all available resources maximally;

iii. To encourage capital formation in cooperative societies;

iv. To develop human resources;

v. To promote greater participation of women in development activities; and

vi. To ensure equitable distribution of benefits of development to all.

Institutional Arrangement for CVDP

In each village, there will be a village-based cooperative called the Comprehensive Village Development Cooperative Society (CVDCS). All the villagers will be the members of CVDCS. The members will be divided into different functional groups. The CVDPSs will be managed by a managing committee having a proportionate representation from each functional group, except that of the children. These are being developed as economically viable and self-reliant institutions by means of resource mobilization and commercial/business activities within the cooperative discipline. The existing cooperative societies and informal groups in the village will be gradually amalgamated with CVDPSs based on the consideration of the extent of their assets vis-à-vis liabilities. No new cooperative societies and groups other than CVDPSs will be promoted in the villages.

Side by side the CVDPSs will have links to their *upazilla* level cooperative associations. The other linkage of CVDPSs will be with local government bodies at different tiers and *upazilla* level nation building departments, the purpose of which will be to develop common village facilities and services (physical, social and economic) and obtaining support services available at the union, *upazilla* (subdistrict) and districts.

Evaluation and Future Directions

Various experiments were carried out with local level institutions, particularly from 1958 onwards, primarily with the objective of establishing a centralized system of administration in the name of devolution of administrative authority, but in fact, to keep the people out of the decision-making process. Thus the people of Bangladesh, particularly the rural people who comprise about 80 percent of the countries population, lost almost half a century during which their participation was virtually absent from the very process of development they were supposed to be the beneficiaries of.

However, in the background of lost opportunity for development and abject rural poverty, growing awareness of the people as well as deeper insight into the miserable plight of the rural poor by the civil society, the concept of decentralization and revitalization of the local level institutions started capturing the imagination of academics and policy-makers. As a result, fresh initiatives were launched during the 1980s for revitalizing local level institutions, at various tiers, and delegating to them some developmental roles along with powers to raise some resources locally. These were, however, rendered dysfunctional, through the extended arms of the Central Government, and the only local level institutions that remain still in place are the union *parishads*.

The fundamental premise of participatory development is development by the people and for the people. Popular participation manifests in the collective endeavor by the people concerned in an organized framework to pool together to attain objectives they set for themselves and action that is stimulated by their thoughts and deliberations and over which they can exert effective control. In this context, the local level institutions become important in providing the institutional fora for both empowerment of people and promotion of participatory rural development in a cost-effective and sustainable way.

In this backdrop, the government, immediately on its installation, established a commission to make, an in-depth study and come up with recommendations on the forms and functions of local government institutions at different levels. Following the recommendations made by the commission, union *parishads* and *pourashavas* will be strengthened both functionally and financially. All these local government bodies will be entrusted with the responsibility to formulate and implement local level development programs/ projects, manage educational institutions, run health and family welfare services and to maintain local level infrastructure. Necessary laws will be enacted to empower these local level institutions to mobilize and raise resources for local level activities thus lessening the burden on the Central

Government. Law has already been passed to strengthen and broad base women's representation in union *parishads*.

To ensure people's participation in the development process, local level institutions will be encouraged to evolve on a spirit of self-help. They will also provide a system for efficient use of voluntary labor in various fields of the rural life, not only in production but also in community development. The government role here will be catalytic and promotional. Using the local government institutions, target groups to promote a back-to-back relationship between policies and felt-needs of the people. An important area will be rural human resource development.

Land is the scarcest resource in Bangladesh. Its proper utilization is a necessity for the success of the plan, as it ensures effective employment of the rural labor force and higher output. Positive steps will be taken to provide an institutional framework for production and employment planning at the local level and ensuring better use of land, water and human resources. It is recognized that local level institutions for promotion of production, employment, voluntary consolidation of holdings, etc. cannot perform readily without adequate policy support and necessary changes in the legal system.

Future Directions

i. The ministries and agencies responsible for development of socio-economic infrastructure strategies must be drawn to develop those in a systematic way without avoidable duplication of activities among different agencies and levels of activity centers. The component activities should be clearly and completely identified and responsibilities properly delineated among different levels;

ii. Formal and informal institutions should be allowed to function so that informal groups, in the course of time may be organized in to cooperatives;

iii. As a part of employment generation strategy, a target-oriented program to promote human resource development including productive skills though formal and non-formal education and training should be implemented;

iv. Poverty alleviation program should be located in distressed areas where incidence of poverty is especially high and government organizations and NGOs have not undertaken any program;

v. Donor agencies should be more involved in rural development and poverty alleviation and finance the rural professional groups;

vi. Donor agencies should provide especial assistance to cooperative societies, as formal groups for their sustainability; and

vii. Appropriate training programs should be developed to support the rural development programs.

References

Ahmed, Junaid, (2007), Local Governments: International Experiences, paper presented to National Workshop on Strengthening of Local Government Institutions, Dhaka, National Institute of Local Government.

Hossain, Zillur Rahman (2001), *Actors and Roles, Community Capacities and Local Governance;* Dhaka: Power and Participatory Research Centre.

Khan Zarina R. and Akther Hussain (2001), *Review/Stocktaking in Local Governance,* University of Dhaka.

Sen, Amatay (1999), *Development as Freedom.* London: Oxford University Press.

Shotton, Roger (ed), (2004), *Local Government Initiative: Pro-Poor Infrastructure and Service Delivery in Rural Asia – A Synthesis of Case Studies,* NY: UNCDF, 2004.

Williams, M; Keith McLean, and Graham Kerr (1998), D*ecentralization and Rural Development: Characterizing Efforts in 19 Selected Countries*, World Bank, September.

7

People Participation in Rural Development : Case of Republic of China

Community-based rural development has been implemented in Taiwan since 1965, and the history can even be traced back to 1955. At that time, the agricultural administration noticed the necessity for developing substantial infrastructure in rural areas. The local communities and institutions, in practice, perform crucial roles in integrating rural resources in the fulfillment of sustainable development. Recently, increased involvement of Non-profit Organizations (NPOs) in local community development not only brought in abundant voluntary human resources, but also contributed to the "re-conceptualization" of rural development.

Institutions in Rural Development

Sustainability is the ultimate goal of rural development in Taiwan. The attainment of economic and social sustainability in rural areas depends on institutional networks with the aid of cultural and social resources. Taiwan rural communities have been experiencing enormous difficulties in recent years due to the increased economic depression, global trade competition, and the continuous natural disasters. As agriculture sector contributes dramatically decreasing proportion of GDP, the rural residents are generally suffering from confidence loss about the future. Local communities, under such circumstance, play the central role in rebuilding their confidence and restoring their subsistence.

The term community stands for different meanings in different countries. A common definition, however, is that a community is composed of a recognized space, a group of inhabitants with intimate relationships, identical local service system, and strong community consciousness.

The total number of *tsuen* is recorded as 7,756 in 2000. Community in rural areas, therefore, is primarily corresponds to a *tsuen*. The *tsuen* residents elect their own chief every four years. A *tsuen* office is setup, along with the election of the chief, within the community and legitimately monitored and financially aided by the offices of township, county, and national administration units.

Primarily three systems are implementing rural development projects in Taiwan. They are official administration system, farmers'/fishermen's association system, and the NPO system, respectively. Among them, the first is government-administrated, while the other two are more non-governmentally administrated or self-administrated. The governmental community development plan in Taiwan was initiated in 1965. At that time the plan was expected to fulfill the missions of improving community residents' education, culture, social welfare, and public health on one hand, and ameliorating agricultural facilities construction on the other. To accelerate community development, the Ministry of Interior encourages existing communities to establish a local institution; namely, "community development association", to assist the *tsuen/li* office.

The community development association, thus, is officially built up and consists of local populace enthusiastic in community affairs. The original objectives proposed to accomplish are to strengthen community infrastructure construction on one hand, and on the other hand to improve the community residents' productivity, income, social welfare, and moral education. A community development association is regularly divided into sections of representative assembly, board of directors, and board of supervisors with differentiated tasks. The members of representative assembly are selected from the community residents and possess supreme authority in determining development policies. The members of the board of directors and supervisors are elected by the representatives and are responsible for managing and supervising the community development affairs, respectively, and its own members designate a chairperson for each committee. An executive chief is nominated by the board of directors to take charge of community affairs and to act as the community speaker.

Despite the continuous decline in agricultural hegemony in many rural areas, the sector still holds significant influence on the shaping of rural communities. Farmers' associations, as well as fishermen's associations, traditionally are local organizations of great importance in promoting rural development, though their major concern is on farmers, fishermen, and agriculture. Since agriculture-related population accounts for the majority of rural inhabitants, this institution, particularly its agricultural extension section, plays impressive role in integrated rural development. The agricultural extension service has traditionally designated the rural community people as its main target populations in need of public assistances, programs, and support to help improve the welfare as well as quality of their lives. In response to impacts resulting from a variety of societal changes and along with the emerging ecological imperative, however, the concept of holistic and sustainable community development nowadays becomes a prevailing belief guiding the transformation of Taiwanese agricultural extension. The agricultural extension system, therefore, is much more emphasizing the training of human resources rather than hardware construction.

After the threatening earthquake in 1999, bundles of rural communities have been haunted by sequential aftershocks and debris flow which consequently leads to increasing NPOs taking part in rural community development. As a great many rural communities faced reconstruction not only in facilities and industries, but also in spiritual phase such as culture and identity, increasing NPOs have actively partaken in post-disaster rural development on the ground of humane and environmental concerns. The involved institutions range from environmental protection groups, cultural rebuilding foundation, local history studio, to associations related to sustainable development.

Given that the cumulative chemicals produced by conventional farming in the past decades have acutely spoiled most of the arable land, progressive numbers of institutions advocating sustainable agriculture or organic culture have risen these years. An NPO, as Wolf mentioned, is defined as a legitimately authorized, self-administrated organization to carryout "public welfare without profit-searching" as the as mission. It is commonly recognized that the existence of NPOs provides solid help to the governmental institutions that a cooperative relation between these two parities shall be the best development policy for the long run.

The NPOs involved in rural development seem to exhibit more momentum, vigor, creativity and concrete ideal in dealing with development affairs than the institutions of traditional two systems, probably due to its independence and better management. Most of the NPOs recruit considerable volunteers and are financed by personal donations or enterprises' sponsor, along with frequent subsidy from the government. The latter usually comes as contributions to rural development.

Roles and Achievements of Local Communities and Institutions

In Taiwan, the community development associations are expected to play the role of a resource deliverer, a coordinator, or a facilitator (Table 1). A resource deliverer possesses a duty to deliver and evenly allocate the resources from government to the community inhabitants. A coordinator rile is played whenever there is conflict to be solved through negotiation involving various parties, whether inside or outside of the community. The role of the facilitator relates to personal learning and improving individual literacy. This is also a role of great importance, since community residents with quality is beneficial for community development in incoming knowledge-based economy era.

Table 1. Roles of Local Institutions in Integrated Rural Development

Institution	*Relational Target*	*Role*
Community development association	Rural residents	Resource deliverer, coordinator, facilitator
Farmers' association	Agricultural population	Resource distributor, trainer, facilitator, management consultant coordinator
Borough/tsuen office	Rural residents	Resource deliverer
NPO	Rural residents	Animator, renovator, facilitator, educator, innovator

Governmental help accounts for the main part of its revenue at approximately 75 percent, most of which were from the township administration office. In addition, about a quarter of the expenditure is drawn from the community itself through personal donation or imposition on inhabitants. Usually, any savings after expenditure are being used to raise "community construction funds" in order to benefit future development plans. The activities and groups involved in rural community development, as a whole, are fairly diversified to accommodate the needs of residents with various ages and characteristics. It is estimated that about 70 percent of the communities have set up activity centers to provide facilities and space for different types of activities. The community development associations, *per se*, are to provide sufficient services and facilities to the residents to empower the community and to bring about the residents feeling of belonging or community consciousness.

Among the NGOs, township farmers'/fishermen's associations contribute a great deal in the past decades pertaining to human resource development within community. The total numbers of township farmers' association and fishermen's association have remained around 300 and 40, respectively since 1970.

With different relations to farmers and rural residents, it simultaneously takes the roles of resource distributor, trainer, facilitator, coordinator, and farm management consultant. In terms of organizational structure, departments of farming affairs, home economics, and youth affairs are divided to take care of farmers, housekeepers, and the youth, respectively. More than a half of the agents, in accordance with the statistics, belong to farming affairs department because of the dominant proportion of farmer in components.

Most farmers affiliated with the farmers association are organized into various crop-specific groups and follow a variety of training programs and management advices. To help the farmers, housekeepers, and the adolescents efficiently learn the skills of interest, the extension agents have to act as facilitators and assist the clients' knowledge transfer and learning process.

Traditionally, most plans are designed and decided in a top-down manner and undertaken passively. The community development associations or the farmers' associations merely obey to what has been determined by the authority. Since the national development policy takes economic growth as the first priority, the development focus has been heavily concentrated on manufacturing, construction and introduction of advanced technology. The environmental and cultural issues, as a result, are overwhelmingly neglected. The emergence of NPOs, however, brings about a whole different picture to these issues with enormous volunteer input and community inhabitants' active participation. Their goals are set to offset the long-lasting loss in ecological resources and traditional culture, and to defend the welfare of the disadvantaged in the rural areas.

Table 2. Statistics of Community Development in Taiwan, 1996-2000

Item	*1996*	*1997*	*1998*	*1999*	*2000*
Total number of tsuen	7,569	7,569	7,755	7,755	7,756
Total number of community development association	4,495	4,747	4,968	5,245	5,497
Households joining community development program	3,447,294	3,816,961	3,993,048	4,296,418	4,930,035
Population joining community development	13,600,735	13,979,483	13,782,603	15,581,542	16,111,715
Membership number of community development association	460,523	509,615	533,370	694,509	801,447
Number of community construction funds	-	-	-	3,341	3,807
Financial resources	49,520,610	45,093,673	46,048,427	57,648,335	55,124,652
From government	39,873,384	35,427,277	36,101,077	42,720,526	41,267,056
From community itself	9,647,225	9,666,395	9,947,350	14,927,809	13,857,595

Table 3. Associations and Community Development Projects

Item	*1996*	*1997*	*1998*	*1999*	*2000*
Community activity centers	3,444	3,660	3,878	3,963	3,899
Training programs for specific topics	-	-	-	435,971	80,152
Community development demonstrations	-	-	-	190,478	157,315
Community aging clubs	3,451	3,672	3,837	3,769	3,804
Community female/housekeeper clubs	3,703	4,019	4,212	4,334	4,326
Community security squads	2,269	2,323	2,259	1,837	1,776
Community voluntary service squads	1,543	1,745	1,743	1,543	1,404
Community libraries	2,308	2,388	2,337	2,100	1,916
Community entertainment squads	2,606	2,585	2,622	2,727	2,456
Community newsletters or brochures	217	254	293	412	388

In 2000, for example, there were more than 1,500 associations related to academic or cultural affairs, among which the majority focused on the cultural or historical issues as their foremost concern. Noticing the quickly vanishing local culture, a social movement with regard to cultural or historical rebuilding is undertaking and rightly pinpointing to the rural communities. Besides, social welfare of the peasants is another issue deserves more attention in rural areas, since the general life quality is deteriorating due to long-term economic and natural resources deprivation. Out of these, a considerable number of NPOs exhibit interest in the issue of rural population. Of grand interest is the rapid rise of NPOs concerned with sustainable agriculture or organic agriculture whose effort gradually awakes rural individuals from environmental ignorance.

An NPO generally consists of paid staff at less than 10 and ample volunteers who are the real activists in empowering the community. In terms of role-playing, an NPO could play the roles of animator, innovator, renovator, facilitator and educator. Being an animator and an educator, the NPO members are supposed to impulse the public awareness toward social justice and hidden reality, and in the mean time to educate them. Along with the awakening of the recognition of environmental deterioration and soil degradation due to chemicals abuse, more and more NPOs set their mission at restoring the agriculture into a more sustainable one or even organic agriculture. Not only they facilitate the conventional farmers learning toward organic farming, but also educate the general consumers to appreciate organic products and farmers contribution. In addition, being creative and renovating in participating in the process, "community development" is an important property of NPO, which precisely differentiates themselves from the other institutions.

Problems and Future Directions

Despite the increasing numbers of community development associations and farmers'/fishermen's associations, the substantial achievements and pace of rural development based on these two approaches in Taiwan is not as expected, probably owing to overwhelming governmental domination on decision-making of community affairs. Successful community development, in reality, requires thorough participation, partnership, and dialogue among actors throughout the community.

At present, dozens of community development associations are established only to obtain subsidy from the government. What have been accomplished most successfully is merely to strengthen the infrastructure construction such as sewage system and road rebuilding. In contrast, little has been done in the agglomeration of community residents' consciousness.

The policy of community development has been so much determined by the Ministry of Interior as that most of the local communities have lost their independence in decision-making. As a result, the participation of community inhabitants in decision-making is limited that the general people frequently exhibit indifference toward community affairs. To leave the local

Table 4. Community Development-related NGOs in Taiwan, 1977-2000

Year	*Occupational Organization Farmers' Association*					*Fishermen's Association*	*Social Affairs Cultural*	*Organization Social Welfare*
	Total	*Total Number of Agricultural Extension Agents*	*Number of Farming Affairs Agent**	*Number of Youth Affairs Agent**	*Number of Home Economics Agents**			
1977	305	1,345	735	311	299	42	280	2,001
1978	305	1,460	843	314	303	42	297	2,132
1979	306	1,624	916	360	348	42	325	2,203
1980	305	1,677	961	364	352	42	347	2,350
1981	303	1,695	972	366	357	38	364	2,526
1982	304	1,694	966	371	357	38	437	2,750
1983	304	1,764	1,003	372	395	38	496	3,037
1984	304	1,791	1,015	381	395	38	532	3,233
1985	303	1,694	1,003	372	395	38	559	3,427
1986	303	1,764	691	333	342	38	566	3,546
1987	303	1,791	754	353	382	38	627	3,677
1988	303	1,770	689	354	376	38	654	3,565
1989	303	1,786	766	264	366	38	562	2,114
1990	303	1,770	770	264	366	38	588	1,695
1991	303	1,807	780	264	376	38	668	1,791
1992	303	1,783	783	269	379	38	671	1,996
1993	302	1,812	784	275	380	38	721	2,298

(Countd)

(Countd)

1994	302	1,896	783	275	377	38	789	2,559
1995	302	1,959	781	275	355	38	874	2,874
1996	300	1,933	845	361	399	38	958	3,073
1997	302	1,904	773	336	364	38	1,035	3,417
1998	302	1,881	737	326	383	38	1,160	3,684
1999	304	n.a.	n.a.	n.a.	n.a.	40	1,343	4,120
2000	304	n.a.	n.a.	n.a.	n.a.	40	1,504	4,535

Source: The Ministry of Interior, Taiwan

Note: * Denotes statistics from farmers' association's annual report.

community more space in deciding development strategy shall be an important direction.

It is affirmed that informing residents of community history or culture leads to higher participation of community residents. Inputs in hardware construction alone cannot bring about residents' substantive participation, if not the cultural and historical reconstruction is undertaken simultaneously. In this context issues such as: how to convert the policy decision-making route from top-down into bottom-up, and how to persuade the inhabitants to recognize their duty in community development and to play an active role in community affairs, are seen as challenges in future. For rural development to be successful, the government-administrated organizations have to work with the farmers'/fishermen's associations and, especially with the NPOs.

References

Day, Graham, (1998). "Working with the Grain? Towards Sustainable Rural and Community Development", *Journal of Rural Studies* 14(1): 89-105.

Kramer, R., (1987). *Voluntary Agencies in the Welfare State*, University of California Press, Berkeley.

Lipsky, M. and S. R. Smith, (1990). "Nonprofit Organizations, Government, and the Welfare State", *Publican Science Quarterly* 104(4): 625-648.

Roling, N. G., and J. Jiggins, (1998). "The Ecological Knowledge System", in N. G. Roling and M. Wagemakers (eds.) *Facilitating Sustainable Agriculture*, p..283-311, Cambridge University Press.

Wolf, T., (1990). *Managing a Nonprofit*, Prentice-Hall Press, New York.

8

Community-based Rural Development in India

There has been substantial progress towards achieving economic progress in the low-and middle-income countries of the world over the last 50 years. However, the gains have not been shared equally amongst various economic groups within particular nations, the losers being usually the poor in rural areas. Such absolute and relative deprivations, in the face of growth, underline the deficiencies in various approaches towards rural development, including the efforts to improve the conditions of the rural poor.

Integrated Rural Development (IRD) as an approach to rural development has been adopted in many developing countries for improving the conditions of the poor by alleviating poverty and improving the quality of life in the rural areas. The concept of IRD, its organization and approach has been undergoing continuous change to meet the emerging demands of the rural poor, concomitant with the political and socio-economic, administrative and physical set-up for its appropriate adoption. It is now being increasingly felt that the goal of growth with social justice can be achieved largely with the active participation of local communities.

The Government of India has always been conscious about supporting or involving local people in development efforts. Ever since independence, the *Panchayati Raj* Institutions (PRIs) were conceived as a local level institution providing for linkages between village, block and the district. However, their growth varied across States, particularly, on account of socio-political reasons. The passage of the Constitution (73rd Amendment) Act 1992 marked a new era in rural development and provided constitutional status to the local bodies (PRIs) in rural areas besides outlining their functional status. Though the 11th schedule to the Constitution of India contains an impressive list of 29 developmental activities, which could be taken up by these local institutions, progress across States in adoption of these activities is at variance. While some of the States have been limiting only to the provision of civic amenities and facilities for elementary education and primary healthcare, others have expanded the horizon of local bodies in the area of land development, agricultural development and irrigation.

Major constraints in broad basing the role of PRIs continues to be the condition of local communities in terms of mass poverty; large-scale unemployment; illiteracy; poor health and nutritional status; widening income disparities and low quality of life. Poor linkages between different institutions and communities further add to the slow pace of rural development.

Local Administrative Systems at Community Level

On the basis of the recommendations of Balwantray G. Mehta Committee a three-tier system of *Panchayati Raj* was introduced in most of the States in the country in order to entrust community development (CD) programs to self-governing elected bodies.

The Constitution (73rd Amendment) Act 1992 has provided for further streamlining the functioning of the *Panchayati Raj* system and Constitutional Status to these local level institutions. The three-tier system of *Panchayati Raj* consists of *Zilla Parishads* (ZPs) (district council) at district level, *Panchayat Samiti* (PS) (federation of village assemblies) at intermediate level and *Gram Panchayats* (GPs) (village assembly) at the grassroots or village level. These PRIs have been vested with powers and responsibilities to undertake various activities to promote IRD.

Proportionate participation of different sections of society with adequate provision (one-third) of the seats for women and weaker sections, i.e., scheduled castes and scheduled tribes is also provided. The States have also passed State *Panchayati Raj* Acts to facilitate the operation of the PRIs as per the State's local situations. The organizational structure and management of these local self-governments, therefore, varies greatly from State to State. Though as early as 1962 a number of States had established PRIs, still a lot of variations exist in the provisions under respective State *Panchayati Raj*

Acts. So is the financial position of these units, few of them being resource rich with a lot of say in their developmental planning, while others are still struggling to establish themselves. At present, there are 232,278 GPs, 5906 PSs and 499 ZPs in the country. These PRIs are being managed by about 2.92 million elected representatives at all levels.

The Smallest Local Government Unit in India

Gram Panchayat is the smallest level of governance in the *Panchayati Raj* system. *Gram Sabha* which is the general body of GP ensures community participation in the decision-making process. The local self-governance through PRIs greatly facilitates in micro-level planning by adopting a bottom up procedure. The grassroots level micro plans are developed by GPs through the *Gram Sabha*, which are later converged at PS and ZP level. The ZPs finally submit the aggregate proposals to District Planning Committee to finalize the District Plan. The State Assembly at State level and Parliament at national level approve the macro level plans at respectively levels developed on the basis of these micro level proposals (Figure 1).

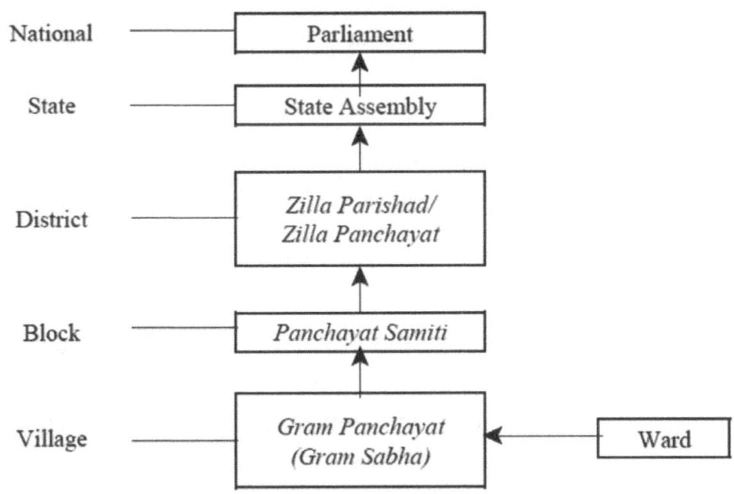

Figure 1. Local Governance Hierarchy for Rural Development in India

1. The Average Population Size of Gram Sabha

The size of population of *Gram Sabha* varies across States. In a number of

States *Gram Sabha* have been established in every village serving a population of 1,000 or more. In areas where there are no villages within 3 miles radius of a particular village, a separate *Gram Sabha* is established for such village even though its population is less than 1,000. If the villages are close by they are combined to form only one *Gram Sabha* even if population is above 5,000. The *Gram Sabhas* that cater for population of more than 1,000 are divided into wards. Average number of villages in a GP also varies from State to State, ranging from 1.0 in case of Tripura to 11.5 in case of Orissa and West Bengal.

2. The Basic Organizational Structure

The executive bodies of the *Gram Sabha* constitute the village *panchayat*. *Panchayats* are elected by *Gram Sabhas* consisting of entire adult population of the village. The number of members ranges from 30 to 51. Seats are reserved for minority community and scheduled castes. Seats are also allotted to each constituency in proportion to its population. The relationship between *Gram Sabha* and the GP is the same as between the legislature and the government.

Each GP is headed by a Chairperson (*sarpanch/pradhan*) and Ward In-charges (ward *panchas*). In some States there is a position of a Vice Chairperson (*up-pradhan/up-sarpanch*) also. In so far as the staff to the *panchayats* is concerned, there is provision of a Secretary in each *panchayat* or a Group Secretary for a group of *panchayats*. He also acts as a Secretary to the *Gram Sabha* responsible for preparing the resolutions of the *Gram Sabha* and placing the same before the GP meeting for follow-up action.

3. Main Role and Functions of the Panchayats

Role and functions are derived from Article 243G of the Constitution which stipulates that the primary role of *panchayats* is in the area of development and planning, whereas implementation of programs of the economic development and social justice are to be the focal point of all their activities. In light of these stipulations each State has prescribed specific functions to the GPs under the respective State Panchayati Raj Acts. Broadly, the functions discharged by the GPs may be classified into:

i. *regulatory functions* like permission for construction of buildings, directing removal of garbage and prohibiting the use of unhealthy water from well or tanks.

ii. *administrative functions* that include management of *panchayat* land, maintenance of pastures, maintenance and disposal of abadi land, preparation and maintenance of panchayat records, etc.

iii. *developmental functions*: *panchayats* are actively involved in a variety of rural development programs/schemes launched by Central/State government and other agencies.

iv. *agency functions*: *panchayats* also discharge some functions as an agency of the State government and the PS.

v. *miscellaneous functions*: *panchayats* are also involved in census and other departmental activities as they are nearer to the villages.

Developmental Activities Entrusted to the *Panchayati Raj* Institutions

The 11th schedule to the Constitution of India contains an impressive list of 29 developmental activities which cold be entrusted to PRIs.

Table 1. 29 Subjects Assigned under the 11th Schedule to the PRIs

1.	Agriculture including agricultural extension
2.	Land improvements, land reforms, soil conservation
3.	Minor irrigation, watershed development
4.	Animal husbandry, dairying and poultry
5.	Fisheries
6.	Social forestry and farm forestry
7.	Minor forest produce
8.	Small-scale industries including food processing industries
9.	*Khadi*, village and cottage industries
10.	Rural housing
11.	Drinking water
12.	Fuel and fodder
13.	Roads, culverts, bridges, ferries and waterways
14.	Rural electrification including distribution of electricity
15.	Non-conventional energy sources
16.	Poverty alleviation programs – IRD Program, *Jowahar Rozgar Yojana* (JRY)
17.	Education including primary and secondary schools
18.	Technical training and vocational education
19.	Adult and non-formal education
20.	Libraries
21.	Cultural activities
22.	Markets and fairs
23.	Health and sanitation including primary health centers and dispensaries
24.	Family welfare

25. Women and child development
26. Social welfare including welfare of handicapped and mentally retarded
27. Welfare of weaker sections and in particular special castes (SCs) and special tribes (STs)
28. Public distribution system
29. Maintenance of community assets

These activities broadly cover the following:

i. Development of natural resources;
ii. Development and maintenance of physical infrastructure;
iii. Poverty Alleviation Programs (PAPs) initiated towards social justice; and
iv. Development of adequate, timely and quality services.

The main areas covered under these activities are as follows:

i. *Programs for Productive Activities* – agriculture, animal husbandry, poultry, fishery, small-scale industries including food processing, cottage industries, fuel and fodder and irrigation;
ii. *Land Development Programs* – land reforms, soil conservation, minor irrigation, water management and watershed development, wasteland development, social forestry and grazing lands;
iii. *Education and Cultural Activities* – primary schools, adult education, technical education and libraries;
iv. *Social Welfare* – welfare of the women and child development, family welfare, care of disabled and mentally retarded;
v. *Provisions of Civic Amenities* – drinking water, rural electrification, non-conventional sources of energy, rural roads, bridges, culverts, waterways, sanitation, rural housing and health;
vi. *Poverty Alleviation and Allied Programs* for social and economic upliftment of weaker sections;
vii. *Maintenance of Community* assets and public distribution system; and
viii. *Organization and Control* of rural markets and village fairs.

Planning for Development by *Gram Panchayat*

The basic objective of the planning at GP is to identify the felt needs and aspirations of the people, which are to be jointly shouldered by the people's representatives and *panchayats*. Such process of planning is expected to be useful in identifying the local problems and local resources, ascertaining the growth potential of the *panchayats* in the light of their resources enabling them not only in choosing schemes from a shelf of projects but properly sequencing the activities in such a way that forward and backward linkages are established. The inputs required for planning are to be collected primarily from the people and by themselves in the *Gram Sabha* meetings.

Decentralized planning process begins at the GP level and all items, which can be taken up by them within jurisdiction, form part of the GP plan. All other items, which cover more than one GP, form part of the plan of the intermediate *panchayat*. Before finalizing the GP plan resources inventory of the village is also finalized.

Sources of Revenue and Budget

Every *panchayat* has a Village *Panchayat* Fund to which all allotments, general and special contributions and donations from the Central and local governments, municipalities, district boards, etc. are credited. The level of budget of different GPs varies drastically. Though a number of constitutional provisions exist to support these institutions to augment their funds, the financial position is not so good with respect to most of the GPs. This is mainly because of poor revenue collection, inadequacy of trained personnel, diversion of funds and misuse of resources and lack of accountability and transparency.

GPs derive their income mainly from the following sources:

1. Taxes

Under the provisions of the Indian Constitution as well as respective State Panchayati Raj Acts, GPs may levy taxes such as: house tax, professional tax, vehicle tax, tax on sold-out village produce, pilgrim tax, animal tax, land cess, entertainment tax, cattle tax, taxes on fairs/festivals/agricultural land/transfer of property/commercial crops, sanitary tax, drainage tax, lighting tax, water tax, tax on fisheries, etc. Types of taxes allocated to respective project implementing agencies drastically varies from State to State.

2. Fees

Under Central and State regulations, *panchayats* have been authorized to charge different types of fees against services extended and also fines and penalties against identified defaults. The fees may include:

(a) fee for services, viz. water supply, drainage, street lighting and conservancy;

(b) license fee on professional buyers, brokers and commission agents;

(c) fee for registration of cattle sold, hides and skins, tea stalls and restaurants, goods on sale in market, new buildings/factories/workshops, cart stand, lodges, for use of common land and community property, fishing and fisheries, etc.; and

(d) fines and penalties on encroachment, failure to take license while dealing with prohibited articles.

3. Communal Income

These include income from fisheries, fairs and markets, fallen trees, cattle dropping and other rubbish, donation of land, money, shramdaan (voluntary labor), panchayat forests, government or community property.

4. Income from Project Funds

Panchayats also receive funds from Central/States and other agencies for implementation of developmental projects/schemes launched by these agencies.

Resource Mobilization by the *Panchayats*

Contrary to the institutional provisions for a broad range of revenue sources, financial position of the *panchayats* in most of the States is miserable. This is largely because of inadequate allocation of tax categories to PRIs under the concerned State Acts. The position is further aggravated with respect to GPs because of small size in terms of population and area. Moreover, the GPs are also not able to fully utilize their revenue resources because of absence of suitable guidelines or rules; lack of secretarial and other staff; unwillingness of the elected *panchayats* in collecting taxes and fees in their locality; unwillingness of people to pay taxes and fees because of poor services in the villages; and inability to pay taxes/fees because of poverty.

Linkage of *Gram Panchayats* with Local Level Organizations and Groups

A closer look at village scenario presents a plethora of local level organizations and institutions operating with multiplicity of efforts. Wherever GPs are active they are able to drive in the programs and priorities of these organizations/groups in there micro plans and extend desired support to these

Constitutional Position with respect to Resource Mobilization by *Gram Panchayats*

i. According to Article 243H of the Indian Constitution, the State legislatures are empowered to enact laws authorizing the *panchayats* to levy, collect and appropriate certain specified taxes, duties, tolls and fees. Such levy, collection and appropriation will be in accordance with such procedure and subject to such limits as may be specified by the State legislatures by law.

ii. Similarly, under item (ii) of sub-clause (a) of clause (1) of Article 243I of the Indian Constitution, the State Finance Commission is required to make recommendations to the State governor the principles which should govern determination of the taxes, duties, tolls and fees which may be assigned to, or appropriated by, the *panchayats*.

iii. State *Panchayati Raj* Acts specify the taxes, duties, tolls and fees, which are transferred to the *panchayats* for their exclusive use. In most of the States, revenue-raising powers are granted by the State legislatures mostly to the village-level *panchayats*.

iv. At present, under the State *Panchayati Raj* Acts of Andhra Pradesh, Assam, Haryana, Himachal Pradesh, Tamil Nadu, Goa, Karnataka, Madhya Pradesh, Maharashtra, Manipur, Gujarat, Kerala, Uttar Pradesh, West Bengal, and Punjab, levy of some taxes and non-taxes by the *panchayats* has been made compulsory. In other States like Bihar, Rajasthan, and Orissa, exercise of the revenue-raising powers granted to the *panchayats* is optional.

bodies. Situation is reverse, where GPs are not so active. With an environment of harmony and cooperation between GPs and different local organizations, the local self-governments could achieve a great deal of development objectives. GPs may collaborate with NGOs in the area of water management, forest management, fisheries development and other categories of income-generating activities. Relevant work done by NGOs in the area of dissemination of latest technology and awareness generation may also be positively utilized by the PRIs. Community-based Organizations (CBOs), cooperatives, private input suppliers, and government departments, all are implementing a large number of programs for rural development. The GPs provide a platform for grassroots level convergence and rationalization of the efforts of these organizations in facilitating a sustained growth and development at rural level.

Local Institutions Involved in Rural Development

Local level organizations and institutions relate to those entities working very closely with the communities at locality levels involving a set of villages/communities, a single village/community associated with it or even smaller groups operating below community or village level. Those involved with rural development mainly concern the overall development of rural areas aimed at improving the living conditions of rural populace leading to poverty alleviation at large.

While formal institutions are well-structured and established systems operating under set norms/work conditions, organizations are a kind of non-formal institution with a very close proximity and dependence on rural community. These local level organizations need a great deal of capacity-building and community participation to be able to extend the expected contribution in rural development.

Major Local Level Organizations and Institutions

Many new institutions emerge; however, only few of them sustain and are able to contribute towards the cause of rural development. Majority of local level non-formal organization fail mainly because they lack clarity in their objectives, lack a balanced organizational structure with poor participation of communities and little or no linkage with other local institutions. Few of the local level institutions /organizations which have made visible impact on the rural development process have been elaborated in the following discussions.

Non-governmental Organizations

NGOs and voluntary action have been a part of historical legacy in India. Though initially operating on a limited area of charitable, social work, these organizations have assumed central place in development process during recent years because of their effective contribution in delivery of services to people, community mobilization and capacity-building of other grassroots level organizations.

The NGOs are registered institutions functioning with missionary approach and focusing on core developmental activities particularly, in agriculture and rural development. The member composition of NGOs is largely as per stipulations of the State Societies Registration Acts. They operate in a limited geographical area and usually in a limited number of fields because of paucity of staff and fund limitations. The most significant contribution of these agencies has been in the area of people's mobilizations for education (extensive literacy), efficient land use, minor irrigation, watershed management, etc. There are a number of good NGOs functioning in different parts of the country viz. Sudguru Water Development Foundation, Dahod (Gujarat); OUTREACH, Bangalore; MYRADA, Bangalore; Seva Mandir, Udaipur, Rajasthan; Rama Krishna Mission, West Bengal.

Rural Cooperatives

The Indian cooperative movement is one of the biggest in the world consisting of around 488,158 cooperatives all over the country. The emergence of cooperative movement has also been almost parallel to the *panchayati raj* movement in the country. It was largely with the resolution of National Development Council during 1958 emphasizing the need for cooperative policy for India, which led to formal beginning of cooperative programs in the country. The Third Five Year Plan (1961-66) also identified the cooperatives and the PRIs as primary agencies for carrying out CD programs. The membership structure of the cooperatives is governed by the respective cooperative rules of the States. While the local level cooperative society in most of the States are headed by a Secretary deputed by the government the cooperatives in Gujarat and Maharashtra operate under the guidance and administration of a general body of members or elected Board of Directors.

The primary functions of the village cooperative are the provision of short- and medium-term credit, supply of inputs for agriculture and allied sector, as well as marketing of agricultural produce. The cooperatives have a vast rural network covering majority of the villages in respect of dairy milk supply. However, the habit of thrift and saving has been the essential objectives of the cooperatives. The Primary Agricultural Cooperative Society (PACS) is the lowest level of credit facility provider to the farmers at the village level.

A comparative study of cooperatives in different State shows that in Maharashtra and Gujarat cooperatives have been doing exceptionally well in the area of sugar cooperatives and dairy cooperatives, respectively. The Anand model of dairy cooperatives in Gujarat has been recommended by a number of international organizations as a replicable model for other developing countries.

Self-help Groups

The emergence of SHGs in the country has been a recent development with the felt need for participatory approach in rural development. There has been growing realization that top-down, inter-personal mode of support during Green Revolution benefitted only the resource-rich and large farmers. The reducing base of the governmental institutions has further justified the need for a group approach in development with the members helping each other as a self-help group. The SHGs are informal institutions and can decide their own membership and the terms and conditions for their working. All the members of the SHGs contribute to group fund were as the matching financial assistance comes through government development programs. The fund collected is rotated as credit amongst group members for their development needs. The SHGs also establish linkages with different financing and developmental institutions and play a great role in creating a culture of self-sustenance amongst the rural communities.

The different government programs under which SHGs have been formed include Watershed Development Programs, Agricultural Development Schemes, and National Watershed Development Program for Rainfed Areas (NWDPRA), Employment Schemes, etc. SHGs have been functioning very effectively in the area of brick making, labor works, household industries, fisheries, sheep farming, poultry farming, silk reeling, collection of minor forest produce, women credit and thrift mobilization, etc.

Interest Groups/Commodity Groups/Activity Groups

The interest groups/commodity groups have also emerged as a major partner in rural development. These are non-formal group of rural people organized together to manage the production and disposal of a particular commodity (both agricultural and allied) or activity. Farmer interest groups (FIGs)/ commodity groups are informal institutions with membership of these groups ranging from 7 to 25-30. Different functions in the group are performed by an informal distribution of work, whereas leader of the group is elected by mutual consensus. Though originally these groups are non-formal at a later stage they may be registered as a society under the concerned State regulation.

Under the innovations in technology dissemination (ITD) component of the World Bank-funded National Agricultural Technology Project (NATP), being implemented in selected States since November 1998. Interest groups/commodity groups have been the main focus for development. A large number of FIGs, women interest groups (WIGs) have been formed and supported to manage the production and disposal of different commodities. The district level Agricultural Technology Management Agency (ATMA) created under the project is engaged in facilitating the formation of these groups. The ATMA also extends needed support to the FIGs/WIGs in the form of technical assistance, capacity-building, linking with the credit institutions or providing revolving funds with an aim to develop these units into sustainable micro enterprises. These village groups are being federated at block level institutions like Farm Information and Advising Centers (FIACs) and further into ATMA Governing Board membership. The objective is to provide the local communities a role space in decision-making and strategic planning of grassroots level agricultural development priorities.

User Groups

The concept of user group has been initiated under the centrally sponsored Watershed Development Program. Under this program, groups of rural community are organized around farmers' farm activities like field crops, water-harvesting structures, pasture plots (sheep growers groups), etc. The main objective of these user groups is to pool their resources and efforts to create assets and then the usufruct or produce generated by these efforts are used by the group. The user group members are essentially land owners and contribute their share of cost in creating field assets like conservation structures (bunds), check dams, farm ponds, etc.

The basic idea behind the user groups is with the sharing of cost of construction. The joint efforts made in the process lead to a greater degree of participation of community in planning and implementation of the activity proposed. Sharing of cost also leads to a sense of ownership in the assets leading to its proper maintenance by the community and rational utilization of usufruct by them.

Farmer Associations/Federations

These are larger groups of rural community involved either with the linkage and convergence of smaller groups engaged in similar activities or, taking up management/ coordination of activities being undertaken by smaller groups. Their area of operation is not limited to *panchayat*. Successful examples of farmer associations/federations are Water User Associations

(WUAs), WAs, *Mahila Mandals*, Commodity Associations/Federations and the larger political lobbies of farmers. Details of few of them are illustrated below:

1. Water User Association

The concept of WUAs has emerged from developments in the area of Participatory Irrigation Management (PIM) involving farmers as a major stakeholder all over the world. PIM through WUAs began in India since mid eighties with the starting of Command Area Development Program. National Water Policy 1987 had further underlined the need for progressive participation of farmers in irrigation management. However, water being a State subject PIM has been progressing in varying degrees across the States. There are a large number of successful examples of WUA in the State of Andhra Pradesh. A WUA is a registered organization with a formal structure. It has a General Body consisting of all the shareholders involving different category of farmers, the number may go beyond 180 in some cases. Area of operation is not limited to a single village. The Managing Committee consists of President, Secretary, Treasurer and farm executive members. Public Works Department is managing very big tanks and other sources of irrigation, whereas medium and smaller tanks are handed over to local bodies (GPs). Management of these irrigation services is transferred over to the WUAs, who maintain all the records, pursue a transparent administration and take up the activities like cleaning of channels, de-silting the tanks and ponds, growing plants on the banks and bunds of the lakes and tanks, fish cultivation in the tanks and ponds, etc. Each shareholder under the WUAs willingly contributes a mutually agreed share of amount based on acreage. Matching grant is released by the government, which is deposited in the fixed deposit in a bank. The interest accrued is used for maintenance of the structure in future. The government provides the constructed field channels.

2. Watershed Associations

This is another form of participatory management, which has emerged concurrently with the WUAs and the centrally sponsored Watershed Development Program. WA is an agency comprising of all the villagers in watershed area. The WAs are responsible for approval of watershed plans and supervision of the execution of plan activities. They are also ensuring collection of contributions, check measurement of works, payment of wages, sharing of usufructs, formation of peoples groups, etc.

3. Federation of Women's Groups

Federation of women's groups into larger organizations has greatly contributed to rural development through empowerment of women. The classical example of such a federation is Mahila Gramin Bank in Andhra Pradesh, which has emerged after federating a large number of credit and thrift groups operating at grassroots level. The *Mahila Mandals* in Himanchal Pradesh have been actively involved in formation of active SHGs of women under different schemes. The ITD component of NATP has also been promoting federation of women group involved in different enterprises viz. production, processing and marketing of produce from agriculture and allied sectors at block level and above. The federation in such situations plays the role of a coordinator, facilitator and capacity builder for the connected groups.

4. Panchayat Samiti

The historical background of three-tier system of PRIs and details of smallest level of PRIs, the GP has been elaborated in the previous section. PS is the block level/intermediate level PRI playing a key role in linking the village *panchayats* with the district level bodies. The 73rd Constitutional Amendment provides that the Chairpersons of all the GPs covered under a block could be the members of PS. In turn, Chairmen of these intermediate *panchayats* could be members of the district *panchayat* (ZP). The Members of Parliament (MPs), Members of Legislative Assemblies (MLAs) can also be members of PS or ZP. The Chairperson of PS is assisted by a Chief Executive called Block Development Officer (BDO) and has supports of Sub-divisional Inspectors, junior engineers and accounts and ministerial staff. In most of the States, unit of planning is PS and ZP acts as a coordinating/ supervisory body. The PSs act as the nodal agency/in-charge for implementing the rural development works assigned to PRIs, funding to GPs, guiding them, supervising and monitoring their work.

5. Nyaya Panchayats

The *Panchayat* Committee of the Local Self-government Ministers Conference 1954 recommended the formulation of a *Nyaya Panchayat* (NP) for the area comprising 4-5 GPs. Each GP elects five persons to be nominated to NP and all the members on the NP are subdivided into five groups, one of them, functioning as a *Panchayat* Court administering judicial function alternately. They further recommended that more powers in terms of criminal and civil limits could be delegated to NPs provided the parties agreed to refer their cases for arbitration to such courts. NPs are functioning in all States except Assam, Andhra Pradesh, Tamil Nadu, and parts of Karnataka, Kerala, West Bengal and Nagaland.

Formal Institutions

At village level, all departments and institutions do not necessarily have in position the required functionaries to implement the schemes and programs in agricultural/rural development. However, a few departments/agencies do have village level functionaries viz., village extension worker, village level worker (*Gram Sevak*), Secretary to GP, agricultural assistant, veterinary assistant, village revenue worker (*Patwari*), Secretary of village level cooperative societies, etc.

Features of Integrated Rural Development

The concept of IRD has had its main thrust on maximization of human welfare in rural areas through achieving a balance between economic growth and social justice. However, inadequacy of resources amongst rural communities because of poverty, unemployment and inequality has been the main concern of all the IRD efforts. It is therefore important to look at the historical developments in order to understand the IRD approaches and strategies initiated to address these issues.

A comprehensive approach to rural development was introduced through CD programs launched in the early 1950s, when the concept of *development block* was brought in. This followed the emergence of PRIs during the late 1950s, which set the tone for rural development through community participation. During 1960-61 Increased Agricultural District Program (IADP) was initiated followed by Intensive Agriculture Area Program (IAAP) in 1964. These schemes propagated improved farm practices and services, which helped to Green Revolution. Because the small and marginal farmers were not able to gain much from the achievements of Green Revolution, the Small Farmers Development Agencies (SFDA) program launched during 1970 had main focus on small and marginal farmers and agricultural laborers. Food for Work program of 1977 and National Rural Employment Program in 1980 again had major initiative towards improving the quality of life in rural areas, by providing income and employment to rural poor. However, the rural poor were still deprived of significant gains because of lack of productive assets and resources needed to generate income. During 1978-79, the IRD program was launched as a major initiative towards addressing these shortcomings.

Table 2. Integrated Rural Development Strategies in India after Independence

Thrust Areas	*Programs and Activities*
Institutional reforms	Community development (CD) Land reforms Cooperatives PRIs Strengthening of District Rural Development Agencies (DRDAs) (1999) Council for Advancement of People's Action and Rural Technology (CAPART) (1986)
Infrastructure development	Minimum Needs Program (MNP) (1974) Basic Minimum Service Program (BMSP) (1996)
Resource Deficient Area Program	Drought-prone Area Program (DPAP) (1973) Desert Development Program (DDP) (1978) Integrated Watersheds Development Program (IWDP) (1989-90)
Poverty Alleviation Program	*Self-employment* SFDA (1970-71) Marginal Farmers and Agricultural Laborers Projects (MFAL) (1970-71) IRD Program (1978) Training of Rural Youth for Self-employment (TRYSEM) (1979-80) Development of Women and Children in Rural Areas (DWACRA) (1982-83) Swarnajayanti Gram Swarojgar Yojana (SGSY) (1999) *Wage Employment* Rural Work Program (RWP) (1970-71) Food for Work (FFW) Scheme (1977-78) Rural Labor Employment Guarantee Program (RLEGP) (1983-84) Employment Assurance Scheme (EAS) (1993-March 2002)

	Jawahar Gram Samridhi Yojana (1999-March 2002)
	Pradhan Mantri Gram Sadak Yojana (PMGSY) (2000)
	Food for Work Program (FFWP) (2001-March 2002)
	Sampoorna Grameen Rojgar Yojana (SGRY) (2001)
	Rural Housing
	Indira Awaas Yojana (IAY) (1985)
	Samagra Awaas Yojana (SAY) (1999)
	Pradhan Mantri Gramodaya Yojana (PMGY) (2000)
	Social Assistance
	National Social Assistance Program (NSAP) (1995)
Empowerment	SGSY, JGSY, IAY, NSAP, restructured Centrally-sponsored Rural Sanitation Program (CRSP) (1999)
	Accelerated Rural Water Supply Program (ARWSP)
	Credit and thrift groups
	DWACRA
	Voluntary action

Source: Ministry of Rural Development, 2002.

Current Scenario

Efforts made so far have created significant impact, however there are still 27 percent of rural poor subsisting in poverty and larger area still deficient in basic facilities needed for improving living conditions in rural India. Since, the beginning of rural development efforts it has been revealed that budgetary support alone cannot solve the problems, unless different concerned agencies and the community at large are involved in the process.

Institutional Reforms

Creation of institutional arrangements, which facilitate effective implementation of IRD efforts, has been a priority initiative since the beginning of five-year plans in the country. It has been envisaged that institutions should be able to:

a) improve local opportunities for enterprise, employment and resource generation;

b) help communities attain greater self reliance in the provision of basic needs and services; and

c) help communities attain self-generated and self-sustained economic and social development.

The institutional mechanisms created for management of IRD over different phases of time have been directing towards the above strategies. While, the initial CD program emphasized involvement of local communities in all kinds of rural development activities, cooperatives have emerged as a strong institutional mechanism, which facilitated socio-economic transformation of rural India. Based on the past experiences, the 73rd Amendment has presented the PRIs as the core local governance mechanisms with a great deal of powers and responsibilities to implement IRD programs at grassroots level.

In the process, the role of local communities has greatly shifted from that of a self-service mode to an initiator, planner, implementer, regulator and a promoter. The GPs at grassroots level are capable of establishing close linkages with various formal institutions (for government support), NGOs (for capacity-building, program implementation) and CBOs (for program implementation). Institutions like DRDAs closely coordinate with PRIs to effectively manage the PAPs. CAPART is also an institution created to promote voluntary action and propagate appropriate rural technologies for the benefit of rural community.

Land reforms have been considered as one of the initial measures for alleviation of rural poverty as these activities addresses the structural parameters of the rural economy, which generate the structural imbalances leading to rural poverty. Though land is a State subject, it has been on the national agenda since independence. The main objective of land reforms has been to achieve an egalitarian social structure which could eliminate the exploitation in land relations, realize the age-old goal of land to tiller, enlarge the land base of rural poor, increase agricultural productivity and infuse an element of equality in local communities. The centrally-sponsored scheme on Computerization of Land Records (CLR) has been able to bring in an element of transparency and effectiveness in land resource management at rural level.

Infrastructure Development Programs

Rural poor's lack of access to basic infrastructure facilities including health; education, food, water supply, etc. have been the greatest constraint in achieving desired results of rural development strategies. MNP was launched to improve the availability of essential needs viz. food, housing, water, etc. for the poor sections. While PDS was one of the major components of MNP, BMSP had the main objective of strengthening social infrastructure in rural areas. Both these programs directly targeted the local communities through closer linkages with various institutions, voluntary organizations involved in infrastructure augmentation.

Resources Deficient Area Programs

A large area of the country in semiarid zone suffers periodic drought situations because of massive soil degradation and water loss, severely affecting the rural poor. DPAP has been launched to minimize the adverse effects of drought on the production of crops and livestock and productivity of land, water and human resources thereby leading to drought-proofing of affected areas. A similar program DDP has been initiated to address the ecological balance of hot desert areas of Rajasthan, Haryana and Gujarat, cold desert of Jammu and Kashmir and Himanchal Pradesh, in addition to few district of Andhra Pradesh and Karnataka. These programs have a direct participation of local communities in planning and development of watershed areas and maintenance of assets. The ZP/DRDA may also select the NGOs as a project implementation agency for the watershed development projects.

Poverty Alleviation Programs

Poverty alleviation has been the main focus of IRD strategies achieved through different mechanisms.

SGSY is the holistic program of self-employment for rural poor covering organization of SHGs, their capacity-building, training, planning of activity clusters, infrastructure build-up, technology and marketing support. This program requires massive interaction between different stakeholders (including PRIs, banks, line departments, NGOs, etc.) for project monitoring and implementation. NGOs are principally involved in formation of SHGs, their capacity-building, credit facilitations and monitoring.

Wage-employment activities have been initiated to help the poor in rural areas as a means of livelihood even during lien period when there is no production. A number of programs, RWP, FFW, RLEGP were initiated after 1970-71 but were closed in due course of time. The ongoing SGRY program has also been initiated after merging two programs, namely; EAS and JGSY. Main objective of the scheme is to create additional wage employment and the creation of need-based rural infrastructure. PRIs are closely involved in implementation of this scheme, ZPs and PSs implement the wage employment component and GPs are involved in creation of infrastructure apart from social audit and monitoring. Another scheme of wage employment, PMGSY has been initiated recently which aims at providing connectivity through good all weather roads to connected habitations in rural areas with a population of more than 500 in plains and 250 in hill States.

Rural housing is a sector, which did not receive the deserving attention, till 1985 when the IAY was launched, which has well integrated community participation mechanism. The scheme provides assistance to Below Poverty Line (BPL) families for construction/upgrading of houses. *Gram Sabha* is empowered to select beneficiaries.

Allotment is in the name of female member (or joint name in the household) and construction is the responsibly of beneficiary. Under PMGY, central assistance is allocated to concerned States/Union Territories (UTs), for providing/improving the outlay of BMSs including 'rural shelter' in rural areas. SAY on the other hand is a comprehensive housing scheme aimed at ensuring integrated provision of shelter, sanitation and drinking water in selected villages. It involves beneficiary contribution of 10 percent in implementing the programs.

Social assistance schemes are aimed at providing social security in case of old age, death of primary breadwinner and maternity. Under NSAP, financial assistance is provided to these categories and the GPs are expected to play an active role in identification of beneficiaries. Disbursement is also held in public meeting such as *Gram Sabha*, GP is responsible for publicity. Another scheme for social security, Annapurna has also similar social objectives as that of NSAP. However, support is provided in the form of free food grains to the beneficiaries. GPs play a similar role as in NSAP, in addition to distributing entitlement cards to the beneficiaries.

Empowerment

In spite of playing a major role in rural development, women continue to be greatly cornered in most of assistance programs. To ensure that women get their share of benefits and opportunities, each scheme has been provided with women component. Particularly, SGSY provides for 50 percent SHGs exclusively of women; under JGSY, 30 percent employment opportunities are reserved for women; IAY houses are allotted in the name of women member or in joint name of household; NSAP has a major focus on women; CRSP provides construction of village sanitary complexes exclusively for women are an active partner in ARWSP; DWACRA (now merged with SGSY) had primary thrust on women.

Credit and thrift groups of women supported under various schemes have greatly contributed to their empowerment. In States like Andhra Pradesh, these credit and thrift groups have emerged as a powerful organization by federating together and operating community controlled rural banks with a large membership.

Future Directions of The IRD Efforts

For many developing economies, IRD need to be revolved around:

i) agricultural growth;

ii) growth of rural non-farm sector; and

iii) human development, population growth and rural poverty alleviation.

With time, thrust of IRD efforts has also been undergoing drastic changes. Agriculture, the backbone of Indian economy, received the desired attention from the Third Five-Year plan, but in the subsequent plans removal of poverty became the central concern. This was, possibly, because of the failure of agricultural growth in making a sizeable impact on rural poverty. As a consequence, the tendency to view agricultural development programs as different from those of poverty alleviation and *vice versa* became quite pronounced. Various PAPs also did not bring the desired impact because of failure of PAPs to integrate with the overall development strategies.

Policy Initiatives

In wake of globalization, economic recession and pressing demand for decentralization, *IRD efforts for the future* would need to focus more on bringing in linkages, integration, market orientation and empowerment of local communities in driving the vehicle of rural development. The path for development will have to be based on the growth of agriculture and allied sector, that too on small and marginal farmers in backward and dry regions.

Increased investment in the upgrading of employment centered and eco-friendly agricultural technologies with adequate focus on technology generation and dissemination, irrigation and water management in irrigated areas, water use efficiency and on-farm water management in rainfed areas would need to be given due priority. Greater involvement of community groups, viz. WUGs, WUAs and WAS would act as a catalyst in the process.

Development of *rural infrastructure* and promotion of non-farm sector in rural areas facilitates greater adoption of new technologies and an equitable growth of rural sector. This would also call for *greater investment in infrastructure*, roads, storage, market, education, health and women empowerment. Land reforms would require to be given due emphasis not only for equity but also for higher production.

There is a need to keep a *rationale between export-oriented agricultural growth and food security for rural poor*. Efforts towards diversification, value addition, post-harvest processing and marketing would need to address the needs of small and marginal farmers. Increased focus on a farming systems approach would be desired step.

In view of funding constraints with the governments, *increased private sector investment in agriculture* has to be encouraged. However private sector would not be inclined unless public investment in infrastructure and human resource development is stepped up.

Public sector capacity towards such investments could be augmented by reducing subsidies in irrigation, electricity and other inputs through appropriate reforms in management of these services.

While sustainable agricultural growth would continue to make a positive contribution towards rural development, non-farm opportunities would need to be enhanced to create greater employment opportunities for the rural poor. This would necessitate massive investment in PAPs to achieve high level of social development and human resource development (HRD) through better living conditions in the rural areas. Unless local communities and grassroots level institutions are deeply involved in these efforts, removal of poverty would continue to remain a dream.

Urgently to Harness Potential of People

With shrinking resource base, increasing burden of manpower in the wake of vast regional disparities, government would no longer be able to drive the vehicle of rural development alone, with desired pace. Sustenance of rural development would, thus, call for large-scale mobilization of local communities, institutions and all those stakeholders who matter for growth in rural economy.

Emergence of PRIs as an effective system of local governance, subsequent to 73rd Constitutional Amendment has created a well-structured system for people's participation in the development process. Following steps would be urgently needed to harness the great potential of people for well-being of the people:

i. A plethora of programs are being implemented by a large number of institutions in the villages. Because of this multiplicity of uncoordinated institutional efforts growth is adversely affected. There is a need for creating an appropriate institutional arrangement at village level where all the programs and activities are directed towards rural development converge. All the stakeholders including institutions, community organizations and the local communities would become a partner in micro level planning at GP level and all the program funds would be directed towards the *panchayat* level plan leading to greater ownership and integration of efforts. The ATMAs established under NATP at district level have created block level institutional arrangements in the form of a FIAC involving both a farmers' body and technical officials body for micro level planning. The grassroots level institutions like GPs may be linked with FIACs to channel multi-agency efforts in agriculture and allied sectors. It is important that an enabling environment is created so that PRIs, other CBOs and institutions work in a symbiotic relationship rather than competing or conflicting interest groups.

ii. Though a large number of programs and activities have been launched by various ministries/institutions, majority of people are not aware of them and hence deprived of the benefits. Massive awareness campaign would need to be organized about ongoing programs and activities at grassroots level. Use of modern communication tools involving print media, as well as electronic media would greatly enhance the efficacy of such measures. Information technology in particular, is emerging as a powerful tool of dissemination of knowledge. Its application needs to be promoted for creating a knowledge-base for rural technology.

iii. As majority of PRI leadership is from weaker sections with inadequate education and managerial capacity, it is important to take up capacity-building of these representations towards management skills in rural development programs, knowledge of development strategies and financing with emphasis on management tools, viz. leadership styles, group dynamics and team work. An attitudinal orientation would need to inculcate, in the *panchayat* in-charges, an understanding that the development strategy has to focus not only on infrastructure creation but also largely on "human development" irrespective of class, caste and gender.

iv. Local level institutions, particularly PRIs are going to drive the rural development process in the future. But unless they emerge as a sustainable entity, it will take too long to achieve the desired progress. Genuine decentralization through adequate devolution of power and resources to PRIs is an essential prerequisite.

v. In order to achieve financial sustainability, it is also important that GPs look into means of revenue through taxes, fees, rents, and tolls and even by owning and or leasing common property resources in a cost-sharing mechanism. Increased initiatives of the government to route all the development programs in a village through GPs would greatly help in expanding their resource base.

vi. Involvement of GPs in reorientation of rural markets to respond to the needs of local communities would greatly help in putting a check on exploitative practices. Greater group mobilization of the local communities in income-generating activities and management of rural resources would need to be strongly supported by these local governments. A close monitoring and capacity-building of these groups would be prime responsibility of the GPs. A systematic federation of various community groups to the levels of local governance would help in ensuring accountability and transparency. Apart from increased involvement of CBOs and NGOs, private sector partnership may also be initiated by GPs for rural development but with due care to safe guard the interests of the rural poor.

Success of development efforts would also depend on the transparency and accountability of political and administrative systems with a strong civil society represented at different levels of governance through strong local institutions and organizations. Moreover, for the development strategies to achieve the desired level of success, upgrading of human resources would be required on a long-term basis. There is no alternative to prosperity except through a knowledge-based society.

References

Choudhury, R. C. and S. Rajakutty, (2000). "Rural Development Charging Focus of Strategy", *The Survey of Indian Agriculture 2000*, pp.213-215, the Hindu, Chennai.

Ekka, Alexius, (1999). Country paper in Dr. Prachanda Pradhan (ed.) *Role of Institutions in Rural Community Development*, pp.154-167, APO, Tokyo.

Hanumantha Rao, C. H., (2001). "Changing Economic Structure of the Rural Economy in Asia and the Pacific" in Dr. C. H. Hanumantha Rao (ed), *Rural Transformation in Asia and the Pacific*, pp.66-80, APO, Tokyo.

National Institute of Rural Development (NIRD), (2001). S. P. Jain (ed) *Emerging Institutions for Decentralized Rural Development*, Vol. I and II, pp. 1-982.

Pradhan, Prachanda, (1999). "Role of Institutions in Rural Community Development" in Dr. Prachanda Pradhan (ed), *Role of Institutions in Rural Community Development*, pp.27-49, APO, Tokyo.

Taha, M., Om Prakash, (1989). *Integrated Rural Development in India*, Center for Integrated Rural Development for Asia and the Pacific, Dhaka.

9

Participatory Rural Development in Iran

Well-planned programs would eliminate ignorance and poverty and help improve health, housing and other socioeconomic aspects.

With a total population about 65 millions, Iran is a populous country in the world with an average density of 35.3 persons/km. Nearly 35.3 million (58 percent of total population) live in urban areas and about 25.3 million (41 percent) in rural areas. The country extends over an area of 1,648 thousand km (16th largest country in the world). In general, Iran is mountainous and semiarid country and only about 51 million ha (31 percent of the total land) has satisfactory potentials for agricultural uses. However, 33 million ha (62 percent) of arable land have not yet been brought under cultivation. And, out of the 18.8 million ha currently allocated to agricultural production, only 50-60 percent is being utilized annually. The irrigated farmland is about 30 percent. The agriculture sector in Iran consists of four sub-sectors; farming, livestock, forestry and fisheries. The farming sub-sector with a 57-percent share in total value-added in agriculture is the largest.

The agriculture sector has a prominent place in social and economic development in Iran. It accounts for 27 percent of GDP, 23.8 percent of employment opportunities, 82 percent of food supply and 35 percent of non-oil exports, plus considerable raw materials for industrial use.

In this country, almost every rural village needs credit, clean seeds, infrastructure and guidance in crops and livestock production. They also need farm machinery, marketing facilities, cooperatives, water supplies and education – both fundamental and vocational. For rapid and efficient rural development, each village must be provided with all of these inputs and functions. Integration of these functions and efficient management demand an active role of local communities and institutions to the highest degree. The governmental and private programs for rural improvement are being launched in Iran and they depend on local communities for their implementation. The emerging methodologies for community development assume that social improvements do not occur until the local communities actively involve and believe that development is possible.

Community people themselves must be sufficiently convinced to take the initiative and the local communities, institutions and people must feel a sense of "ownership". Community development is a social process by which human beings can become more competent to live with and gain some control over local aspects. It should comprise of group methods and help in the growth of personality as well. Such a process could occur when neighbors work together to serve themselves. It involves cooperative and group thinking and decisions, collective action and joint evaluation.

Local Governance System in Iran

Iranian civilization had never been limited to cities. Settled and nomadic villages have always contributed significantly to the cultural characteristics of the country. According to the Constitution of the Islamic Republic of Iran, all branches of the governing bodies, executive and legislative are responsible for implementing development programs. For administrative purposes the country is divided into 29 provinces 252 districts, 680 sub-districts, 624 cities and about 70,000 settlements and villages. Divisions of administration system in Iran are as follows:

1. Total population of Iran: 65 million
2. Province (*ostan*): 29 (each with an average population of three million)
3. District (*shares – stan*): 252 (average population: 258,000)
4. Sub-district (*bakhsh*): 680 (average population: 40,000)
5. Village settlement (*dehe – stan*): 1,400 (average population: 17,000)
6. *Abadi*: About 70,000.

Process of Rural Development in Iran

The objective of the government's rural development program is to address the rural-urban drift. Iran's population has gone up rapidly and most of the increase has been in urban areas. The First National Development Plan was launched in 1948. This seven-year plan was basically focused on the production and export. There was no direct emphasis on rural areas or societies. Instead, the main goals of rural development had been expected to achieve through agricultural development.

The Second National Development Plan was prepared in 1955 for another period of seven years. That plan too, did not have significant goals and policies for rural development. Again, the goals of rural development had been considered within the agriculture sector. Despite the fact that it lacked significant goals and polices for rural development, specific legislature had been introduced to improve "social affairs" and to "rehabilitate" rural villages. The following priorities were assigned for services in the rural areas:

i. Provision of clean water, road development, establishment of schools and public baths.

ii. Efforts against herb pests.

iii. Installing a "Rural Cooperative Fund". iv. Installing electric power stations in rural areas.

These goals and efforts could be considered as a "good experience" in rural development for the system centralized planning. The Third National Development Plan was launched between 1963-66. An important step in the development of rural society of Iran had taken place during the implementation of this plan; namely, the "land reform". This reform was launched in 1962 and could be regarded as "turning point" of rural villages in regard to capital relations. Market-orientation of agriculture commenced at this stage and the landlord system was abolished and, therefore, villagers became the owners of the lands.

Based on the new definition the rural development, three main objectives had been considered by the Plan:

i. Operations aimed at agricultural product promotion.

ii. An effective program for the well-being of the rural people and rehabilitation of villages.

iii. Social welfare and training of villagers.

Along these three main components, there were specific policies for rural development. This approach was followed in the Fifth National Development

Plan as well. Finally the approach of Rural Development District (RDD) was adopted during the five-year period, 1974-78.

After the revolution, there were no National Development Plans in Iran for 10 years, from 1978 to 1988. Rural development efforts during these years were mainly focused on escalating social and physical infrastructure and services, mostly clean water, electricity network, roads and medical facilities.

The First National Development Plan of the new government, after the revolution, was prepared in 1989. One of the most important rural development strategy launched in Iran was the Rural Rehabilitation Program. This program was mainly focused on physical planning in the large villages of rural districts. This program could be regarded as a "spatial improvement" in the village physical structure, using the tools of "land use program". One of the other major changes in the rural development strategy after the revolution was the centralization of the operational activities of rural development into one organization; namely, the Ministry of Jihad-e-Sazandegi. This institution was responsible for rural development operations. Due to the non-bureaucratic nature of this institution at its foundation in 1979, it was successful in the implementation of rural programs.

The Second National Development Plan after the revolution started in 1995 and ended in 1999. In this Plan, rural development was seen as a clear program with the following objectives:

i. Implementing rehabilitation program in 900 central villages.
ii. Centralizing and composing a large number of scattered villages.
iii. Preparing 75 rural comprehensive plans for 75 rural districts. iv. Making 33 "Rural Manufacturing Zones".

In this respect, people's participation should be considered as a necessary requisite.

In the recent past, the status of social services in rural areas has rapidly risen. For example, access to safe drinking water has gone up to 83 percent in rural areas and over 80 percent of the rural areas now have access to primary healthcare services. Over 49,000 km of rural roads have been paved and the rural electrification program has covered over 15,000 villages. The literacy rate has reached to 67 percent. This was 37 percent during the First and Second National Development Plan periods.

Role of Agricultural Bank in Rural Development

The first financial institution with clearly expressed responsibility for the agriculture sector commenced its operation as a wing of "*Bank Melli Iran*" (The National Bank of Iran) in 1930.

The nation's awakening and strong desire for socio-economic development instigated the decision to establish a specialized bank to provide the private sector with institutional financial means and guidance and to channel their concerted efforts towards the national economic development goals. Thus, "Agricultural and Industrial Bank" was established in 1933 as an independent bank.

In 1969, this Bank was expressly commissioned to regulate the organization and management of the rural cooperatives. So the Bank was renamed as "Agricultural Cooperative Bank of Iran" (ACBI). Its main function was to improve the state of the rural cooperatives. In 1973 it was converted to a development bank called "Agricultural Development Bank of Iran" and in 1979 was again renamed as the "Agricultural Bank".

Rural Development Objectives of the Agricultural Bank

The ultimate objective of the Bank is to facilitate rural development and to ameliorate the standard of living of the rural population through increasing agricultural production and productivity and the development of small rural industries and local traditional arts and crafts.

In pursuit of these objectives, the Bank is empowered to grant loans to individuals and legal entities and to share, participate and undertake direct investment in agriculture-related industries.

All real persons or legal entities that are, or intend to be, engaged in one of the following activities can use the Bank facilities:

- Farming
- Horticulture
- Fishing, bee-keeping and sericulture
- Agro-related industries
- Rural industries and handicrafts, especially carpet weaving
- Agricultural marketing services
- Animal husbandry, poultry and sheep farming.

The role of the Agricultural Bank in rural poverty alleviation, rural development and the safety programs are some of the policies of this Bank. Related to this role, the main activities are as follows:

i. Simplification of collateral conditions for small farmers;
ii. Provision of financial services to the deprived regions;
iii. Family supporting and rural women's scheme;
iv. Carpet weaving workshops and improvement program;
v. Agricultural products insurance fund; and
vi. Relief fund for the loss-incurring farmers.

Role of the Cooperative System in Rural Development

Iran has a very extensive network of cooperatives in rural areas. The most widespread form is the rural service cooperative (RSC), of which there are 4,200 branches, 24 provincial associations and a national federation called the Agricultural Cooperative Company (ACC). The provincial associations provide administrative, logistical and marketing support while the ACC issues branch licenses and coordinates policy-making and operations of the provincial associations. The system covers 90 percent of the total villages in Iran and has 4.5 million members. The RSCs are Multi-purpose Cooperatives (MPCs) whose main functions are as follows:

i. Input and equipment supply;
ii. Purchases of support price commodities;
iii. Sale of consumer goods; and
iv. Credit distribution.

The second form of service cooperative is the Agricultural Cooperative Society (ACS). The total membership of ACSs is 562,000. Each ACS is specialized in a particular activity such as poultry production or machinery services. The RSCs and the ACSs are supervised, trained and backed up by a central organization for rural cooperatives.

Moshaa Production Cooperatives

Moshaa Production Cooperatives with 12,800 societies and 100,000 members provide common services to peasants, who had benefitted from the land reform. Efficient production in small plots is being promoted by the Ministry of Agriculture through the cooperatives, but these cooperatives are not common (only 76 societies with 12,500 members).

The cooperative system in Iran's hand-woven carpet industry was introduced after the revolution. Carpet cooperatives were established in an attempt to organize and bring together the carpet weavers. The carpet weaving workshops which are scattered nationwide, supply the raw materials, upgrade the quality and quantity of the carpets, train new weavers, control the work environment, address health issues, market the products of members and promote the exports of hand-woven carpets. In addition to such cooperatives, the unions across the country have been brought together under the "Nation-wide Union of Hand-woven Persian Carpet Cooperatives".

Rural Islamic Councils

At present, the Rural Islamic Councils are the main local institutions for rural development. The first election of the Rural Islamic Councils was conducted in March 1999.

It covered 33,000 villages and 108,000 representatives were elected; out of them, only 559 people were women and the rest were men. This new people's institution has now become the major tool of the rural development process in the country, especially in terms of village management.

At present, there are 33,000 village councils in different parts of Iran. The main activities of Islamic Village Councils in Iran are as follows:

i. Study and identification of village needs and preparing projects for rural development;
ii. Involved in people's participation and connecting them with ministries and organizations which are related to rural activities;
iii. Supervising and looking after the application of rural development projects;
iv. Cooperation with authorities for the establishment, maintenance and the use of public establishments and looking after socio-economic and welfare of rural people; and
v. Improving health and environmental conditions in the villages.

Government and Administration

Iran's population was 60.05 million in 1996 (Census, 1996). About 60 percent of the population lives in cities and 38 percent in rural areas. The remainder is the tribal and moving people. The population growth between 1986 and 1996 was 2.3 percent, compared to 3 percent in the previous decade. The Central, North and Northwest regions of the country are of the most crowded regions. The Central region with about 19 percent of the surface area contains 32 percent of country's population while the East region with about 50 percent of the surface area has only 19 percent of the total.

For administrative purposes, the country is divided into 29 provinces, 252 districts, 680 subdistricts and more than 70,000 settlements and villages. The Ministry of Interior appoints the heads of provincial and district administrations.

Rural life in Iran, which has a long history, has undergone some transformations, both in terms of economic and social, just over the past few decades. These transformations are manifested in human resources development, increase in the participatory organization, rural dwellings and villages, ownership of water resources, irrigation and farming systems, production tools, and also in the use of manpower as well as in the economic and cultural relation with urban societies. In parallel with these changes, the structure of rural population has changed. Based on 1996 census, the total rural population of country was 23,026,293 persons in 68,125 villages. In spite of the absolute growth of the rural population in the recent decades, the proportion of rural population in comparison with the total population has decreased due to increased village-city migration and the increasing trend of converting rural centers into cities. Nevertheless, nearly 40 percent of the country's population is still living in rural areas, something that underlines the importance of paying more attention to these areas.

Major economic activities of Iran's villages include cultivation, gardening, animal husbandry and handicrafts. About half of the active rural population of age 10 and above is engaged in the agriculture sector, nearly 27 percent in the industrial sector and 22 percent in the services sector. The cultivated surface area of the country is about 18 million ha and the number of domesticated animals in the villages amounts to 92 million. Historically, soil and water resources as well as economic, social, political, security and cultural conditions have influenced the spatial distribution and form of Iran's villages.

According to the constitution of the Islamic Republic of Iran, all branches of the governing body – Islamic laws under the supervision of the "*Valieh – Faqih*", the great Islamic jurist, govern executive, legislative and judiciary. The president, the second highest authority, is responsible for implementing and safeguarding the constitutions provisions and coordinating all three branches of governing body.

Ministry of Jihad for Agriculture

After the revolution, one of the actions adopted by Imam Khomeini's directions, the Great Leader of Iran, was the formation of a foundation named Jihad-e-Sazandegi (Jihad for Construction) worked in Iran's villages with the aim of agricultural and rural development and alleviation of poverty, especially in the villages.

This action was developed and could attract rural people's reliance by encouraging them to participate in activities, decision-making and considering their ideas in respect of program development, solving existing problems, budgeting and accessibility to resources. Such developments resulted in the conversion of this foundation into a ministry namely, Jihad-e-Sazandegi in year 1983. And, in the year 2002, this was combined with the Ministry of Agriculture as the new Ministry of Jihad for Agriculture.

The important duties of this ministry are as follows:

i. Determination of policies, strategies and required plans for development of the rural and tribal regions of the country;

ii. To provide possible and active participation of people in rural areas in social and development activities;

iii. To provide the required energy for the villages and constructing and maintaining rural roads;

iv. To improve and perform the education and extension courses suitable for the rural entrepreneurs;

v. To protect the watersheds, stabilize the movable sand and reduce the deserts; and

vi. To regulate and control the market of domesticated animals, meet and other protein productions.

Deputy for Extension and Popular Participation

The major role of this Deputy is to support the activities of other Deputies and organizations through extension, training and attraction of people's participation. It plays an important role in integrated rural community development of Iran.

The Deputy's major strategies include the following:

- Revising and reorganizing the departments' plans with emphasis on increasing the quality and effectiveness of respective missions;
- Reviewing and designing the internal establishments in terms of organizational structure; and
- Reorganizing manpower and staffing.

The relevant policies are listed below:

- Supporting private sector participation in the agriculture sector;
- Developing extension network;
- Designing and implementing a needs-assessment system;
- Organizing and promoting local grassroots institutions; and
- Encourage people's participation, design appropriate organizations for rural women and human resources development.

The long-term qualitative objectives are as follows:

- Develop human resources and productivity;
- Promote organized participation among producers and beneficiaries of the sector by taking advantage of local and regional capacities;
- Optimizing the utilization of extension's infrastructure resources and services;
- Providing basic information and technical knowledge to for producers and beneficiaries;
- Upgrading the knowledge level as well as theoretical and technical skills of both beneficiaries and producers on a constant basis;
- Stabilizing appropriate sustainable employment opportunities in rural areas; and
- Improving organizational structure of the skilled human resources (both producers and beneficiaries) in various sub-sectors of agriculture.

The duties of the Deputy include: improve cultural and social development of rural communities; increase and develop the technical skills in order to improve rural people's power for using their facilities to optimize production and economic condition of the villages; create and develop rural organizations and foundations in order to ensure effective people's participation in the management of villages; mobilize and use facilities and public resources in the rural development programs; and develop the cooperative works at production, distribution as well as in services.

Deputy of extension and popular participation includes some offices such as studies and planning, extension, popular participation and mobilization, training of rural people, women affairs and organizing and supporting the headquarters of extension. Each of these sections undertakes specific duties.

The authorities of the Ministry of Jihad for Agriculture believe that integrated and sustainable rural development could be achieved only if the planning is made from lower to upper levels with active participation of people. The authorities and governmental experts would then play the role of supervisor, supporter and facilitator.

Role of Grassroots Organizations in Rural Development

A "needs analysis" is required to facilitate the regularization of policy-making and planning activities so as to make better use of local human resources and capacities and, as a result, to break down macro-level development in to local areas. The current concern is "bottom-up development" with emphasis on the significant role of people. Following this, grassroots institutions as well as local and indigenous organizations should play a significant role as organized and effective establishments.

Besides governmental and nongovernmental organizations a great number of such traditional organizations have been active through local leadership and "co-thinking". Because of their simplicity and adaptability to available resources, properties and the community-based socio-economic system, these types of participatory organization or institutions can comparatively meet the needs of the community in a more effective way.

However, due to characteristics such as traditional simple structure, poor communication system and the like, not only their efficiency cannot be increased, but also they are less likely to expand their capabilities beyond local levels. Nevertheless, at present emergence and expansion of modern popular organizations, including NGOs, have facilitated bottom-up development or participatory development in a new path. These organizations often come into existence spontaneously or voluntarily by local and indigenous people with related capacities for decision and action. In some cases governments also establish and develop such organizations.

Presently new types of grassroots organizations are being created and developed which are actively involved in development process alongside the cooperatives and other kinds of governmental organization and establishments.

Characteristics of Grassroots Organizations and Establishments

The major characteristics of grassroots or popular organizations at local level (including cooperatives and community-based organizations) as well as those of NGOs can be summarized as follows:

1. Voluntary Formation

Most often, these organizations tend to form in accordance with the common felt-needs of local people. People themselves come together and undertake common activities on a voluntary basis. Apart from the fact that how they are formed, these organization might be considered as establishments where the individuals tend to maintain their membership voluntarily.

2. Independence and Autonomy

Grassroots organizations are managed and controlled by people themselves and through their own initiatives. In some particular political, social, and economic contexts, however, their independence is faded away to the extent that the government deems it imperative to intervene in controlling or conducting their affairs.

3. Popular Funding

Capital and assets needed by grassroots organizations are mainly provided by their members and people of the community.

4. Close Proximity to the Community

Grassroots organizations take their roots from the community. No other institution is thus as much near to the community as they are. Also, local people tend to have a sense of belonging and attachment to these organizations.

5. Non-profit Nature

Contrary to commercial institutes or agencies, grassroots organizations are not looking for economic benefits; rather they are dynamically directed towards either fulfilling local needs or accomplishing development objectives. The latter is particularly in accordance with national overall policies. Viable group activities, legitimate objectives, innovation, creativity, and lack of political affiliations/interests, are among many other characteristics of grassroots organizations.

Due to their strength and popularity, grassroots organizations perform important functions that cannot be ignored by development programs. Some of these functions are given below:

1. Information Delivery and Promotion of New Ideas

Rural areas in developing countries have been always recognized as less-developed areas. As far as development of rural areas is concerned, the major role of governments has been limited to the one-sided implementation of plans and projects on a top-down planning basis. Such a trend, however, would not be workable according to the new approaches to development, in which a great deal of emphasis is laid upon the participation of people. Improvement of this process, thus calls for intermediary agencies to provide development programs and the related qualitative or quantitative objectives with the flexibility needed for corresponding them to local community's requirements and circumstances. From this point of view, grassroots organizations not only are capable of transferring new ideas of the development programs, but also are able to create a culture appropriate to new ideas along with the transferring of needed know-how (both technical and non-technical).

2. Communication Facilitator

In establishing relations with communities, grassroots organizations tend to use interpersonal communication methods so as to win the confidence of people. In addition, worldwide experiences show that these types of organizations take advantage of peculiarities that would allow them to recognize and understand objectives, functions and characteristics of other organizations. They are also well familiar with the community's norms and values as a system. Accordingly, they can serve effectively as either intermediary institution or as appropriate communication channels to link government and NGOs together at both vertical and horizontal levels.

3. Counseling and Research

Giving advice and conducting research on characteristics, potential capacities and the community's socio-economic living standards as a whole, is another important role-played by grassroots organizations. Since they are deeply rooted in the community and are created by people from the same community, grassroots organizations can come up with efficient information on the manner of living or cultural dispositions of the community's individuals. They may as well gather the same information on natural and economic capacities or generally about the community's status so as to enrich the development planning process in an effective manner. Some of these organizations can conduct feasibility studies for development projects under their expertise domain. They may as well provide important basic and analytical information for drawing up and launching development projects through deliberated studies utilizing their ability to recognize the exact needs of communities and obtaining relatively adequate knowledge or information about potentialities and available resources.

4. Planning

Because of limited activity span, simple structure and lack of complicated linkages, grassroots organizations tend to have simple and sometimes indigenous system for decision-making and planning. However short term and small scale, their planning process is in compliance with the recognized felt-needs of local people. As a result of the simple and limited nature, this sort of planning process is easily understood and grasped by people, which in turn, cause the programs or activities to be carried out with the least problems. This would allow grassroots organizations to break down any macro planning, so as to correspond with local conditions.

5. Implementation

Grassroots organizations possess good performing or implementing ability in some aspects. According to the specific objective and the assigned task, they may deal with activities, which can, at the same time, be regarded as development objectives. Infrastructure construction activities in rural areas are among such activities that could benefit from the participation of grassroots organizations and local people in intellectual, financial and physical terms. Some of these activities include, for instance, building public facilities such as general baths, schools, clinics or road construction.

6. Training

Some grassroots organizations, particularly cooperatives and NGOs can be effective in training related to their areas of skills and in transferring of technical knowledge and necessary information about economic, environmental, social and cultural issues. They may as well provide the setting for improving the awareness level of people through employing a variety of media.

Grassroots Organizations and Institutions in Iran

Local traditional institutions have long been in existence in Iran mainly for mutual help. These sorts of "mutual help" have been embodied as cultivating groups or commodity exchange (like "*boneh*" or "*vara*") in economic terms, and as temporary collective actions (such as participation for providing expenses needed for marriage, etc.) in social terms. Following the emergence of cooperatives and NGOs in the new era, Iran has also witnessed development of such organizations.

The country experienced cooperative system as the first formal form of grassroots organizations. Since 1935, this system took its shape progressively by establishing agricultural and rural cooperatives. Land reforms in 1960 replaced the former landlord-peasant system. These organizations are mainly involved in producing and supplying agricultural inputs as well as in other supportive activities such as granting credit or offering training and instructions. Cooperative system has, thus, a longer history as compared to the other types of formal establishments. Currently some 5,120 producer, service and distribution cooperatives are actively involved in agriculture sector.

As the second type of grassroots organizations, NGOs are generally active in urban areas and mainly deal with urban issues or problems. Recently these types of organizations have emerged and developed in rural areas as well. Depending on the type and field of activity, they often take measures such as offering instructions and information services or managing activities. Indigenous or local establishments have developed and evolved according to economic, social, and cultural settings of rural communities without being guided by urban intelligence or governmental agencies.

Islamic Councils are another form of grassroots organizations in Iran. They are expected to play a key role in integrated rural development. A brief account on selected institutions/groups is given below:

1. Rural Islamic Councils

After the omission of the traditional foundations concerning the management of the villages (such as "*Khans*", "*Katkhoda*") and due to the inefficiency of foundations such as "justice house", there was a vacuum in public foundation at village level. This was removed by the Islamic Revolution and the subsequent formation of the Rural Islamic Councils. Members of Islamic Councils come directly from the community. Major tasks of these councils include: identifying rural needs; encouraging popular participation; cooperating with other governmental agencies; etc. At present there are 720,742 and 32,836 units of Islamic Councils at town, division, and village levels.

The members of Islamic Councils played the important role in transferring the villages' problem to the authorities and supporting social and development projects of the villages during the last two decades. This was possible because of the suitable "public base".

One of the important problems of the Islamic Councils is the weakness in their legal position. Some of the duties of the Islamic Councils are as follows:

- To identify needs and problems of the villages;
- To attract people's participation and associate with the executive authorities;
- To supervise and pursue the performance of the plans and development projects;
- To elect an efficient person as the village assistant for a period of four years; and
- Introduce the said person to the governor of the district.

To attract people's participation for the rural development operations, it would be appropriate if the Rural Islamic Councils are entrusted with some planning and village-management responsibilities. Also, the councils may undertake educational services, supervision and support.

At present there are 32,826 villages in the country with Islamic Councils. The number of members of these councils is 102,800 (about 500 are women). The Councils are working under the supervision of the Ministry of Interior so their training is entrusted to this Ministry.

2. Rural and Tribal Extensionists*

Rural and tribal volunteer extensionists are one of the most important elements for facilitating the country's rural development process. Based on their activities they are considered as the promoters of animal husbandry, watershed management, crop production and social aspects.

The total number of extensionists is about 7,100. They are working in villages and in tribal regions of the country. These extensionists are from rural and tribal communities and are familiar with the culture, traditions and attitudes of their societies. They can successfully transfer the modern methods of utilization of natural resources, animal husbandry (including domesticated animals) and health and nutrition to the rural people. Moreover, they are capable of communicating problems in rural areas to the higher authorities.

In many of the villages a place called "extension house" has been established to organize the activities of extensionists. This place has a meeting hall, library and educational facilities, which help extensionists to implement their work. At present, there are 385 extension houses. In villages where extension houses have not been established yet, the extensionists use other public places such as rural libraries, schools and mosques.

3. Co-helpers

Rural co-helpers are considered as facilitators of rural development. In general, they are educated youths of age above 25 years and elected by the Islamic Councils. These co-helpers are in-charge of rural co-help houses. Their objectives/aims are as follows:

i. To organize the existing resources of the villages, especially human sources;

ii. To provide suitable grounds to transfer local affairs to the people;

*Extensionist: a person who is the local and technical leader of the village.

iii. To rank the rural needs through organizing rural people and promoting participation; and

iv. To reinforce the cooperation and association spirit of rural people.

At present, there are 210 co-help houses in the country. In general, a co-helper heads each one and there are several associates. These persons are independent in terms of managing and financing their work. They encourage rural people to construct and maintain infrastructure. The Ministry of Jihad for Agriculture only undertakes the supervision, support and training of co-helpers. Therefore, the formation of co-help houses and employing co-helpers are considered as an appropriate step towards the institutionalization of rural development in Iran.

4. Rural Librarians

Enhancing community information and knowledge level of rural people can be considered either as one of the development ends or as a requisite thereof. Therefore, the Ministry of Jihad for Agriculture took the initiative of constructing rural libraries and the training of rural librarians in the villages. The rural librarians are volunteers and motivated youths of the villages and they attempt to enhance information related to socio-cultural, religious aspects. They focus on the rural people, especially the youths. There are 2,500 libraries and 5,000 rural librarians at present and about half of them are women. The rural people, especially the youths, welcome the libraries.

5. Construction (Sazandegi) Groups

The construction (*sazandegi*) groups are a collection of volunteer forces of rural people who have been gathered based on social motivation and the needs of the rural community. They have a common program and goals and they work under the same leadership in order to develop the villages. The objectives of such groups are as follows: i. To pave the way for labor and group activities in the village; ii. To provide confident and strong power for the executive units in the village; iii. To utilize people's participation in performing rural development programs; and iv. To utilize the human sources and the existing financial facilities.

Presently, there are 830 construction groups throughout the country. On average, each group has about 30-40 members.

Role of Facilitators in Rural Development

Promoting self-reliance of rural communities and the internalizing of integrated rural development could be facilitated by well-trained and motivated facilitators. A lot could be learned from the conditioned prevailed and the management styles and strategies of local and native people. These may include: identification of problems and needs; perception of rural people towards authorities; more effective innovations and better methods of production; conservation of the environment; observing sanitary principles; etc. If this learning process is followed, there is no need to impose development programs. Instead, rural development could be conformed to the reality of the rural community. Moreover, people's participation in the identification of the problems, planning, executing and evaluation could be realized. Rural development facilitators could facilitate such a process. In general, these are from the rural volunteer forces and the Ministry of Jihad for Agriculture help these facilitators in their activities through organizing, supervising, supporting and training.

Training of Rural Development Facilitators

Training of development facilitators is crucial for integrated rural development. Hence, the training of relevant facilitators in subjects such as facilitating principles and skills related to the duties of each of the above mentioned groups and institutions has been a major policy initiative of the Ministry of Jihad for Agriculture. The Ministry is utilizing training, supervision and support to make communities self-reliant and to internalize rural development within communities. During the period 1998-2001, the training input was equivalent to 475,000 person-days and involved Islamic Councils, directors of the cooperatives, rural librarians and rural extensionists.

Other statistics shows that, in the same period, 450 meetings and national/regional training workshops have been held for librarians, co-helpers, extensionists and the members of the Islamic Councils.

The educational and training needs of the facilitators are being determined on the basis of the duties entrusted and expert opinion. After the educational needs have been determined, they are examined by the experts based on their subject type, standards of the educational courses, duration, subjects/topics, training venues, etc. Training tools include video, slides, radio, television, pamphlets and educational catalogues. Correspondence training and educational meetings are also used for further information.

Rural Development in Iran: Historical Background

In ancient times, Iran was governed by a decentralized system called *Satrap*. Without damaging the local structure of the regions, both within the "Iranian Empire" and in newly conquered territories, the rulers only appointed the local chiefs as the heads of regions. The Chief had sovereign power over all regional affairs except some highly critical matters, like going to war or paying tribute, which were coordinated and decided by the central empire/ government. Due to their minority, the Moslems and the Moguls conquerors established a highly centralized government. When the Safavid dynasty came to power, economic growth and social development spread all over the country. But the tribal structure of the administration led the system towards a centripetal rule. For example, when constructing dams or digging subterranean canals (*qanats*), which recorded a significant increase in this period, the new cultivated lands were taken by the monarch (*soltan*) or his governors or endowed (*waqhf*) to special personalities (*sadat* and religious jurisprudent) or special places (holy shrines and religious schools).

Since those who were working on such lands were not the real owners, they were not attached to those lands and did not have the motivation for developing or improving productivity because any endeavor to increase production would lead to more exploitation by the owners. On the contrary to lessen the pain and avoid multiple exploitations, the farmers destroyed effective factors of production to suggest to the owners that the output or the production had decreased. Thus the owners were content with what was available and the farmers were busy with their daily routine life. Consequently, no one was bothered about growth and development.

During the Qajar era the above-mentioned procedure reached its peak. In this period not only the villages but also cities were exposed to destruction. The *Qajari* kings put up to auction the administration and offered the princes the governance of their territories. Instead of trying to develop the acquired territories, they were only eager to exploit the people as much as possible. This was one of the causes of social unrest and domestic tension in the *Qajarera*.

This practice continued up to the Pahlavi dynasty. Until this period, the villages were traditionally governed. Through the above-mentioned system, the *Khan* owned one or more villages, which were acquired, inherited or bought. However, there were villages, which had been flourished and cultivated by the *Khan*. He ordered via *Kadkhoda* because he lived in the capital city or at the provincial center. In each village, *Kadkhoda* was responsible for determining the timing and the type of plantation and also for managing the irrigation system, division of duties, supervising farmers labor and activities, issuing and payment related to land rights and the regulation of social relations such as security, arbitration, prosecution and punishment, management of rites and ceremonies.

Unfortunately, it was too late when in the middle of the 2nd Pahlavi era the land reform policy was put to practice and the obstacles removed. Although villagers were attached to their land and earned livelihood, lack of saving and modern methods and techniques of production exceeded their ability to survive against cheap imports of agricultural products, a policy which was being pursued by the former regime. Division of agricultural land into small pieces eliminated the remainder of cooperative and collective work and management done by *Kadkhoda*.

In 1963, the Act on "Establishing Village Associations and Reforming the Social and Developmental Affairs" was passed. This has gradually paved the way for the abolition of traditional system of management enforced by *Khan* via *Kadkhoda*. Because of the change in ownership by land reforms programs, it was not enforceable. In 1975, sanction "The Act of Organize Rural Association and Village Center of Governor *(Dehbany)*" created a new radical change. It divided power and authority between several institutions like rural cooperatives, rural associations, house of justice, and *Dehban*.

Developments after the Victory of the Islamic Revolution

After the Islamic Revolution the foundation called Jihad-e-Sazandegi was established. It tried to rehabilitate the rural area and improve living standards in the countryside. The young revolutionary forces and engineers were busy to create basic affairs in villages. Such developments included roads, drinking water supply, electricity, telephone, hygiene-related affairs, libraries and teaching new methods of farming. Because of American economic sanctions, climatic problems, civil war in several provinces and "imposed war" to which human and material resources were allocated, it took 20 years to do such improvements.

Interior management was left to the people via councils of province, city, district, and village. This goal was not fulfilled until 1999. Considering the necessity of establishing rural councils to improve living condition in villages, in 1982 "The Act of Islamic Councils Organization" was passed in Parliament. Jihad-e-Sazandegy was charged to execute this Act. Thus rural council elections took place, members were elected and they started managing villages, in cooperation with Jihad. In 1987, Low of "the Islamic Councils Elections" charged Interior Ministry to execute elections in all categories. However, because of the continuation of the "imposed war" the council elections were not held.

According to official statistics, Jihad organized about 33,500 rural councils in 3,600 villages in which at least 20 families were living. In the end of this term the new elections was not held and an interregnum commenced. The authorities demanded the former elected members to continue their duties. But many of the councils have been terminated.

Jihad proposed the bill of "*Khaneh Omran* and "*Dehyar*" to protect establishments and to be in charge of village affairs. The Cabinet approved the temporary execution of above-mentioned bill. This condition continued until the general elections of Islamic Councils in 1999. Therefore, during the period from the Revolution until the general elections of councils, the rural elections had been executed by Jihad. Rural management was collective and during the interregnum elected members continued their duties. When *Dehyar* was in charge of village affairs he was protecting public facilities like water and electric nets. He also coordinated with Jihad in governing the village affairs.

General Elections of Islamic Councils

By the end of the reconstruction of the damage caused by the war and with the "Five Years Economic-Social and Cultural Development Program", Mr. Khatami and his political development policy were voted at the Presidential election by an overwhelming majority of voters. Later, the general election of councils was held all over the country and under four categories: city, town, district and village.

On the basis of census of 1997 there were 4,405,603 rural families. And the total rural population was 23 million. In other words, 40 percent of country's population lives in 60,000 villages, and they produce 35 percent of GNP.

According to the law of "Rural Councils Election" any village with at least 20 families or 100 people is permitted to organize a council. Elections were held in 32,826 villages and 107,293 members were elected. Out of these, 2,564 are women. Also 22,298 persons or about 13 percent of members are Sunniest, 10 are Zoroastrian, nine members are Christians and the remaining majority are Shieaa Moslim. According to 4th article of law, in the villages with less than 1,500 people, three members had been elected. In villages with over 1,500 people, five members had been elected.

.Rural management was strengthened when rural council came to play its role. It focuses the scattered viewpoints of national, provincial and local government units. Rural council as an official institution carries out its official missions. Meanwhile the administrative council consists of all local government units. It plans and classifies the village's needs. For example, hygienic house is unable to prevent contagious diseases unless other institutions do their duties such as the supply of healthy water, cleaning passages, handling sewerage and waste. Only the councils that are native and better informed than government agents can coordinate efficiently, e.g. *Nosrat Abad* and *Choobeendar* in the province of Qazvin.

Present Status of Iranian Villages

Portrait of a typical Iranian village is as follows: There is a main road, hygienic drinking water, hygienic house, electricity, telephone, school, cooperative societies, bank, veterinarian, *Bassij* base. This means the villagers enjoy basic needs. They are grateful to Jihad personnel and feel that they require of two programs:

i. Protection, maintenance and management of what have already been built in order to continue on acceptable living in rural areas; and
ii. Carrying out the objectives of Economic, Social and Cultural Development Programs. These include health services, standard buildings, widening and paving/asphalting of public passages, improved sewerage system, projects to increase employment and productivity and income.

In the first case it will continue on the basis of citizens right, which have been stipulated in the constitution. The relevant Ministries shall allocate adequate funding in respective annual budgets to protect them.

For the second program the leadership is very important. Leadership at the center should concentrate on governmental and non-governmental aid and programs by paying attention to planning and implementation. Through the organization of councils, leadership has been created at that level. Leadership, infrastructure and appropriate programs are the (three) key factors of rural management, like the three sides of a triangle. It is necessary to explain that council election is the process of choosing leadership. And, it is necessary for the candidates to present their programs during the election campaign. Such a process would automatically specify the future program of the council.

The members of the council then consult each other and make decisions in a participatory manner. Also, special commissions could be established by the council to deal with specific matters such as security, culture, education and economy. The council convenes the experts and selects one of its members as the secretary of every commission. The council can utilize those commissions for planning and assessment like it is happening in the village of Qoroq in Golestan province and in the village of Segze Abad in the Qazvin province.

In addition, official sessions could be held with government agents in the village like those in charge of water, electricity, telephone affairs and hygiene, director/manager of the village cooperative society, school masters and the banker. These persons could offer counsel to the village council and at the same time, transfer/link council policies to their respective offices. Finally, *Dehyar* is appointed by the council to implement its decisions.

It is noteworthy that the governor of the district (*Bakhsh*) links this group to the executive and also offers counsel to them. Even in some small provinces (Shahrestan) governor convenes official sessions with the village council, like it is happening in Mahabad, a small province in western Iran.

References

Agricultural Bank of Islamic Republic of Iran, (1998). *Role of Agricultural Bank in Rural Development.* APERI, 1996. *Iran Agriculture at a Glance.*

Cernea, Michel M., (1997). *NGOs and Community Development*, translated version by Gholam H. Salleh Nassb, Ministry of Jihad, 1376.

Jabbari, Habib, (1997). "NGOs: Concepts and Practices", *Municipalities Magazine*, Vol.6, 1376.

Ministry of Interior, (2001). *Symposium on the Role and Status of NGOs*, in national and international version, first print, Tehran, 1380.

Patnam, Robert, (2001). *Democracy and Civil Traditions*, translated version by M. Taghi Delforouz, Ministry of Interior, first print, 1380.

World Bank, (1996). Report No. 11956 – IRN/*Islamic Republic of Iran, Services for Agricultural and Rural Development.*

10

Integrated Rural Development in Nepal

The majority of Nepal's population resides in rural areas. They are confronted with enormous problems like hunger, disease, illiteracy, etc. The immediate need is, therefore, to improve the socio-economic lives of the rural masses that are economically weak and numerically large in overall spectrum of development and growth by combating poverty, disease, and ignorance. In order to achieve these basic objectives, several developing nations including Nepal are giving priority to Integrated Rural Development (IRD) approach. It has been recognized as an effective approach to combat against the multidimensional problems of the rural areas of developing countries.

Integrated Rural Development: Concept and Approach

Keeping in view nature of rural problems, the planning for rural development must be multipurpose, the objectives and contents of different programs must be in mutual harmony and their implementation must be coordinated. This approach stresses integration of different programs in a relatively smaller area to make it manageable and effective. The approaches and methods for rural development strategy could differ from country to country. Many factors, such as: the country where it occurs; the stage of development of that country; the skill and wisdom of its planners and administrators; and the extent to which its citizens are informed, consulted and encouraged to participate would determine the shape it takes. Despite the considerable efforts in the past, alleviation of poverty in the rural areas has posed intractable problems. In general, the growth models tried in the past have failed to make trickle-down mechanism to reach the hardcore poor. A consensus has been reached that Integrated Rural Development Program (IRDP) is the right policy strategy for rural development in Nepal, assuming the effective enactment of decentralization bill followed by the evolution of new institutional structures.

Evolution of Integrated Rural Development in Nepal

The concept of rural development emerged in 1940s when development programs were operating through community participation. After the establishment of United Nations (UN), developed and underdeveloped nations formulated community-based development processes. In a changing political environment during 1950s, Nepal initiated *Tribhuban Gram Bikash Karyakram* (Tribhuban Village Development). With the establishment of one party system "*Panchayat*", the program was renamed *Panchayat Bikash Karyakram.* In the 1970s, Small Farmer Development Program, Productive Loan Development Program and other regional relevant programs were operated as key IRD programs in Nepal. In the 1980s, the slogan of

"Self-reliance for Rural Development" emerged. This approach was developed during the period to circumvent different characteristics of rural poverty through analyzing local community characteristics, needs, situation and, dividing them into different groups through mobilizing activated local community-based organizations (CBOs).

Role of Local Institutions in Integrated Rural Development

Local self-reliance institutions need to be mobilized in order to recognize and mobilize the dispersed community resources which can construct small projects, identify more needy sectors and for self-evaluation of its capacity for IRD. Roles of local institutions and organization for IRD are:

i. increase the affection and reduce the cost of projects as the members of local organizations would work as volunteers;
ii. follow participatory approach for rural infrastructure development and diagnosis of marginalized people in the society;
iii. motivating the communities by coordinating and recognizing community needs, benefits, and capacity for project development and implementation sustainably;

iv. appropriate mobilization and recognition of local resources and means; and

v. utilize rural community people's knowledge, working system and capacity for their own betterment.

In Nepal, the Village Development Program (VDP), which started even before launching the First Five-Year Plan (1956-60) with the donor's interest, primarily that of the World Bank; led to adoption of the IRDPs. The IRDP has been implemented to improve the living condition of the rural people by providing different goods and services in a coordinated manner and to develop rural infrastructure. In the Ninth Plan (1997-2002), the high-priority areas were: poverty alleviation; productivity increment by promoting people's participation; strengthening institutional capacity of the local bodies (government); and the employment-generating projects which were constructed and maintained by the users' groups. The projects focus in backward regions and communities and the poor people. The projects have been selected under the priorities determined by District Development Committee (DDCs).

During the Ninth Plan, four IRDP projects have been implemented in five districts: Gulmi and Arghakhachi Rural Development Project; Gorkha Development Project; Lamajung Development Project; and Dhading Development Project.

In Nepal, special emphasis is being given for the last few years, to the participative development efforts, based on the concept of decentralization for all-round national development. Development programs based on enabling self-government and people's empowerment at the local level have been pushed forward. To accomplish this mission, resources and means have been made available to the village level through the government sector as well as non-governmental institutions. Also, emphasis has been given to mobilizing local resources on the basis of people's participation through consumer groups. In order to make local development programs sustainable and effective, local institutions have been made fully accountable for the management of resources and means, thereby moving forward the process of their spontaneous mobilization and management. In this way, in order to promote, motivate and encourage local development in line with decentralization process, His Majesty's Government has formulated acts and regulations relating to local institutions.

Development practitioners must believe that rural people know what is their requirement for their own development and they have the potential to participate in efforts to improve their lives. Development policy-makers, bureaucrats and front-liners/agents must believe that the rural community, however naïve, simple and uneducated, do have the latent talent to seek both local alternatives and outside possibilities to solve their own problems and devise designs for their own development.

Future Directions of Integrated Rural Development Programs

At present, increasing people's involvement in deciding development activities is the most challenging task for developing countries. For any project to be effective, the people/ farmers, local institutions and organizations must participate in deciding project activities required to increase productivity, to improve access to markets and to improve sustainable management of farm/forest recourses and product/market systems. Rural development through such strategies could be one of the important vehicles to achieve following basic objectives:

i. Increased access to resources, their control and opportunities for income by local people;
ii. Increase local investment in development;
iii. Mobilization of local resources;
iv. Creation of local employment opportunities;
v. Increase the local sources of income;
vi. People's active participation in development process;
vii. Women's active participation in the development process; and
viii. Effective implementation of decentralization at local level.

Salient Features of Integrated Rural Development

- Improving the life standard of local communities;
- Development of different social aspects like education, health and sanitation, drinking water, employment and skills. Training and other essentials services;
- IRDP must be complete within a fixed time period;
- It must be community-based; and

- It should be coordinated with grassroots level and there must be participatory and decentralization local governance policy.

Village Level Local Administration System

The Act of Local Government and Local Autonomy has provided legal rights to mobilize local resources. The Act has given more power to local governments to decide themselves in diagnosing problems, determining priorities, implementing, evaluating and arranging provisions to coordinate municipality and Village Development Committee (*Gaon Bikash Samitee*) (VDC) with local government DDC. At present, VDC plans are being formulated annually through *Gaon Parishad* (Village Assembly). In this, they consider VDC plan, DDC grant plan and the NGOs plan. All the ward members and NGOs representatives participate in the latter. Plan is implemented through different line agencies, users groups, NGOs and local CBOs. VDC play the role as the village development entity and ward members coordinate settlement issues with the VDC Executive Board. VDC collect revenues from local road services, approve house maps and various other documents and, manage district grant, nation subsidy, etc.

Role of Users' Committees

The users' committee is the grassroots level organization that ensures people's participation in IRD work. Users' committee is formed from the mass meeting of the local beneficiaries of the concerned project. Local Governance Regulation has made it compulsory that the participation of women members in users' committee should not be less than 30 percent of total members in a users' committee but the number varies depend upon the size, duration and cost of the project and the area.

Users' committee can be a useful link between the technical office and the people. Before construction they can act as a source of information about the needs of the people and existing problems in the village. They should be consulted before designs are prepared so that their valuable inputs can be incorporate into the designs. Careful consultation with the users' committee during the feasibility stage and site selection will help to eliminate future problems and bring to light special conditions and situations at the project site that might not be noticed by an engineer or technician.

Besides the practical value of their advice, it is important to involve the users' committee early in the life of the project so that they feel that the project is truly theirs. Without this feeling, it will be more difficult to get necessary cooperation of the users' committees. Part of the cost of construction is often met through volunteer labor provided by the users' committee. When this is the case, the person in-charge of the site must maintain contact with the users' committee to keep them informed of the amount of labor required to keep the project on schedule and all other matters relating to the work.

After construction is completed, the users' committee is responsible for maintaining the system, whether it is a drinking water supply system, irrigation projects, suspended bridge, roads, trails, buildings or other projects.

In the past, the users' committees were more like informal bodies, and were previously called construction committees. The Local Governance Act has made formal provisions for the users' committees.

Role of Non-governmental Organizations

Many Nepali communities and ethnic groups have a long tradition of *Guthi* (Trust) for public interest through CBOs. A *guthi* can be private or public. The purpose of traditional *guthi* is charity or welfare of clan or community. Some *guthis* have been in existence for centuries with some of old traditions and customs still in practice. The written history of civil society organization dates back to 1926, when "*Kamdhenu", Nepal Gandhi Smarak Charkha Prachaarak Guthi* (the Gandhi Memorial Spinning Wheel Propagating Trust) was founded by Tulsi Mehar. It was the first modern Nepali NGO for social reform and citizen's self-reliance. In different places, religious societies like *Bhajans* (group of singing religious song) used to function to make the people aware of their rights and duties.

After the establishment of democracy in 1951, different efforts were made for the development of NGOs. In the early 1950s the government took the leadership to launch the community development movement with the assistance of U.S.A. and India and initiated the "*Tribhuvan Gram Vikas* Movement" to improve the conditions of the rural areas. This effort led to the formation of some people-based organization. Some of the CSOs like Family Planning Association, Nepal Red Cross Society, *Paropakar Sanstha* were established with the initiation of the people to help the needy people.

Reorientation of development activities is a process of transfer of decision-making and command over resources to people's organizations and institutions, both from donor agencies and governments. But the national and local NGOs of the developing countries need to play a much larger catalytic role in fostering people's participation and empowering them.

In this era of globalization and unbridled market forces, local CBOs and NGOs are the only institutions that can advance the interest of people as a group. As the agencies of IRD, local NGOs can play an important and effective role in the delivery of services like community health and drinking water, income-generating activities and skill training to uneducated and marginalized rural communities. The greatest advantage in NGOs is that they are flexible in methods of communication, timing of interventions and in the mode of operations.

Successful NGOs use to begin a close dialogue with people, identify their needs and work with the people for the fulfillment of qualitative targets, especially when they are not dependent on external donor funding. The process for awareness raising and confidence building in itself is recognized as a development goal. Successful NGOs have worked through organizing communities into groups for self-help, and self-development, which would help in building solidarity of the community members and empowering them.

Mobilization of Non-governmental Organizations

The role of NGOs has become increasingly important in making various activities of people-oriented IRD and also in extending services and facilities to the grassroots level. In a liberal administrative environment created after restoration of democracy, NGOs have become involved in large number in various sectors. However, the services and the scopes of activities of those NGOs, which are actively in operation, are limited and small in terms of coverage.

The major problems involved in effective mobilization of such organizations include: the lack of coordination among different activities of these NGOs in conformity with social, economic and cultural characteristic and lifestyles of concerned communities; and the lack of proper record-keeping system to monitor and record activities and achievements of NGOs. In this context, NGO will be mobilized in a way to make their work complementary to the development activities carried out by the government.

The important contribution made by local NGOs in socio-economic development will be objectively identified and; the nature, scope, resources and capabilities of such local community-based NGOs will be judged and they will be encouraged to work in backward communities and especially in underdeveloped remote regions. They will also be motivated to work as facilitator vis-à-vis local institutions including DDCs and VDCs, educational institutions and various community organization (CO) and consumers. A facilitating environment will thus be created to mobilize local NGOs for IRD. An appropriate criterion will be developed for positively evaluating, monitoring and supporting the works, scope and role of NGOs.

Institutional Coordination and Network in Local Governance

DDC and VDC should coordinate the activities of the NGOs in their working areas so as to avoid duplicate of programs and activities. NGOs mobilization strategies play a vital role to achieve this task. CBOs, i.e., cooperatives, consumers' committees, self-reliance organizations, saving and credit groups, etc. have been working in coordination with local governance to solve their own problems.

Village Development Through Social Mobilization

VDP is one of the Participatory District Development Programs (PDDPs) integral components and the main channel of implementation for participatory and sustainable local governance/development. As a people-centered program, VDP's main thrust is improving livelihood at the household level for alleviating poverty. It uses social mobilization as a tool for urging local people to form their own organizations, to promote their development through their own and other resources, and to actively participate in decision-making process for improving their lives and their surroundings.

VDP builds on the lessons learnt from Seed Grant Fund (SGF) activity. SGF had successfully demonstrated the value and effectiveness of the user groups as channels for managing participatory and community-based projects. The Fund had also illustrated the validity of establishing and strengthening an operational partnership between the DDCs and the targeted VDCs.

Social mobilization works on the basic premise that poverty is a form of social, political and psychological disempowerment and occurs when people lack access to social base of power and productive wealth. Thus, enhancing people's access to the social power reinforces their political power too, and an increase in productive wealth leads to improved livelihood. When people are socially empowered the atmosphere is conductive for them to group together into organizations. These organizations, through capital generating and skill enhancement activities, work for the collective benefit of the community.

Components of the Village Development Program

PDDP's social mobilization has two components: institutional development and economic development. The underlying assumption in the social mobilization process is that people get organized to work together if they live in close proximity and share common interests for community development. The foremost requirement in the institutional development process is that people organize themselves into COs. A CO is created around activities of maintaining importance to most of the villagers, whose continuing economic interests are best served by organizing themselves as a group. Active participation is sought from all households, without any restrictions or discriminations. This is essential for the whole society to move together in consensus and to build community-level social capital. When individuals organize themselves into broad-based groups, they have the control with which to address and tackle problems that they alone could not have done.

Once the social capital has been mobilized, the COs work to build up their economic capital. The people in the community need an incentive to remain organized. They require high returns from any social innovation to offset the risk involved in change, and to compensate for extra effort often required in terms of labor.

Economic development provides the COs with a mechanism to capture the potential benefits of social change. To build up their economic capital, the group members deposit monetary contribution into the group's savings account during their regular meetings. The COs also supplement their income by upgrading their skills to conduct income-generating activities. COs can have access to credit capital facility established in the "Local Trust Fund" (LTF) to fulfill their credit needs for establishing micro enterprises and other income-generating activities.

When they organize themselves, save and upgrade their skills, the COs can have access to a one-time investment through "seed grant" for increasing productivity, improving infrastructure, as well enhancing the CO's resource management capacities. As an essential element in VDP, a seed grant is matched with cost-sharing contributions from the DDCs and VDCs (cash) and COs (kind).Figure 1 illustrates the VDP process.

PHASE 1.
Formation of Community Organizations

⇩

PHASE 2.
Graduation of Community Organizations

⇩

PHASE 3.
Activating Community-based Entrepreneurial Skills Service

⇩

PHASE 4.
Implementing Priority Productive Investments

Figure 1. The VDC Process

Phase One: Formation of Community Organizations

The first phase of VDP implementation is community mobilization and the formation of a broad-based multipurpose CO. The average duration of this phase can vary from one to two months. The formation of COs is initiated through a sensitization program or a series of "dialogues", which forges partnership with the local communities. The aim is to mobilize and get CO members to work together to make their organizations stronger and to develop an alternative local institution to support local development.

Phase Two: Graduation of Community Organizations

The second phase, with an average of less than a month, tests the maturity and formation of the COs and encourage to initiate program activities which do not require external inputs or costs but which can bring the members to work together for a common cause with their own resources and inputs. These include small village development activities, literacy classes for illiterate CO members, family planning activities, formation of cultural groups, clubs, etc. During this phase, each member of the CO is also encouraged to make plans for undertaking at least one farm and non-farm entrepreneurial activity that will contribute to both economic and social well-being of their village.

Phase Three: Activating Community-based Entrepreneurial Skills

In this phase, which takes about three months, the COs can access the LTF to undertake individual as well as collective entrepreneurial activities of their choice. During this phase, the COs can start utilizing their savings for small-scale credit purposes and can also tap on LTF credit support for initiating community-based entrepreneurial activities. Such credit support is provided to the COs based on the amount of savings they have accumulated and based on the principles of social collateral. The plan prepared and approved by the COs under phase 2 activities form the basis for identifying entrepreneurial opportunities. Support from LTF is provided to COs who have graduated or demonstrated towards self-reliance and social empowerment.

Phase Four: Implementing Priority Productive Investments

During this phase, which lasts for three or more months, the COs finalize the VDC plan and productive infrastructure priorities. Support is offered through the SGF to fund local investments of the COs such as irrigation projects, drinking water supply schemes, micro-hydro, development of higher levels of cooperative enterprises, commercial forestry and others. Where possible, it also assists them in accessing markets and enhancing their sustainable resource management capacities. Grants are only given to those projects that are sustainable and provide common benefits for all members of the CO, enhance the productivity of COs. These grants are therefore provided as a means to get the CO members to work together to make their organization stronger and to develop alternative local institutions to support local development.

Horizontal and Vertical Linkages for Village Development

An intensive efforts is made to establish working relationships between COs and sectoral line agencies at the district level, as well as to tap their resources in the social mobilization process. Once VDP is fully functional, the COs should be transformed into self-governing grassroots institutions. These institutions, in the long run, will act as permanent-receiving mechanism of various resources directed for local development.

Public-Private Partnership

A participatory approach to development entails that there must be a non-central but polycentric process of development. This approach stresses on a multiplicity of sources for initiatives and decision-making, allowing a wide range of alternative institutions and funding mechanisms for IRD. The decentralized and sustainable participatory development advocated by PDDP argues that development efforts, in order to be relevant to local needs, as well as sustainable, must be an integrated effort of all the stakeholders involved: the government line agencies, the local bodies, private organizations, NGOs and COs. Nepal's rural development

policy, like most other developing countries, has so far relied extensively on government agencies to implement projects that provide social services and infrastructure development. The demands, however, far exceed the capacity of the government agencies to deliver. On the other hand, the private sector has more resources, and the NGOs and women's organizations have the capacity to deliver on a sustainable basis. Contribution of the private sector is especially significant for the generation of employment and income in the non-agriculture sector and in the post-production stage in the agriculture sector. In the absence of organized institutions at the community level, these communities have not been able to exploit the resources potentials of both these sectors.

Partners in Progress

It was clear that the resources available in the private and public sectors should be linked and coordinated. Also, the community-level institutions should be strengthened to exploit the potential exist in the districts that PDDP has been promoting. Public-private partnership should be established among DDCs, VDCs, private organizations, NGOs, and CBOs. This partnership should focus on promoting rural investment opportunities by tapping into the production capabilities of the rural communities, linking them with existing capital resources of the private sector and by exploiting existing market potentials. Such partnerships between local authorities and private sector will have a synergistic effect on the overall development of the district's joint efforts, which would be complementary to each other. This would be demand-based and pre-planned to achieve the objectives of economic development. Through public-private partnership, PDDP aims to initiate and support the mechanism for building confidence amongst the public and private sectors for the promotion of coordination, planning, and implantation of DDPs. It also aims to initiate and support the mobilization of the private sector producers, investors, marketing people and other planners together with the communities to form institutions for the enhancement of local governance, rural investment and development. Based on the success of the district and VDP, PDDP emphasizes on people-oriented, cooperative self-help efforts to implement public-private partnership in selected districts to support rural investment opportunities and also to strengthen local governance. This program envisages joint efforts by the DDCs and the private sector organizations to promote rural investment opportunities by tapping into the production capabilities of the rural communities; linking them to existing capital resources of the private sector; and by exploiting existing market potentials. Partnership between local authorities and the private sector will have a synergistic effect on the overall development of the district, as these joint efforts are complementary to each other and will be demand-based and preplanned to achieve the objectives of economic development.

Support Organizations

The public-private partnership is implemented through "Support Organizations". The local Chambers of Commerce and Industries (CCI), which have representations from various types of private sector organizations operating in the districts, which also possess sound knowledge of the problems and opportunities for economic development that exist in the districts, are the ideal institutions as "Support Organizations".

Participatory Planning and Monitoring

PDDP assists the DDCs to implement a "trickle-up" planning and monitoring process, based on the principles of participation, transparent decision-making and coordination between political bodies, technical agencies, NGOs and the communities. These Plans are then forwarded to the central level to be incorporated into the National Annual Plan to receive central funding.

References

Acharya, Umesh, (2001). *Decentralization and Local Governance.*

Gelal, Mani Ram, (2002). *Participatory Rural Infrastructure Development in Nepal.*

PDDP, (2000). *Making A Difference*, PDDP Impact Series: 01/2000.

UNDP and NORAD, (1998). *Putting People First, The Year in Review*

11

Participatory Rural Development in Pakistan

The total area of the Islamic Republic of Pakistan is 79.61 million ha and the cultivated area is 20.96 million ha. Out of the total population of 140.5 million, about 67 percent is living in the rural areas. At present, the population growth rate is 2.15 percent per annum. The total labor force of the country is nearly 41.2 million (28.4 million in rural and 12.8 million in urban) and the unemployment rate is estimated at 5.9 percent. Nearly 33 percent of the population is living below poverty line. Agriculture contributes about 25 percent to GDP, 44 percent of the country's workforce and sustainability of export earnings.

The non-agricultural GDP, however, grew by 4.3 percent as against 3.1 percent last year. Besides agriculture, the value addition in electricity and gas distribution has also been adversely affected by drought. Pakistan presents a unique picture of experiencing a relatively stronger economic growth with poor social indicators. In other words, Pakistan's growth performance and the state of social indicators appear to be incongruous. In most cases, Pakistan's social indicators are not comparable with those of developing countries. It is endeavored to improve its social indicators for both economic and equity grounds.

Pakistan is primarily an agriculture economy with a network of canals irrigating a major part of its cultivated land. Wheat, cotton, rice, millet and sugarcane are the major crops. Among fruits, mangoes, oranges, bananas and apples are grown in abundance in different parts of the country. The main natural resources are natural gas, coal, salt and iron. The country has an expanding industry. Cotton textile, sugar, cement and chemicals pay an important role in its economy. It is fed by cast hydroelectric power.

Pakistan witnessed a prolonged and sustained period of economic growth with an annual average rate of more than 6 percent in the past three decades, fastest in the South Asia. But this economic advance has not been translated into the betterment of lives of rural poor. The income gap between the poor and the rich household has widened. Growth has failed to tickle down to the poor. Arising income inequality and poverty with other factors have accompanied the slowing down of growth in the 1990s. The incidence of calories based poverty, despite increase in per capita income of above 1 percent, almost doubled from 17.4 percent in 1987 to 30 percent in 1999-2000. The position become more delicate if a broader definition of poverty (basic needs) is taken into consideration.

Rural Development Scenario

The importance of the rural sector of Pakistan in the national economy is evident from the fact that it produces bread and butter for the entire national contributes nearly 24 percent to the GNP, earns about 50 percent of foreign exchange, employs about 46 percent of civilian labor force, provides raw material for industries and serves as the main market for a large proportion of industrial products. In this respect, rural Pakistan may be legitimately termed as the backbone of the country's economy. However, the rural poor who hold small landholdings could not produce any tangible effect on redistribution of physical assets and labor productivity.

Rural development is a challenge as well as a promise. It is a challenge that baffles the policy-makers and administrators and puts their initiative, ingenuity and resourcefulness to severe test. At the same time it holds out a promise of better future and new vistas of development, modernization and progress for the vast multitudes who stand condemned to a life of poverty, disease, ignorance and the concomitant maladies that plaque an underdeveloped society. However, rural development has no magic remedy for the multifarious problems that afflict the rural people. It is, on the other hand, a painfully slow process that calls for collaborative effort of the entire community and the pooling and integration of all recourse, human and material, to combat and surmount the problems that have accumulated over centuries. It is a dynamic program that requires the development of innovative techniques and new strategies to meet the ever-changing demands of a development-oriented society. It is not concerned merely with providing a package of services and inputs leading to an improvement of physical infrastructure which constitutes the outer surface of the system, but also involves the change of attitude and the replacement of the anachronistic values and traditions with a progressive and enlightened out look and behavior patterns.

Objectives of Rural Development in Pakistan

The principal aim of rural development in Pakistan is to improve the quality of life of the rural people by improving the rural economy and living conditions in the villages. The main objectives of growth-oriented rural development strategy are the following:

i. To improve the rural infrastructure
ii. To provide the social amenities to rural people
iii. To undertake such productive projects as will satisfy the felt-needs of the people
iv. To combat unemployment and underemployment by enlarging opportunities for gainful work
v. To mobilize local resources create the spirit of self-help and motivate the people for participation in rural uplift programs
vi. To meaningfully integrate rural development with the national socio-economic development effort and further development of existing infrastructure.

The objective of the rural development strategy is to provide infrastructure and social amenities like construction of roads, supply of water, village electrification and provision of health and educational facilities. The strategies and approaches adopted/advocated so far can be grouped under the following major categories:

- Growth strategy
- Welfare strategy
- Integrated rural development approaches.

1. Growth Strategy

During 1950s and the beginning of 1960s, national and international development efforts focused on "growth" criteria to achieve the rapid economic development with an assumption that the benefits of development will trickle down to the poor and disadvantaged groups. The strategy could not be able to achieve its desired objectives because of peculiar technical, geo-political and socio-economic reasons. It rather resulted in intensifying the gap between the rich and poor besides creating regional imbalances.

2. Welfare Strategy

Basic needs approach was adopted afterwards for socio-economic upliftment of the society or alleviation of rural poverty under the "Welfare State" concept. The underlying idea was to provide basic necessities of life such as food, shelter, clothing, medical and educational facilities, etc. to the poor segments of the society.

The basic assumption was that the poor did not have the capability to stand on their feet so the government should help them in every sector of life. This assumption created attitude among the poor who later got the tendency of looking upon the government to solve even their petty problem. However, the limited resources of the government led to new way of thinking which focused more on involvement of people in the development process.

Community-based Rural Development Approaches

The lessons learnt from thè failure of the past development strategies led to better understanding of the nature and complexity of rural society. Rural poverty was then the main concern of the development experts in 1970s. The causes of rural poverty were considered multiple and inter-dependent so an integrated or holistic approach involving all the relevant sectors was adopted for achieving the objectives of rural development.

The present government has initiated Local Government Plan – 2000 to evolve "Good Governance" though the empowerment of civil society from district to *Tehsil* and village level. The reconstruction process aims to utilize to bottom-up methodology, be people-centered, transformation all segments of the society are be included as potential partners in the national reconstruction process.

The government announced a strategy for the reconstruction of local government that addresses the agenda point on "Devolution of Power" at the grassroots level. This process involves the devolution of power through introduction of new "District Government System" for empowerment of local communities at grassroots level and the tenderization of the government and NGOs functionaries at various tiers. The new system is primarily:

(i) people-oriented;

(ii) right- and responsibility-based;

(iii) right to development;

(iv) right to participation; and

(v) right to information.

The government attaches high priority to strengthening of local government institutions for ensuring effective and maximum participation of beneficiaries in the development process at grassroots level. The government believes that objectives of decentralization can be realized by associating the local government institutions and the local community organizations in planning and implementation of development programs and strengthening local leadership capabilities.

The essentials of this "Devolution/Local Government Plan" is based on five fundamentals:

i. Devolution of political power;

ii. Decentralization of administrative authority;

iii. De-concentration of management functions;

iv. Diffusion of the power authority nexus; and

v. Distribution of resources to the district level.

Presently the administrative set-up of local government comprises the districts, *tehsils*, and villages under the provincial governments. There are district councils, *tehsil* councils and union councils at district, *tehsil*, and village levels. The elections of the local councils were held in May 2001. The structure of the local administration system is as follows:

(i) union;

(ii) tehsil;

(iii) town;

(iv) district; and

(v) city district.

A union comprises one or more census villages with more or less a uniform population. Its boundaries do not cross the limits of a *tehsil*, or a town in a city district. A town may be as declared by the government a whole number of contiguous unions to be a town in the city district. A city district/district may be one or more *tehsils* within one or more adjoining districts as a city district with a population exceeding one million people having commercial industrial economy and existing administrative and municipal.

The new system of local government installed on 14 August 2001 provides an integrated three-tier local government structure ranging from the smallest unit – union, *tehsil* and district levels. The unions are organized in rural as well as urban areas across the whole district. Unions have directly elected union councils consisting of 21 member including Union *Nazim* and *Naib* Union *Nazim*. Union *Nazims* are also members of the respective district council. Likewise *Naib* Union *Nazims* are members of respective *tehsil* council. They provide vertical linkages between the three tiers of local government.

The middle tier, i.e. the *tehsil* has *Tehsil Nazim* with *tehsil* municipal officers working under the control of the *Tehsil Nazim*. The *Tehsil* Council consists of *Naib* Union *Nazims* and indirectly elected *Tehsil* Councilors against the reserved seats of women, peasants and workers and minorities. At the top tier the district government consists of a District *Nazim* and district administrator. The district administrator is responsible to the District *Nazim*. There is just one line of authority from the district down to unions but with adequate checks and balances to ensure that it serves the people and not to rule them. The district council consists of Union *Nazims* and indirectly elected district councilors against the reserved seats of women, peasants, workers and minorities.

For the first time in the history of Pakistan, women have been guaranteed representation of at least 33 percent at every tier of local government. This would allow empowerment of the traditionally marginalized sections of the society.

The local government system envisages that large cities will be declared city districts in a phased manner. The peculiarities of these large urban centers call for variations in the administrative, municipal and police structures. These structures have already been installed in the provincial headquarters. The plan effectively addresses the specific needs and problems of urbanized districts in future.

The proposed "Local Government Plan" integrates the rural areas with the urban local governments on the one hand, and the bureaucracy with the local governments on the other, into one coherent structure in which the district administration and police are answerable to the elected chief executive of the district, citizen monitoring by elected representatives, the civil society's involvement with development, and a system of effective checks and balances, completes the hard core of the political structure and system of the local government.

Role of Local Communities in Integrated Rural Development

To involve people more actively in community development, grassroots organization like the village councils and citizen community boards are introduced to ensure effective integrated rural development. Village and neighborhood councils provide direct interface between the people at the grassroots and the local governance for changing attitudes and promoting community drives. The new approach in community participation enables proactive citizens to participate in community development/service through creating voluntary organizations called citizen community boards.

Selected Rural Development Programs in Pakistan

The Agha Khan Rural Support Program

The Agha Khan Rural Support Program (AKRSP) is a private, non-communal, nonprofit company, established by the Aga Khan Foundation to help improve the quality of life of the villagers of northern Pakistan. It was established in December 1984 with a mandate to focus on income generation in collaboration with government departments, elected bodies, national and international development agencies and commercial institutions. In particular, diversified, sustainable and equitable economic development is promoted through building the competence and confidence of local organizations and individuals, and through the provision of economic resources and opportunities. AKRSP acts as a catalyst for rural development, organize resources so that local institutional structures are gradually developed to sustain the process of development.

Local institutions and NGOs fostered in the region exist and function at various levels. At the village level, a network of more than 3,973 village organizations and women's organizations has been capacitated to undertake local development initiatives. These organizations are today successfully managing a range of activities including local infrastructure creation, natural resource management, savings and credit, and small-scale enterprise development. Finally, at the local area level, AKRSP has helped develop local NGOs and other development organizations charged with yet broader sets of functions including helping build capacity of smaller village institutions, operating and managing social sector facilities, protecting and enhancing common property resources, and working with government line departments to help influence local development outcomes. To this end, capacity-building services provided to these NGOs include intensive trainings in management, financial accounting, proposal development, and fundraising; linking them to possible funding sources, and exposure visits and workshops for there enhanced sensitization and awareness.

AKRSP commenced its activities in the Gilgit region of the Northern areas in 1982, and extended its activities on a trial basis in 1983 to the Chitral district of the Northwest Frontier Province (NWFP). During 1986, the complete range of AKRSP programs were introduced in Chitral and the Baltistan region of the northern areas. The six districts of the program area have a combined population of approximately one million, consisting of about 111,000 households, in over 1,100 villages, settled on an area of 74,200 km. The region is rugged and mountainous, located among the four of the highest mountain ranges – the Himalayas, Karakoram, Pamir, and the Hindukush.

National Rural Support Program

National Rural Support Program (NRSP) was established in 1992 to set up a countrywide program for poverty alleviation. The program aims at setting up a network of grassroots organizations (community organizations) through social mobilization. NRSP's strategy is to "harness peoples potential to help themselves" for which NRSP provides social guidance to the organized communities.

Social mobilization is the core of NRSP's philosophy. It is based on the concept that the community is the center of all development activities. It is only informed and enlarged community members who can plan and undertake sustainable grassroots developments.

NRSP extends micro credit to the poor who do not have tangible collateral. In order to facilitate the community organizations and its members in the repayment of their loans in difficult times, NRSP encourages them to generate a matching saving before requesting NRSP for a loan. However, in order to ensure that this does not discourage the poorest community organization members, NRSP has set flexible ceilings for such mandatory savings. NRSP facilitates the community organizations in developing new enterprises or improving the existing ones through its vocational training program and natural resource management program. As part of the Village Improvement Program (VIP), the community organization members also receive training in business development and financial management.

Balochistan Rural Support Program

Balochistan Rural Support Program (BRSP) is the second province after NWFP, which accepted the modality of community-based development of rural support programs. In Balochistan where community mobilization efforts are far more difficult than the other province, BRSP performed fairly well in its initial years of operation. Village organizations were formed in 13 districts out of 26 in the province. There has been reasonable savings in these village organizations, which demonstrated the interest of the communities for the development work under participatory methodology. However, due to internal difficulties, BRSP could not continue its pace of progress and it is almost dormant for the last two years.

Integrated Area Development Programs in Pakistan

The concept of area development implies an integrated development of the program area covering all aspects of its socio-economic life, including productive sectors, which include natural resource management, social sector services and physical infrastructure. The area development approach facilitates seeking such solutions. The approach requires that the area selected for program implementation is large enough so that adequate coverage of all aspects is possible and the majority of the area's needs are met in a practical way. Besides, the size of the area should be sufficient to create economies of scale. The extent of the area to be covered by the program, at any one time will depend on the resources available.

The integrated development approach would necessitate a focus on several broader issues to adequately development the area. Some of these may not be of immediate concern to ordinary villager, but may determine the extent to which local initiatives stand a chance of success. Good examples of such issues are:

- lack of all weather access roads;

- degradation of rangelands and loss of biodiversity;
- low productivity of the crops and livestock production systems;
- rapidly dropping groundwater levels; and
- unexploited or untapped mineral resources.

Some of the important integrated area development programs implemented in Pakistan can be summarized as follows:

Chitral Area Development Program

The Chitral Area Development Program (CADP) jointly funded by International Fund for Agricultural Development (IFAD) and the Government of NWFP has been a first major intervention in Chitral for integrated area development after the AKRSP. The main purpose of the CADP was to eradiate poppy cannabis cultivation from the program area and to provide alternate means of livelihood.

Dir District Development Project

The Dir District Development Project (DDDP) is an integrated area development program for the district of Dir. This project is in place for over a decade now. It was designed for five years with the financial and technical assistance of the United Nation Fund for Drug Abuse Control. The Government of NWFP is a partner in funding the project. The goal of the project is to eliminate poppy cultivation and providing an alternate livelihood to the people of the district. Initially in the first phase, there was a project management unit (PMU) and a technical support unit (TSU).

The PMU consisted of national staff and the project manager headed the unit while in the TSU, all the technical advisers were expatriates. Now in the second phase, the TSU has stopped functioning. The DDDP transformed gradually from a government implementing status to the formation of community organization. Initially the communities used to be consulted and now they are participating with a community development approach. The project is multi-sectoral in nature.

All the sectors being dealt by the line agencies are also the focus of the DDDP. In the first phase the major interventions included construction of roads, electrification in the poppy growing valleys provision of subsidies on fertilizer seeds and introduction of improve varieties of crops and seeds. Sixty-five km of metalled roads leading to the poppy growing valleys was constructed in the first three years of the project life. These valleys though far flung and deep into the rural areas were also electrified with a huge investment.

Area Development Program Balochistan

The Area Development Program Balochistan (ADPB) is one of the major interventions planned under sustainable livelihoods; with the resource poor rural people of the province as its target beneficiaries. The ADPB is planned to be a model of community-based poverty eradication and is aimed at executing people's choices and opportunities for a secure and sustainable livelihood.

The program approach being used in formulating ADPB replaces the stand-alone projects made of development support and covers a broader spectrum of integrated and area specific activities. Learning from the past experiences, this approach tries to overcome the problems, which stood in the way of creating the desired impact on the livelihoods of the target beneficiaries. It is based on analysis of an area's human needs and priorities and its physical resource base and focuses on people's participation as the main tool to increase production and productivity on a sustainable basis. The program approach is thus essentially based on two fundamental principles of area development and Pakistan.

Informal/Social Institutions in Integrated Rural Development

The term institution is by no means clear and does not convey the same meaning to everybody. It is probably one of the many misunderstood words, especially when one tries to interpret its technical meanings. The dictionary meanings of the word are "an act of organizing, setting up, or founding". It is also defined as "an established practice, law or custom". The institution has also been indicated as a society or cooperation, especially of a public character and may also include the building, which houses it. The social scientists generally agree that rural communities are different from other communities in many respects. People in rural areas tend to live in a village type of settlement. A village may contain between 20 to over several hundred families, depending upon socio-cultural and natural factors. The population density in rural areas, on the average, is lower than in the urban areas. The low population density makes it possible for agricultural occupations to continue. In rural areas, most people, therefore, earn their living through agricultural work. Only a small percentage of population is engaged in other occupations.

The social relations in rural areas revolve around kinship and friends more than with other members of the community. Kinship and friendship are thus very important aspects in rural area. This does not mean that other institutions are not important. In fact, the geographical and other conditions may look similar in rural areas; they could be radically different from the socio-cultural point of view. Therefore, the socio-cultural conditions of rural community need a more comprehensive and detailed discussion especially in terms of family type, group formation and function and types of rural social relations.

The social institutions in rural areas are effective means for rural community development. These institutions are numerous and different. Depending upon particular cultural trepidations of the rural society it is important for any development initiative to examine and study the particular institution in a specified rural environment. It will be wrong to assume that the rural conditions and particularly the rural institutions are the same.

The major social institutions as identified in rural areas are family, kinship, education, health, economic and profession, political and administration, and belief and religious institutions. It is generally assumed that all these institutions behave jointly and independently to support promote and perpetuate the existence of the society as a whole. To identify and mobilize rural institutions for development it requires a vast amount of knowledge skill and effort including knowledge about human behavior culture and psychology skill and communication and efforts to improve human conditions.

Since the institutions do not operate in isolation, linkages must be forged and established not only between the institutions but with the environment as well. Four such linkages have been identified:

i) enabling linkages;

ii) functional linkages;

iii) normative linkages; and

iv) defused linkages.

The structure and working of different government institutions presently working in rural areas differ so widely. It is very difficult to propose general strategies for making structural improvements in these organizations. When one complains that "local institution are not working" one usually means the newly established institutions. The rural development specialists have indicated three alternatives which are:

(a) to oppose and try to undermine the existing institutions;

(b) to ignore and work around them;

(c) to try to use and work through them; or

(d) to try to work with and build on them.

The last two options generally make more sense. The third alternative corresponds to a promotion mode where persons in traditional social institutions are opted to work on activities essentially defined and determined from working on the pattern of organizations already familiar and accepted. Examples of such institutions could be the formation of large cooperatives for credit services from irrigation being carried by an informal cooperative system for generations. The government institutions established to provide various services can and should operate through the existing social institutions in rural areas.

Sustainable development is greatly dependent on the political will of the governments, mode of governance, the capacities of a state and the abilities of its people. It also requires a legal environment under which communities are empowered to pursue programs/projects. It is a universally acknowledged fact that people are both the means and the end to development.

References

APO, (1999). *Role of Institutions in Rural Community Development*, proceedings of the Study Meeting on Role of Institutions in Rural Community Development, 21-29 September 1998 held in Colombo, APO, Tokyo

National Reconstruction Bureau, (2000). *Local Government Plan*, Chief Executive Secretariat, Government of Pakistan.

Pakistan Academy for Rural Development, (1990). Local Government for Rural Development in Pakistan.

Planning Commission, (2001-2002). *Progress Report on PSDP Projects*, Government of Pakistan.

12

Role of Local Communities in Rural Development of Philippines

Agriculture remains the critical economic sector in the Philippine economy. Half of the labor force is engaged in agriculture. Moreover, 80 percent of the nation's wealth is controlled by the richest 20 percent. Around 50 percent of the population in the countryside is below poverty threshold. This situation is the result of inequality in the distribution of productive assets (land, income and opportunities) and powerlessness among the population in the countryside. This also causes the high level of in-migration from the rural areas to the big cities like Manila, Cebu, Cagayan de Oro, Davao, Iloilo, etc. Thus, the poverty in the Philippines is largely a rural phenomenon – and that *the redistributive reform holds the key to rural development.*

Inequality and growth are the two big challenges that necessitate to vigorously push sustainable rural development. In order to realize this, the following must be addressed/ considered:

a) distribution of the productive asset (land) to the landless farming families;
b) strengthen public participation, cooperation and accountability;
c) active participation of the people in the designing, planning and implementing projects and in the delivery of basic services;
d) enhancing and strengthening the capabilities of people's organizations (POs), cooperatives and local institutions;

e) improvement of rural infrastructure and appropriate technologies; f) facilitate investment and marketing tie-ups and opportunities;

g) ensure participation of major stakeholders such as the local government units (LGUs), civil societies and business; and

h) provision of basic social services such as education, health, potable water supply, etc.

To ensure the sustainability of rural development programs/projects, it should be anchored on the expressed needs of the rural poor and their participation in the planning, implementation and monitoring.

Local Administration in The Philippines

Local governments are defined as political units or instrumentalities constituted by law, the peculiar or unique characteristic of which is their subordinate status to the central government, which has substantial control over local affairs and likewise the power to tax. Agriculture includes fisheries and forestry as well.

Before the entry of the Spaniards in 1521, the Philippines were comprised of independent socio-economic units called the *barangays* and *sultanates*. A *barangay* was headed by a *datu* who served as head of the government, as well as legislator, judge and executioner. The Spaniards cut the powers of the *datu* and imposed a centralized system of local government. The Royal Decree of 1583 organized the islands into *provincias* (provinces), *pueblos* (municipalities), *cabildos* (cities) and *barrios*. Power was centralized in Manila, a set-up characterizing "national-local relations" for the whole Spanish era.

During the declaration of independence in 1989 by Emilio Aguinaldo, a local government plan was drafted organizing the towns to be supervised by commissioners and election of officials. The central government exercised full control of these towns.

During the American occupation, municipal councils were created. They were composed of president and the headman of the *barrios* within the town. A blueprint for town organization was developed which included the election of the presidents through *viva voce* by the residents. The powers include the creation of police force, collection of taxes and enforcement of regulations on market and sanitation, schools, and lighting facilities among others. The centralist relationship between local and national remained.

LGUs performed services for their own behalf but only acted as agents of the national government.

Efforts to expand and focusing on the role of local government were undertaken in 1970s. After the declaration of Martial Law, four cities and 13 municipalities were integrated under a political region and metropolitan system of governance known as Metro Manila. Changes in local government structures were made such as: change in the function of the Ministry of Local Government, creation of the Ministry of Human Settlements under the First Lady which took over the role of community development and the transfer of cooperative function to the Ministry of Agriculture. These changes resulted in greater centralization of structures.

The EDSA Revolution in 1986 which brought an end to the Marcos dictatorship, paved the way to new democratic processes. The resurgence of NGOs, POs and non-traditional politicians paved the way for the enactment of the 1987 Constitution which provided new emphasis on the local government and the passage of Local Government Code (LGC) of 1991.

The Code provides for a more responsive and accountable local government structure instituted through the system of decentralization. Under decentralization, LGUs shall be given more powers, authority, responsibilities and resources. The main feature of LGC is decentralization in three forms: de-concentration; devolution; and de-bureaucratization. It provided LGUs autonomous powers in four areas: agriculture, health, environment and local infrastructure. LGU as defined under the LGC includes the provinces, cities, municipalities and *barangays.*

Barangay is the basic political unit and serves as the primary planning and implementing unit of government policies, plans, programs, projects and activities in the community, and serves as forum wherein the collective views of the people may be crystallized and considered, and where disputes may be amicably settled.

As embodied in the Code, a *barangay* consists of a contiguous territory with a population of two thousand inhabitants in the rural areas. Within Metro Manila and in other highly urbanized territories a *barangay* may contain certified populations of least five thousand inhabitants. The *Sangguniang Barangay* is the legislative body of the *barangay* composed of *punong barangay* (*barangay* captain) and seven *sangguniang barangay* members (*barangay* council), and *sangguniang kabataan* chairman (*barangay* youth chairman) elected at large. As legislative bodies, they enact *barangay* ordinances relative to discharge the responsibilities conferred upon by law, promotion of general welfare of the community, tax, revenues and budgets in accordance with the provision of the LGC.

Barangay budget is sourced through the collection of taxes, fees and other charges and contributions accruing to the *barangay* and the internal revenue allotment (IRA). However, income generated from fees and taxes must be deposited with the city or municipal treasury. Budgetary requirements of the *barangay* are based on the annual *barangay* budget for legislation of the *barangay* council. The total annual appropriation for personal services shall not exceed 55 percent of the total annual income. The IRA is the share of the LGU in the national revenue taxes based on the collection of the third fiscal year preceding the fiscal year as follows:

a) Thirty percent on the first year of effectivity of the LGC;

b) Thirty-five percent on the second year; and

c) Forty percent on the third year and thereafter.

The share of the LGUs to the IRA for provinces, cities, municipalities and *barangays* is 23 percent, 23 percent, 34 percent, and 20 percent, respectively.

In the Ninth Rapid Field Appraisal (RFA) findings showed that significant participation of civil society in local governance continues. The extent of civil society participation in local government programs and decision-making varies from one jurisdiction to another. There are local governments that can be categorized as having achieved the high level of civil society participation in governance because they actively sought partnership with NGO and PO in the planning, implementation, monitoring and evaluation of programs.

Many local governments have also explored involving civil society beyond code mandated advisory local special bodies (LSBs). Respondents agree that NGO participation in local planning and localization of national programs has resulted in stronger partnership that improves the delivery of basic services. However, participation in some jurisdictions begins and ends with the accreditation of NGOs for inclusion in LSBs or initial consultation on specific initiatives, after which the LSB or the local government relationship become dormant or inactive. Instances remain where participation is determined by the attitude of the local chief executive towards NGOs/POs. The concern to be clarified constitutes meaning participation.

Local Level Organizations and Institutions

After the EDSA Revolution, there has been a paid growth of the NGOs and POs because of the new democratic space after 20 years of the Marcos dictatorship. The participation and involvement of NGOs in development is guaranteed by the Constitution.

NGOs refer to private non-profit organizations that are committed to the task of sociopolitical and -economic development and established primarily for services. NGOs arc acknowledged as organized, competent and knowledgeable about community problems and issues. Some, however, were scored for their weaknesses – parochialism, inconsistence in implementing plans, narrow mind-set, power struggle and ideological differences. Victor Jose Peñaranda, Secretary of Council for People's Development (CPD), sums up the seeming difference between NGO's development efforts vis-à-vis the government:

a) NGOs-POs operate with limited resources;
b) the government unlike NGOs, does not perceived development problems as interrelated; and
c) NGOs have an advocacy component as part of their concern, not simply the delivery of basic services.

Because of the complexities of the issues on the rural development, usually NGOs and POs form networks depending on the issue/s at hand. As an example, a coalition composed of 22 different networks was formed called "National Coordinating Council on Local Governance Code (NCC-LG)". The 22 networks are as follows: Association of Foundation (AF), Congress for People's Agrarian Reform (CPAR); Convergence for a Community-centered Area Development (Convergence); Council for People's Development; Ecumenical Center for Development (ECD); Green Forum Philippines; Kapipunan ng may Kapansanan sa Pilipinas, Inc. (KAAMPI); NGO Council for Cooperative Development (NGO-CCD); Nationwide Coalition of Fisher-folks for Aquatic Reform (NACFAR); National Confederation (NATCCO); National Council of Churches in the Philippines (NCCP); National Council for Social Development (NCSD); National Secretariat for Social Action (NASSA); Partnership of Philippine Support

Service Agency (PHILSSA); Philippine Business for Social Progress (PBSP); Philippine Federation of People's Economic Council (PFPEC); Philippine Institute of Non-government Organizations, Inc. (PINOI); Philippine NGO Council (PNGOC); Philippine Partnership for the Development of Human Resources in the Rural Areas (PHILDHRRA); Salinlahi; Women's Action Network for Development (WAND); and the Caucus of Development NGOs (CODE-NGO).

POs usually are formations composed of local organizations in terms of structures. POs uphold the wider participation of its mass membership expressed through collective leadership and collective action. Generally, POs form alliances with similar organizations and accept conflict-confrontation and action-reflection methods in transformation of society.

Other local institutions working at the grassroots level are cooperatives (categorized as primary, secondary and tertiary), irrigators' associations, farmers' associations, and women's associations.

- Cooperatives have a minimum of 30 membership, operated and managed business enterprises providing services to its members and acquire legal personality through the Cooperative Development Authority (CDA)
- Irrigators' associations, all are water users, operate and manage an irrigation system, acquires legal personality through registration to the Security and Exchange Commission (SEC)
- Women's association composed all women usually engaged in livelihood project to augment family income.

Other forms of organizations in the *barangay* include informal groups such as auto-savings group, religious organizations, clubs, etc.

Salient Features of Integrated Rural Development

Rural development remains the key towards the 21st century. Its impact on the poverty alleviation, food security and sustainable growth promises to be far-reaching. Unleashing the potential inherent in the vast majority of the rural poor who rely on agriculture for employment and income can accelerate poverty reduction. A steady step towards eradicating poverty in a sustainable manner begins by empowering the rural poor and small farmers in redressing glaring rural disadvantages.

Agrarian Reform Community Development Program

While limited in some respects, CARL is the most progressive law on land reform in the country's history. Its key features includes: coverage of all agricultural lands regardless of crops or tenurial status of the tiller; recognition of all workers of the land as beneficiaries provided they are landless and are willing to till the soil; provision of delivery of support services to the beneficiaries; creation of an inter-agency body to coordinate program implementation; provision of arrangements (such as distribution, leasehold and production-and-profit sharing); ensure tenurial security of farmers and farm workers; creation of an adjudication body to resolve agrarian disputes; creation of an inter-agency body to coordinate program implementation; and the creation of provincial and *barangay* level coordinating mechanism such as provincial agrarian reform coordinating committee and *Barangay* Agrarian Reform Committee (BARC).

The Ramos administration carried the task of completing the implementation of agrarian reform. The Department of Agrarian Reform (DAR) pushed for a faster, fairer and more meaningful agrarian reform. In 1993 DAR pursued a strategy for developing viable ARCs as key strategy for sustainable rural development. The ARC strategy will serve as critical link between agricultural growth, rural industrialization, and household welfare.

ARC framework, as a strategy for sustainable rural development, entails the development of ARCs with active participation of civil society and critical partnership with the state and the market in order to mainstream in the area-based initiative. It espouses a development alternative where the balance of economic, political power will be in the hands of the ARCs. The program emphasizes sustainability through the following:

Key Players Partnership

The ARC development approach is anchored on the active participation of civil society and principled partnership with the government and business sector. It shall link the ARCs to the changing economy, transforming both civil society and market forces into vehicles for civic entrepreneurship.

Scale Intervention Approach

Identification and selection of ARCs shall be based on:

1. Ecological Considerations

In order to allow for ecological integration and sustainability, an ARC may comprise of one or two ecological zones from among the three major types of ecosystems (lowland/ agricultural, upland-forest).

2. Socio-political Considerations

Physical and demographic characteristics of the *barangays* comprising a cluster is a critical factor in ensuring that there is a critical mass of people and community resources that can be marshaled for sustained area development.

3. Economic Considerations

Economies of scale; sound practices of resource sustainability; potential to serve as building blocks for agro-industrial development; conducive terrain for wide private investment, etc.

Focused Program Beneficiaries

i. Primary focus of interventions are marginalized groups, comprising of small farmers, farm workers, agricultural lessees, subsistence fisherfolk, indigenous people and rural women in the ARCs;

ii. Special focus be given to women's groups to mainstream them in the development process hand in hand with their male counterparts; and

iii. Other members of the ARCs (professionals, small rural entrepreneurs and youth) will also be mobilized to support development initiatives.

Gender-sensitive Program

i. Drawing in the under-represented and marginalized population into the mainstream of development processes, especially the women's sector; and

ii. Seeks to achieve gender equity in all the stages of community empowerment processes.

Integrated Area Development

i. Establishment of closer linkages between and among communities belonging to the same economic and ecological systems; and

ii. Harmonious integration of a sound and viable economy, responsive government, social cohesion of the communities and ecological integration to ensure that development is a life-enhancing process.

Key Components of the ARC Development Program

i. Land Tenure Improvement (LTI) is a basic component in ARC development that spells the difference over other rural development programs. The Land Acquisition and Distribution (LAD) involves the physical transfer of landownership and control to the farmer beneficiaries in order to emancipate them from the clutches of the landowners;

ii. Social infrastructure and local capacity-building is geared towards establishing groups, structures and social institutions that will catalyze popular participation in ARCs. These social institutions will serve as avenues for accessing support services that are necessary in improving ARC households' productivity and income;

iii. Sustainable, area-based rural enterprises are concerned with the improvement of agricultural production for food security and self-sufficiency in basic needs and eventually increase in farm income and improvement in quality of life of ARC households. To achieve this goal, it is necessary that ARCs have capital, appropriate technology, information, physical infrastructure and market. The key intervention points under this sub-component are: sustainable agriculture; construction and/or rehabilitation of physical infrastructure facilities; rural industrialization; investment and marketing assistance; credit assistance; and community-based resource management; and

iv. Basic social systems development promotes the establishment of community-based social services systems like primary healthcare, potable water supply, recreational activities, disaster management and popular education, among others.

The ARC Development Players

There are various people who play vital and complementary roles in the development of a viable ARC. Central to the development processes are the people in the community who would take the role and responsibility in charting their own development. People's participation is an essential element within the process that seeks to bring better quality of life. Participation at a more dynamic level is meaningful when it involves active partnership of various development players. The DAR and other agencies, government organizations and NGOs merely play supporting roles.

i *ARC Development Facilitator*: acts as the initiator, enabler and facilitator in ARC development process. Usually, she/he is the agrarian reform technologist. The development facilitator is complemented with the partner NGO called development worker and the PO in the area. The DAR shall not take direct community organizing where there are NGOs/POs doing community organizing. The development worker shall take the lead in organizing activity;

ii. *The ARC Development Managers*: The Municipal Agrarian Reform Officer (MARO) (head of the municipal agrarian office) and the Provincial Agrarian Reform Officer (PARO) act as the area development managers at their respective level. Their major role is to orchestrate the development processes in the ARC; and

iii. *ARC Task Forces at Various Levels:* created to provide overall direction on ARC implementation:

   a. *National ARC Task Force*: overall direction and provides technical support to the regional and provincial task forces;

   b. *Regional Task Force*: overall supervision and direction in the ARC development in the region; and

   c. *Provincial Task Force*: overall direction in ARC implementation at the ARC level.

Role of Rural Communities in the ARC Development Program

Participation of local community even at initial identification of any agrarian area (to become an ARC) is critical. An area to be considered as an ARC must pass the "must and want criteria" and must be endorsed by an LGU and PO through a *barangay*/municipal and PO resolution.

NGOs are tapped to focus on the institutional development of the organizations in the ARCs. The NGOs' engagements in the ARC development work varies and include community organizing, enterprise development, training, advocacy work, etc. They work in

ARC *Must Criteria:* area has large land with high potential to be distributed within two years, high density of potential and actual farmers, area is economically depressed, NGOs or POs are presently operating in the area; *Want Criteria*: farmers and farmer workers clamor to participate in Comprehensive Agrarian Reform Program (CARP) implementation, support services have been initially provided and LGUs and other institutions support

CARP implementation.tandem with the development facilitators of DAR. In most of the foreign-assisted projects, the services of NGOs, POs, institutions and universities are tapped to focus on the institutional development component of the project. Most of the foreign donors require the services of NGOs in institutional development components.

At present there are 1,415 ARCs (nationwide) located in 1,002 municipalities over 5,098 *barangays*. The average number of *barangay* per ARC is four while there is one ARC in every municipality.

Land distribution in the ARCs is 592,745 ha out of a total of 1,285,323 ha. The total land scope in the ARCs is only 30 percent out of the total target of 4,290,453 ha to be distributed, nationwide. The bulk of the lands for coverage are those in coconut, sugar and other plantation areas. Farmers especially those in these areas are strong advocates for the coverage of these lands.

One of the community-based local institutions is the BARCs. These are composed group of farmers, farm workers, PO/cooperatives, NGO, and LAs. BARC is playing a very important role in the CARP processes. They represent the farmers in the LAD processes and have the access to support services. Some of their functions are: land and landowner identification; mediation in land disputes; and coordination of support services. There is a total of 4,117 organized BARCs in 1,415 ARCs.

The ARB organizations such as cooperatives, irrigators' associations and farmers' associations/organizations are the critical partners in the ARC implementation. The delivery of support services to ARBs shall be through a unified development approach. Support services are provided to the ARBs through these organizations. Generation of their own internal resources is through capital build-up and savings mobilizations. These internally generated resources are utilized in their own business enterprises, health insurance, trading, micro finance organizations (MFOs), irrigation services, etc.

These cooperatives/irrigators' associations likewise are tapped as conduits for foreign-assisted projects. Like for instance, in the construction and rehabilitation of irrigation facilities, cooperatives/irrigators' associations generate counterpart fund as equity for them to operate and manage irrigation facilities, post-harvest facilities, etc. They also serve as credit conduits for farmers through their re-lending scheme. Out of 3,523 organizations in the

ARCs, 1,745 have availed some form of credit or financing from formal sources such as Land Bank of the Philippines (LBP), Development Bank of the Philippines (DBP), Department of Trade and Industry (DTI) and DAR. These loans are in the form of fixed asset, livelihood, and production loan. Investment and marketing assistance activities are likewise the focus of the organizations in the ARCs. Market matching and linking are undertaken by the organizations with agribusiness firms and other markets. Results of the market matching are market tie-ups with the agribusiness firms and traders.

Most of the infrastructure projects, whether foreign-funded projects or locally-funded projects, are through contract or managed by Department of Public Works and Highways (DPWH) for Farm-Market Road (FMR) or by National Irrigation Administration (NIA) for communal irrigations. For the irrigation projects, farmers organizations' participation starts during the construction, cost reconciliation and operation and maintenance (O&M) of facilities. During construction, they provide labor and materials and this also a means for generating equity. In the construction of FMR, farmer's participation is very limited or none at all. Participation of LGUs, specifically in foreign-assisted projects, is limited to counterpart equity for the construction of these facilities.

Basic social systems and services such as potable water, health and education, power supply and recreation facilities are critical to viable communities. While in most cases DAR does not provide these services, it is however, a good indication of the impact of agrarian reform to the ARBs. Provision and access to basic needs such as health can be a community effort. Health insurance for the rural community through community efforts can be a good strategy for encouraging community participation. In the pilot testing of DAR-*Agraryong Pangkalusugan*, health and community-based health insurance schemes in 18 ARCs show a very promising strategy for health in the rural areas. This scheme utilizes indigenous way of pulling resources for health needs. They plan and develop their own insurance policy, implement it and monitor. This is a social security and risk management strategy among the rural poor.

In the final analysis agrarian reform and ARC development is worth pursuing as an integrated rural development strategy.

Future Directions

Efforts have been made to respond to the centuries-old problem of inequality and poverty among the rural communities. Despite the impressive economic and social gains, poverty and inequality continues to be a major challenge. The main lesson drawn from the experience in agrarian reform and rural development is that the involvement of people, local community, organizations and institutions in the implementation of any integrated rural development program is not shaped by the mere existence of a blueprint for development, policies, and coordinative mechanism.

On the part of the LGUs, participation in agrarian reform does not limit by endorsing an area to become an ARC and allocating their IRA as equity counterpart in infrastructure project. In a study conducted in relation to the LGU's participation in the implementation of CARP defines that there are specific conditions, which facilitate or hinder LGU participation in agrarian reform. These factors are: a) the leadership of the local executive; b) coordination efforts between implementing agency and LGU; c) presence or absence of social pressure of the ARBs, POs and NGOs; and d) landownership structure.

On the part of the POs, their full potential must be developed and capability-building interventions must be anchored on their needs. Self-organization must be enhanced. The people are not merely recipients of development projects but rather the key players in the whole development cycle.

For DAR, readiness of the whole bureaucracy to undertake a comprehensive rural development program must be considered. For the past 20 years, DAR's main work was distribution of land. Most of the DAR personnel are new to the rural development work. Hence, skills and capabilities of the relevant personnel must be upgraded to enable them to handle rural development work.

References

Antiporta, D. B., (1999). *Agriculture and Rural Sector in Regional Perspectives: Growth, Food Security and Poverty Alleviation*, M.C. 5 series of 1999, DAR.

Blessing, Garcia-Glova. *Local Governance and Agrarian Reform: A Focus on Two Municipalities.*

Sosmeña, Guadioso, Jr., (1991). *Decentralization and Empowerment*, Local Government Foundation, Manila.

Tapales, Proserpina D., (1992). "History and Evolution of Philippine Local Government Administration", in *Strengthening Local Administration and Accelerating Local Development*, UP College of Public Administration, Quezon City.

Villarin, Thomas S., (1994). *KAISAHAN*, Occasional Paper No. 94-02.

13

Participatory Rural Development in Sri Lanka

The economy of Sri Lanka is predominantly based on agriculture and related activities. Currently the share of the agriculture sector as a percentage of GNP is about 20 percent, which has been decreasing over the recent years due to the expansion of the manufacturing and the service sectors. The population, which has been growing at 1.4 percent per annum, was about 18.7 million in 2001. Nearly 80 percent lives in rural areas and, the population density is 283/km overall and 1,063/km in cultivated lands. The real growth rate of Sri Lanka's GDP, on the average, was almost 5 percent per annum from 1990 to 2000. The estimated GNP per capita at current prices is Rs.73,528 (US$899).

The Sri Lanka society was primarily based on the family and the village. The village was considered to be the focal point for economic and other socio-cultural activities. The country was predominantly rural and the arrival of western powers radically changed the situation in terms of political, social, cultural and economic conditions. As a result, the country became a multi-racial, multi-religious and multi-cultural society. Due to the commercialization and modernization of the agriculture sector, urban centers began to spring up resulting in vast disparities in economic and social conditions. The urban-rural differences have mainly driven the policy-makers to pay more attention to rural development for the spreading of economic benefits to poor farmers and village people.

Importance of Rural Development in Sri Lanka

In the past, Sri Lanka demonstrated the characteristics of a dual economy composed of two sectors; the traditional agriculture sector and the modern estate sector. The latter produced crops for export such as tea, rubber and coconut and received adequate financial services, insurance, communication and infrastructure. On the other hand, the traditional sector predominantly confined to rural areas with subsistence crops such as paddy, vegetables, fruits and minor exports crops. This sector has undergone certain changes in the recent years and is being "modernized" to some extent. However, even today, in many rural areas, *chena* cultivation, irrigated and rainfed paddy and highland farming are the principle methods of cultivation under small farms. Apart from these, the traditional sector also includes cottage industries, blacksmith, inland fishing, etc. And, in contrast to the modern estate sector, the traditional sector does not receive many of the required facilities.

The traditional sector centers around villages. There are over 10,000 villages in 24 districts in Sri Lanka. In many villages, the Buddhist temple (spiritual development) and the tank are the two main features depicting the life of the rural people. The family, which is the nucleus of village society, is the socio-economic unit of production in the traditional agriculture sector. Most of the rural/regional development policies therefore focused on the family as the basic unit in the rural areas.

The continuous history of more than 2,500 years under the Sinhalese kings was broken in 1505 after the arrival of the Portuguese, the first colonial power. Since then the Dutch (1658-1796) and finally the British (1796-1948) radically changed the social, political, cultural and economic life of the rural people. The colonial powers mainly focused their economic activities in the urban and plantation sector resulting in considerable neglect of rural-area development.

The urban sector had all the required facilities, services, infrastructure and material well-being thus creating a large disparity between urban and rural sectors. In addition, the colonial powers introduced new technology, new religion, new education system, financial services, modern transport and communication mainly in the urban sector; thereby heightening the differences in the country. This transformation in society under the colonial powers left behind problems for the people of Sri Lanka when they gained independence in 1948. Therefore, the successive governments after independence in 1948 had to adopt specific policies to deal with the socio-economic disparities and underdevelopment in rural areas.

Decentralization of administrative powers to sub-national level has been pursued in order to disperse the power and authority to local governments to make decisions on development activities. The process of transferring the power away from national government to local government had positive impacts on the planning and implementation of rural development. It helps to incorporate local needs into development plans, reduced delays in decision-making, increased the flexibility in administration machinery and ensures the participation of beneficiaries in development work.

Integrated Rural Development in Sri Lanka

The Integrated Rural Development (IRD) is a novel idea, which was to Sri Lanka in the 1970s though it had been in use in several other countries in the region. The IRD program was initiated as a vital innovation for accelerating socio-economic development in rural areas. Its rationale derives from the long felt-need for sub national level development of those districts, which are not benefitted by lead projects such as the Mahaweli Development Project, the Free Trade Zone and urban development programs. The main intention was to minimize the possible inter-district imbalances. The IRD program as a supplement to the national program consolidated the ongoing process of decentralization of administration and development. It is now regarded to be almost the fourth lead project of the country. The key influential factors leading to the introduction of the concept include:

a. increasing rural poverty not being checked as envisaged by the top-down planning approach based on the trickle-down effect;

b. uncoordinated rural development policies and programs taking place in the rural areas and their failure to recognize linkages within and outside the rural economy;

c. the multidimensional and multi-sectoral nature of the rural development problems;

d. importance of beneficiary participation and integration of rural development projects and programs so that their full benefits accrue to the poor segments of the community;

e. ensuring popular participation in planning and implementation of rural development projects and programs; and

f. the inefficiency of the techno-economic approach to address the complex issues of the rural sector.

There are two distinct approaches in the IRD program concept:

i. Related to traditional area-based, sector-oriented "place-prosperity" approach; and

ii. Mainly concerned with target group-oriented, poverty reduction "people-prosperity" approach.

The key strategies of the former approach are infrastructure development and improving the service delivery mechanism. On the other hand, the latter approach pursued basic need provision, human resource development, income and employment generation, poverty alleviation and social mobilization.

However, the IRD concept is not consistent; it is vague and complex. Although the IRD concept is an extended and improved version of the conventional community/rural development framework, it recognizes the need for social change, mitigation of disparities (group/gender/regions), combines human and economic development, environmental protection, institutional development, poverty reduction, women in development and improved coordination and integration of development activities with other ongoing and parallel projects and programs for optimum resource utilization and maximum benefits.

However, the IRD program of Sri Lanka has not attempted to address the fundamental constraints in rural development, which are at the bottom of rural poverty. Since the IRD program was originally designed by the profit-oriented multilateral donors, they were more concerned with high rate of return, a large positive Net Present Value (NPV), and quick payback period. Therefore, most of the IRD projects did not really address the core problem of rural poverty. The macro policy framework, project environment and the social structure of the country was not given due recognition. Therefore, in some districts, the IRD program has become nothing more than a "shopping list" type sectoral activity rather than a carefully designed development plan with far-reaching consequences.

The broad objectives of the IRD program are to bring about a significant increase in income, employment, production and living standards of the rural people; reduction of inter-district imbalances of socio-economic development; elimination of underutilization and wasteful use of resources; elimination of bottlenecks and constraints believed to prevail in the rural areas affecting the development negatively; strengthening the institutional capacity to plan and implement rural development projects; and promotion of participation of the rural poor in development.

There are mainly two different planning approaches could be identified in the IRD program framework of Sri Lanka:

1. Blueprint versus Process Planning Approach

The blueprint (top-down sectoral approach) planning approach implies that identification and planning is oriented from the center. This approach has been mainly used by the first generation of IRD started in 1979 with Kurunegala project, followed by Puttalam and Matale projects. The blueprint-planning model was considered to be somewhat rigid in that there was little room to modify the design, project activities and structure by the recipient district. The whole planning process, implementation and project management was done by technocrats in Colombo or by the donor representative. The participation of people in the development process was very limited. They participated in the project, more as beneficiaries rather than partners of decision-makers.

2. Target Group Approach

Most IRD projects are target group-oriented. A target group is a defined and identified segment of community. The target group of Sri Lanka IRD program is generally the rural poor and criteria had been developed to select the "poorest of the poor". These include income level, food-stamps holders, *Janasavi/Samurdhi* beneficiaries, disabled, unemployed and women, etc. The target group approach implies that the project strategy is designed to ensure that the defined target group will become the beneficiaries of the project intervention.

Community-based Organizations

The following local level institutions and community-based organizations are discussed here to explain how the rural development activities carried out to ensure the prosperity of rural development.

District Secretariat/Government Agent Office (*Kachcheriya*)

The oldest decentralized administrative system of Sri Lanka is called the "*Kachcheri* System" and was introduced by the British. During the early years, this system mainly performed tax and revenue collection and maintenance of law and order. It also coordinated the implementation of development activities in the districts. However, the power of Government Agent (GA) in making decisions in development work was somewhat limited. Hence the first attempt in the decentralization process of Sri Lanka, which took place in the late 1960s, was the strengthening of the plan implementation and coordination machinery in the districts. Under this move, GA was made the chief coordinator of the government's development work in the district. GA had the authority equal to the Deputy Head of all public sector departments operating in the districts. These measures were initially taken to speed up the implementation of agricultural development programs. However, as far as beneficiary participation in the decision-making and development work was concerned, there was very little evidence of any improvements during this period. The second stage of decentralization began in the 1970s with a view to minimizing the technical drawbacks in the *Kachcheri* system. The development projects and program, which are identified by the central government for the district to be implemented and the Divisional Secretary is the key person to launch such projects and programs at the grassroots level on behalf of the District Secretary.

The District Political Authority System

Another decentralized administrative mechanism is the District Political Authority (DPA) system. The establishment of the DPA system in 1973 was a significant landmark of decentralization of administration to sub-national levels in Sri Lanka in order to enhance the living condition of the rural people. It could also be considered as an attempt to ensure the participation of beneficiaries in the development and decision-making process. It was envisaged that the DPA system would enhance the participation of people in planning, implementation and monitoring of district development work. However, the immediate objective of the DPA system was to provide political leadership to the district administration and development program.

This move of the government witnessed not only the increasing politicization of the district administration, but also of "over influence" by politicians directly or indirectly over administrative matters. This process, in some cases, was extreme and undermined the normal functioning of the public service. Because of political support and backing some subordinate staff disobeyed superior staff making the system unworkable. However, the DPA system provided the rural poor some access to public organizations through their representatives and ensured relief for their grievances. Though there were drawbacks in the actual implementation of the DPA system it provided a means to obtain quick solution to most of the rural problems.

The District Minister System

In the process of the decentralization of the power of government, the District Minister System (DMS) was introduced in 1978 to replace the DPA system. Under the "open economy", the government removed the subsidies and people had to fend for themselves by engaging more in economic activities. Therefore, it was the responsibility of the government to bring the people into development process in the country at all levels. One of the strategies in realizing this objective was to make the administrative system more flexible. The objective of DMS was to provide political directives to all development activities in the districts. The District Ministers were entrusted with the following functions in the districts:

i. Formulation of district development plans;

ii. Monitoring and evaluation of implementation plans;

iii. Identification of implementation constraints and bottlenecks;

iv. Identification of remedial action to speed up the implementation of development work;

v. Supervision and coordination of development work and departmental activities in the district; and

vi. Resolve immediate problems of the district.

The notable achievement of the DMS was the greater degree of coordination and quick decision-making at district level, since the District Minister, as the representative of the president, had a good control over the functions of almost all the public sector departments at the district. Sometimes conflicts between the Cabinet Ministers and the District Minister and between members of parliament were experienced which affected the functioning of the system negatively. But in the implementation and planning of development work, this system certainly had some positive impacts.

Decentralization of administration system in Sri Lanka was considered to be necessary not only for development needs but also for ethnic considerations, particularly during the 1980s. The early decentralization packages such as the political authority and the DMS were introduced mainly to help the district development process. However, early in the 1980s, ethnic conflicts emerged with the demand for "Eelam", a separate state for Tamils. Therefore, the government had to give greater importance to ethnic considerations in its decentralization agenda.

Thus, the District Development Council was established under the provisions made in the District Development Council Act of 35 A 1980 in which stipulates that "*The state shall strengthen and broaden the democratic structure of the government and democratic rights of the people by decentralizing the administration and by affording all possible opportunities for the people to participate at every level in the national life and in government*".

The District Development Councils

The district development councils was in fact a political body comprising of Members of Parliament of the district. The function of the district development councils included the village committees thereby making the beneficiary participation in the development activities very limited. During its three-year period of existence it had a number of difficulties in discharging the duties:

i. Lack of adequate commitment by the council members to development activities;

ii. Lack of clear demarcation of functions between ministries and departments;

iii. Conflicts between the council and the District Minister and Members of Parliament;

iv. Problems with prevailing procedures, practices, rules and regulations in the public sector;

v. Little involvement in the implementation of the development program; and

vi. Available funds were not adequate to prepare a comprehensive development plan for the district.

The Provincial Council (*Palath Sabhawa*)

The setting up of provincial councils (*palath sabhawa*) was purely done as a solution to the growing ethnic problems in the country. The idea was to devolve some of the powers of central government to the provinces within a unitary State. The provincial council comprises of elected members while a Chief Minister heads the provincial administration and its executive powers rest with the board of provincial ministers. There are five ministerial portfolios in a province including the chief ministry. In the provincial council the central government is represented by the Governor appointed by the President.

The provincial council was expected to be the framework for devolution of powers between the center and the periphery. In order to keep Tamil-speaking areas together, the northern and eastern provinces have been amalgamated temporally forming a total of eight provincial councils in the country. Powers of the provincial councils were stipulated clearly in the 13th Amendment to the Constitution. Accordingly, all devolved subjects are the sole responsibility of the provinces while concurrent subjects are the responsibility of both the central government and provincial councils. However, the weak financial base, high administrative cost, party politics conflicts, lack of planning and implementation capacity, unclear producers and responsibilities made the provincial councils ineffective some provinces. It is not yet mature enough to access the effective step in the provincial and regional/rural development in Sri Lanka.

The next level of the decentralized system consists of the local authorities comprising urban and municipal councils in the urban areas. The recently established *Pradeshiya Shaba*, an elected body, looks after the interests of the rural areas. For administrative purposes the central government has appointed Divisional Secretaries to each Division. A *Pradeshiya*

Shaba may comprise of one or two Divisions. The lowest administrative level is the *Grama Niladhari* [Village Officer] Division with about 20-30 *Grama Niladhari* Divisions per Divisional Secretary Divisions. Villages and hamlets are the smallest spatial unit where 50-300 families live. Most of the rural development activities are planned for implementation in these spatial units with the active involvement of beneficiaries.

The Divisional Secretariats (*Pradeshiya Lekam Karyalaya*)

Divisional Secretariat Divisions have been established under the Act No. 42 of 1987 and the 13th constitutional reform to avoid the failures of former Assistant Government Divisions that was coming from the British colonial time, which was administered under by GA of the district. In the past, assistant GAs implemented the policy decisions and development plans formulated by ministries/central government. However, after the introduction of divisional secretariat system, all development programs implemented in rural areas were handed over to the Divisional Secretary. Therefore, the Divisional Secretary had become the coordinator and the supervisor of all development activities, which were launched in the Division by other divisional offices of State institutes.

The Divisional Secretariat Divisions again subdivided to *Grama Niladhari* Divisions by incorporating three-four villages. The *Grama Niladhari* is the leader of this division and he/she looked after all government activities, which were implemented in villages by the government. The *Grama Niladhari* Division system is the main and important existing local level lowest administrative unit of the State and it has a very sound reputation among the public. This is because it covers the major administrative requirements of the local community that are powered by the legislative and financial mechanism of the central government handled by the Divisional Secretary. This is the wider potential system in dealing with local community in grassroots levels.

Objectives of the Divisional Secretariats

The major objectives of the Divisional Secretariats are listed below:

i. Providing the services required by the local people;
ii. Implementing, planning and monitoring of development projects and programs within the division to enhance the socio-economic condition of the local people;
iii. Coordination of government officers of other institutions, local communities and institutions and, NGOs in the area to integrate the rural development activities in the division;
iv. Providing subsidies to eradicate the poverty in the division, e.g., *Janasaviya, Samurdhi*, food-stamps, dry food, materials for housing and sanitation improvement for lowest income families of the division; and

v. Providing incidental subsidies for refugees from natural disasters such as floods, cyclones, droughts, earth-slips, etc.

Income and Financial Sources of Divisional Secretariat

The major sources of income of the Divisional Secretariats are given below:

i. Annual budget allocations of the central government;
ii. Development projects and programs funded by national and international organizations; and
iii. By issuing of permits to transport timber, driving license, registration fees for new vehicles, marriages, births, etc.

Divisional Councils (*Pradeshiya Shaba*)

The latest development in the evolution of regional planning took place after the devolution of powers under the 13th Amendment of the Constitution and the Divisional Councils Act of 1987. It is a major landmark in the evolution of political and social institutions in Sri Lanka, as it constituted an exit from the highly centralized system to system of governance in the country. The Divisional Councils are the authority to plan, make decisions and manage public functions in respect of subjects assigned to the providence. Subjects and functions reserved for and shared between the government and the Divisional Councils have been set out in three lists under the under the 9th Schedule of the Constitution. The subjects and functions of Divisional Councils are mainly matters of regional concern and focus directly on the daily life of the people. The Divisional Council then becomes the provider of basic services to the community in the following areas:

i. Public order and local government;
ii. Planning and implementation of provincial economic plan;
iii. Economic and social services such as land development, industries, health and education;
iv. Institutional, human resources and rural development including employment, employment planning and manpower development;
v. Infrastructure, urban development and environment; and
vi. Trade and commerce, etc.

Although the above is not an exclusive list of domains in which the Divisional Councils have a primary responsibility, it covers the major areas and is indicative of the wide range of powers and authority vested in a Provincial Council powers and functions which had hitherto remained with the center.

The *Janasaviya* Program

The "*Janasaviya*" program introduced in 1989 focused on the poorest families receiving less than Rs.700 per month as its target group. This program shifted from mere provision of consumer goods towards promoting self-reliant development among the recipients through community mobilization, income generation and education of beneficiaries.

The *Samurdhi* Movement

The *Janasaviya* movement was replaced by the "*Samurdhi* (or 'prosperity') Movement" after the People's Alliance Government came into office. Even though the envisaged intention is to provide greater opportunity to the poorest of the people to plan and implement their economic development, the operational framework or the implementation procedures are still being worked out. The new program stresses on "family development" rather than community development because other programs do the community-based development work. The families, after their improvement to a certain level, will be linked to other development projects and programs operating at different levels: divisional, district, provincial and national. Similar to the social mobilization program of the IRD program, the community mobilization process of the *Samurdhi* Movement will organize poor people into producer groups, create awareness, generate savings, promote income-generating activities through skills development, access to credit and markets.

The *Janasaviya* Trust Fund

Another program to support poverty alleviation is the *Janasaviya* Trust Fund (JTF), established in 1991 and financed by the World Bank. The JTF provides credit to *Janasaviya* holders and other poor families earning less than Rs.1,500 per month in the rural areas. Among the four sub-funds of the JTF, the credit fund lends money to partner organizations for on lending to poor people to start up small enterprises and self-employment. The partner organizations are NGOs such as rural development societies, thrift and credit cooperative societies, etc.

The Change Agent Program

The Change Agent Program (CAP) was first initiated on an experimental basis in the search for a suitable strategy to reach village and mobilize people in order to educate them to be partners in development. Indicators such as increasing rural unemployment, production and income, increasing malnutrition among children and disparities in income distribution, show that the past development efforts aimed to bring about an improvement in the living standards of the rural poor have not been realized. The CAP was launched in 1978 by the government with the assistance of the UNDP and started village level action in several areas to "release and mobilize the creative energy of the people".

In terms of socio-economic development in rural villages, the CAP concentrated on creating and working with groups of 10-15 poor villagers to improve the cooperation among members and build confidence towards self-reliance through self-help in the group. This was achieved through an agent who lives and works with groups in the village. The focus of the program was to educate the people about the deep roots of socio-cultural, political and economic causes and relationships that made the persons poor. They were now told to make effort to extricate themselves from this vicious circle of poverty. In the context of villages where various external factors operate, it is difficult for trapped persons to get out of the circle. Therefore, the CAP attempted to awaken the rural poor by building self-reliance and confidence on their ability to create and negotiate.

Social Mobilization Program and IRD Program

The participatory model in IRD programs was first introduced in Hambantota as the *Gramodaya Mandala* Development Program in 1983 and the Assistant Government Agent (AGA) level development program in Katuwana in 1985. Further expansion took place in Ratnapura as "Key Area Planning" and in Matara as "Backward Area Development Program".

Under the participatory model, a village is considered as the basic spatial unit for planning and implementation. The poorest families of the village earning an income of less than Rs.700 per month (food-stamp holders) have been taken as the target group of the poverty reduction programs. From 1985, social mobilization was introduced as the means of mobilizing the poorest section of society. Drawing experience from the CAP and the Grameen Bank Program of Bangladesh, the social mobilization process was looked upon as the most appropriate and effective approach for reaching the target group.

The Agrarian Services Center

Agrarian Service Centers (ASCs) are the regional offices of the Department of Agrarian Services under the purview of the Agricultural Ministry in Sri Lanka. The main purposes of the establishment of these centers are to provide assistance for farmers in terms of technical, economical and social services to enhance the productivity of agriculture. Actually this is the place that provides services and support for farmers to increase their harvest with help of the government technical/extension officers such as agriculture instructors and agricultural extension officers (KVS). Head of the ASC is the divisional officer of agriculture. Main services provided by ASCs are as follows:

i. Seeds and seedlings at the lowest rate of prices;

ii. Fertilizer and chemicals (pesticide, fungicides, etc.) for lower prices;

iii. Technical know-how to improve the productivity;

iv. Credit for lowest interest rates;

v. Infrastructure development in agricultural areas; and

vi. Establishment of farmers' societies.

Farmers Organizations (*Govisanvidanaya*)

These organizations are informal communities in village level formed by the ASCs. All members of the organization are farmers. The main objectives are to share experiences, work as a team by sharing labor and avoiding the intermediate interferences/exploiters when selling the output as the intermediaries earn more profits than farmers and entrepreneurs. As a community, these organizations can receive low interest loans from banks and other financial corporations with the assurance of ASCs.

Death-aid Societies (*Maranadhara/Awamangalliyadhara Samithiya*)

Almost all the families of a typical village in Sri Lanka are members of the death-aid society and nearly all the villages have separate death-aid societies for their welfare activities. Though these societies are informal, the structure of societies and functions are keenly formal and objectives are very keen because of such a society has a carder of volunteer officers such as the

Chairman, Secretary, Treasurer, etc. At least once a month a meeting will be commenced to discuss the progress, events took place and collect the membership fees for the month. The main purpose this community is to help each other when a funeral occurred in the village, as these poor people have no served money to spend such an incident happened. Each and every activity of a funeral will be carried out by the members of the society and covers the financial requirements under a certain limitation. *This system is a vital, most famous and efficient mechanism among villagers to assist among others when encountered unexpected incidents.*

Salient Features of IRD Efforts in Sri Lanka

i. Government institutions involved in IRD are not in a position to continue support for rural people due to the influences of politicians;

ii. As most of rural people are less educated, first of all they must be aware how their living conditions could be improved;

iii. The most important and significant feature in the rural development in Sri Lanka is that all regional level State organizations are integrated in implementing development projects and programs through the Divisional Secretary or *Grama Niladhari*. Therefore, the Divisional Secretariat is a key institute involved in IRD; and

iv. Well-organized and well-coordinated development programs could be found as a joint intervention in the region and the efficiency depends on the attitudes and characters of the officers' dealing with such projects.

Future Directions for IRD Efforts

The following are suggested as important aspects to be considered in future IRD efforts:

i. Enhance the socio-economic standards of the rural people by providing employment, new sources of income and introducing new technological know-how to improve productivity;

ii. Integrated effort as a team and effective coordination of projects, programs and activities to reach the ultimate goal;

iii. Infrastructure development should be a major responsibility/role of community level organizations as well as NGOs; and

iv. Instead of providing food and subsidies, facilitation and the provision of appropriate technical know-how related to the improvement of the quality of life and productivity should be taken as the new concept and strategy.

References

Central Bank of Sri Lanka, (2001). *Annual Report of the Central Bank*, Colombo, Sri Lanka.

Dahlen, A., (1992). *Comparative Evaluation Study of the Sri Lanka Integrated Development Program*, Ministry of Policy Planning and Implementation, Colombo, Sri Lanka.

Gunarathne, L., (1987). *The Poorest and the Poor in Sri Lanka and the Alleviation of Poverty in Sri Lanka*, Central Bank of Sri Lanka, Colombo.

Ministry of Finance, Planning, Ethnic Affairs and National Integration, (1995). *Integrated Rural Development Program: 15 Years Experience in Sri Lanka*, Regional Development Division, Sri Lanka.

Morapaya, R. B., (1986). *Integrated Rural Development in Sri Lanka*, Sterling Publishers Ltd., New Delhi.

Ramakrisnan, P. S., (1987). *Some Aspects of the Integrated Rural Development in Sri Lanka – Past Experiences and Further Perspectives*, Regional Development Division, Ministry of Plan Implementation, Colombo, Sri Lanka.

14

Participatory Rural Development in Thailand

Thailand occupies an area close to 514,000 km and has a population of 62 million. Bangkok has a population of eight million. Thailand is the only country in the region that has not been colonized by a western power. Since the foundation of the Thai Kingdom in the seventh century, the country, under successive dynasties, had maintained its independence and a strong identity with the hinge, nation and religion, as the cornerstone of the Kingdom.

Thailand is a country currently undergoing rapid changes. As a primarily agricultural nation, Thailand is expected to propel into the ranks of the newly industrialized countries (NICs) with annual economic growth rates of around 7-9 percent. Thai economic progress has undoubtedly been accompanied by social costs. For instance, the increasing gap between rich and poor has placed considerable pressure on the livelihoods of the 75-percent of villagers who occupy rural areas, leading to an increase in rural-urban migration. Obviously, there are approximately 42 million villagers earning their livelihood from agriculture and agriculture-related industries. Over 10 million of these live in poverty. The average per capita income in the capital Bangkok is US$1,000 per annum, while in the rural northeastern part of the country, where most of population are farmers, living at a subsistence level, the average is US$235 per annum.

Role and Strategies of Local Institutions

Development, both rural and urban areas, is very important for improving the quality of life of the grassroots groups in Thailand. The aim of community development is to improve the economic and social livelihood, particularly that of the poor. In the past, the traditional thinking has been that only the government must attend to the welfare of villagers. However, the role of NGOs in Thailand has dramatically increased and become significantly established.

One of the large Thai NGOs or local institution working in community development is the Population and Community Development Association (PDA). It consists of 600 staff and 16 community development centers nationwide implementing 20 development programs both in urban and rural areas. Mechai Viravaidya founded PDA in 1974 in Bangkok. PDA's programs are based on the belief that local people are best suited to shape and sustain their own development. Furthermore, PDA was first active in promoting family planning in urban and rural Thailand and successfully recruited 12,000 volunteers and utilized several mobile health units to distribute contraceptives to over 16,000 villagers.

Achieving the aims and promoting villagers' participation in development programs are not easy in rural areas. However, PDA has used various strategies such as:

1. Participation

PDA staff promote both villagers and official staff joining the programs since the beginning to end of the programs. Participation includes villagers sharing costs in cash and in kind to run the project and also joining the project for improving their lives. These lead to a sense of belonging.

2. Having Fun

PDA staff also try to promote villagers who participate the programs having fun or entertainment. Certainly, the easy dialogue and easy understanding words have been used. Moreover, various joyful events have been organized such as condom contest, condom night, vegetable bank sport day, vasectomy tour, and so on.

3. Appropriate Technology

This strategy promotes villagers looking back to use local materials, local technologies and local wisdom holds. Villagers, certainly, can save their money and earn more incomes from using appropriate technology. PDA has been implementing and promoting this strategy nation wide for 25 years.

4. Easy and Convenient

Be easy to understand and be convenient for using are the main, good and appropriate strategies that PDA have implemented for various development programs. For example, when PDA staff explain about family planning; like how to use condoms or how good vasectomy is, it is easier for the villagers to understand, when compared to medical doctors describing. Moreover, the condoms and vasectomy service are very convenient. PDA has promoted 12,000 family planning volunteers in Thailand and all can provide condoms 24 hours service.

5. Revolving Loan Fund

The idea of "nothing free in the world" is basically promoted in PDA's development programs. Thus, the participants must pay back the loan to the project, while the very poor villagers can pay through labor instead of money.

6. Promoting Private Sectors and Business Companies Joining the Development Programs

The concept of promoting private company involvement in rural and urban development has been created and developed by PDA since 1986. Furthermore, various people had agreed that, the basic idea is to mobilize the relatively untapped private companies to participate actively in rural development, especially to help in the development of basic business skills of villagers, create new jobs, and provide opportunities. The roles and appropriate strategies to convince business sector participation in development projects are as follows:

a. *Concept presentation*: Basically, this is an in-depth explanation about the concept of "private company helping villages to develop". This concept is presented to the executives of selected private companies.

b. *Study tours*: After agreeing in principle to join the rural development program, the PDA suggests the private company to form a task force plan and develop ideas on how the company can help the village. This team should then attend a study tour of the area and work out the plan. The PDA can assist the team in identifying potential program villages.

c. *Target area village*: The task force visits potential villages to meet community leaders and the village headman. Together they can access villages' needs and potential, discuss possibilities and jointly plan activities. In some of development programs, a project coordinator may be hired to implement the project in the village.

d. *Project planning*: When the target village is selected, the task force works with villagers to develop a simple workplace. Various issues, such as time-line, budget, and coordination with many other development agencies will be scheduled.

e. *Sponsor approval*: The senior management of the company or board of the organization approves the work plan and corresponding resource commitments before the project is formally launched. Funds for rural development activities spent by the private company are tax-deductible through the PDA.

NGO Promoting Local Institution Strengthening

The NGOs basically promoted activities both in household level and village level and supported activities at subdistrict and district levels. Local NGOs such as PDA have been implementing Community-based Integrated Rural Development (CBIRD) for 20 years. The activities included income generation, primary healthcare and educational programs. Firstly, it addressed the household level. Next, the village-groups were strengthened. PDA tries to stimulate villagers in implementing the activities by themselves. Various groups, including cooperatives and women groups have been established and registered. Few examples are discussed below.

Local institutions such as NGOs demonstrated that there are two main goals for national rural development. The first goal is to increase productivity. For example, in an irrigation project conducted in Thailand in 1990, it was found that the area under second rice crop had increased significantly from 377,600 ha in 1976 to 704,000 ha in 1985, while yield increased from 3,250 kg/ha to 3,725 kg/ha over the same period. Interestingly, the level of yield of the second rice crop was about two times higher than the yield of the first rice crop. The increase in area and production of the second rice crop has been made mainly by the expansion of the irrigated areas.

The second goal was to encourage equity and eradicate pockets of rural poverty. The study was implemented in two villages in northeast Thailand, one irrigated rice village and one rainfed rice village, and found that farm incomes of farmers in the irrigated village were higher than farm incomes of rainfed areas. Moreover, the same research showed that the living standard of irrigated households was high and they had electrical appliances such as refrigerators, color televisions, radio, motor cycles and pick-up trucks. The rural development of Thailand has concentrated on the development of infrastructure facilities to promote land productivity. These measures have improved productivity and in consequence, raised living standards in large areas of the country. More clearly, they have been supplemented by various programs, such as water supplies, animal husbandry, crop production, training courses for poor farmers, and community development programs – all aimed at opening up employment opportunity for many villager groups.

It was also examined other countries, such as the Philippines, where the government has favored integrated rural development, and Indonesia where the government has carried out a program of intensification of rice cultivation. These programs have been supplemented by the provision of agricultural credit to farmers, partly in kind and partly in cash, and programs of social education. In addition, it was found that India and Nepal have emphasized on multidisciplinary approaches and active participation of local government agencies.

Many authors have discussed various outcomes of rural development programs and their effects on both villagers and implementing organizations. The benefits from private company participation in rural development programs could be categorized into five areas:

i. Improved quality of life;

ii. Village-based work opportunities and additional income;

iii. Significantly improved business skills;

iv. Institutional development and communal village structures; and

v. Expanded markets for village products.

Village organizations and local institutions promote income-generating activities. Local village organizations are a vital part of the rural development process because a village group can mobilize communities and maximize the impact of program inputs that are coming from outside the village. These local organizations include Lam Sai Yong (LSY) and Nong Sai (NS) cooperatives, Nong Ta Kai (NTK) silk production group and Rai Kok vegetable bank group. The local village organizations lead the community to unify and strengthen the power (all of them are in northeast part of Thailand).

There were only 107 members when it was first established in 1989. Similarly, in the case of the NS cooperative, the number of members increased from 80 in 1989 to 511 in 1997. In another case study, it was found out that only two women in NTK village made silk clothes earlier for sale, but currently 55 women participate in the silk group after PDA and American Express extended support. There were 24 villagers jointly in the vegetable bank activity in Rai Kok village at the beginning of the CBIRD program, and in mid-1998, there were 90 members. In addition, two other private companies sponsored two other (new) deep-well irrigation systems in the same public land.

From direct observations and from group meetings, it appeared that the village committees manage the village organizations. This fund allowed villagers to borrow at 2 percent interest rate a month. However, this fund was not allocated to all the villagers, and only those who have close contacts with the committee members had borrowed money. When repayment date arrived, borrowers tended to continually ask to borrow again without paying back the money. The committees actually did not get the cash from those borrowers.

The net profits from shoemaking business had been dramatically reduced (90 percent) from1995 to 1996, and 150 percent from 1996 to 1997. This was caused due to the Thai economic crisis, which gave a serious warning signal at the end of 1996, and really happened in the mid-1997. However, the net profit is not the prime concern of the cooperative. Instead, providing good jobs, good incomes, low interest rate, appropriate knowledge, agricultural inputs and marketing sources for members are considered as cooperative's significant roles. *Despite the fluctuations in incomes, the two cooperatives survived the crisis, unlike many other businesses both in urban and rural Thailand.*

The incomes increased sharply from 1995 to 1996, but declined slightly in 1997. The reason was the cooperative operated a new shoe production line, made new shoe styles and expanded the capacity. The profit in 1996 was low since the cooperative bought new machines and reduced orders for shoe-sewing servicing causing the cooperative to operate the business without buying the raw material and facing the high risk of marketing.

In the case of NTK silk weaving production, women's committees manage the group. By creating an income-generating activity for women, the ICD program empowered the participants through financial independence. Even though initially the American Express Company and the PDA supported it, the management of the activity was absolutely under the control of village women. Interestingly, the NTK silk group has its own funds, which increased slightly every year. This fund was allocated annually for the members who borrowed to invest on silk production. Although, the interest rate was quite high, 2 percent per month, all the members satisfied since they wanted the fund to be increased rapidly. However, it was still cheaper than interest rate of the rich person's loans, which were 5-10 percent a month. The group has annually paid a dividend of B/ 70 for each principal share (of B/ 100). It was actually higher than the bank saving interest rate in Thailand, which was 4.5 percent per annum (The Nation, 1998). The NTK silk production group has not yet gained legal status. Therefore, some governmental services are not yet extended to such groups. The observation from field research show that the bookkeeping system needs to be improved.

However, the committees do understand and work on the bookkeeping smoothly and they can also explain the accounts, etc. to members during the annual meeting.

In the Rai Kok vegetable bank, the villagers began to grow the vegetables in 1997. Thus, the group's fund has not yet grown much. However, S.C. Johnson and Son had primarily donated an amount of B/ 60,000. All members can borrow money to buy agricultural inputs, such as fertilizer, vegetable seeds, fungicides, and pesticides. Each member initially paid an amount of B/ 500 for a membership fee and for the irrigation system including the water cost. This income will be used for electricity, irrigation systems maintenance costs, including the running costs, such as training, reports, promotion, and gasoline. In the near future, the vegetable bank group hopefully could survive and also have its activities managed by villagers like the two cooperatives and silk weaving production groups discussed above.

The villages supported by the CIRD program have obviously increased individual and village organization-level incomes. Prior to the project they seldom had jobs after the rice-harvesting season. After they joined with the CIRD programs, they got more income, which helped them to live more comfortably in the villages. In addition, some of them support their children's study at a higher level. All the villagers interviewed had incomes more than the poverty line. Although a few participants earn income less than their previous jobs, they are happy with the current situation as they have money to save, live with family, work in the village, and strengthen their organizations.

Moreover, for village organizations, they enjoy incomes and benefits from implementing their business. The Thai economic turndown since 1997 directly affected these organizations, but they are still running business. Hence, these organizations are different from many companies in the country, which have already collapsed due to economic crisis. Higher level of net profit is not the prime concern of these village organizations. Instead, supporting members' well-being is more important. Three village organizations, with more experience, have reached a self-reliance level, while one new group, the vegetable bank, still needs to be supervised and supported closely by both private company, NGO and government organizations.

NGO Activity and Rural Development in Thailand

There are increasing the number of NGOs in the world. The aims of Thai NGO activity are largely classed as follows; promotion of human rights of women or children, health care and medical relief, promotion of slum life, relief of refugees, rural development, NGOs coordinating, and advocacy activity. While Japanese ODA has been criticized, NGOs have been estimated in these activities in the worldwide.

In general, the ideals of NGOs may be said the pursuit of humanistic right, the coalition of people, the orientation of universal value, and tackling rural poverty. NGOs have worked to solve these problems. First, NGOs have been well estimated in that NGO workers promote a project discussing with villagers how to develop. In short, when they make a development plan, they have peasants participate in making a plan, and promote a project. NGO workers have peasants motivate to develop their village. One of NGOs roles is to have villagers participate in the process of a planning and implementing of development Second, it can promote a project, rapidly, flexibly, and economically. Third, it can provide an adequate technique for natural environment. Fourth, it can develop respecting the cultural orders of villages.

The number of rural development NGO has been increasing in Thailand. Nowadays, rural development NGO has numbered much more than 200 in 1992. Rural development might be said one of the most important activities of NGOs. NGOs have the above-mentioned merits. On the other hand, you must notice that NGOs' activities have the demerits as the followings. Rural development NGO workers often look down upon peasants, and compile their projects to villagers without consulting with them. But you should recognize that villagers could solve their problems by themselves. NGO workers had villagers participating to develop their community . Thai NGOs has the characteristic of conducting rural development by promoting a spirit of "self-reliance" and integrated agriculture..

Brief History of Thai NGOs

The Thai government conducted many rural projects such as "Master Plan for Solution to Poverty Problem" consisting of four projects; Rural Employment Creation Project, the Village Activities Promotion Project, the Basic Service Provision Project and the Production Project. But these projects did not improve the conditions of peasants' lives. They instead come to be in debt in fact NGOs might be said to provide alternative rural development idea.

Since Prime Minister Sarit Thanarat started the First Economic and Social Development Plan from 1961. After then the national plan has been succeeded, and now the seventh national plan is carrying out. Prime Minister Sarit is famous politician as conducting a paternalistic policy, for instance he implemented the national development plan as a kind of paternal grant. National Economic Development Board (NEDB) was founded in 1959, and later National Economic and Social Development Board (NESDB).

Furthermore, Thailand Development Research Institute (TDRI) was established in 1984 to conduct the policy research and disseminate results to the public and private sectors. NGO Coordinating Committee on Rural Development (NGO-CORD) was established in 1985. This committee, which served NGOs, worked to coordinate among NGOs as well as between NGOs and the government. The present King, Bhumipol Adulyadej, also promoted development programs through the royal development plan since the 1960s. The King and his royal family have often endeavored to develop poor villages in rural areas.

The King and government have arranged the infrastructure, which was mainly equipped through the modernization, namely the national economic and social development plan and the royal development plan: e.g. constructing roads, the bridges built, dams, irrigation and others equipped. There have been prevailing cultivating machines, mobilization, cash crops in the whole country, and the wage labor became to take the place of the exchange of labor. Then the strata of peasants have polarized, which means rich peasants are richer, while poor peasants are poorer.

Besides, the difference of incomes is increasing between residents in rural areas and ones in urban. Nowadays, the wage of rural peasants is one of twelve compared with that of urban labors. Then, peasants are going to work in Bangkok etc. The big capital prevails in rural area, for example rural peasants have to buy seeds, fertilizer, agricultural chemical, selling products to big companies, which export them. In short, the Thai farming structure partly changed from self-sufficiency to cash crop farming, while most peasants still remain self-sufficient.

Thai NGOs started to overcome the problems brought out by the modernization. Rural development NGOs work to struggle with the most basic problems in rural areas above all. First rural development NGO was Thailand Rural Reconstruction Movement (TRRM), called the munnithi buruna chon-nabot in Thai, which founded by Dr. Puey Ungphakorn in 1967. Another important NGO was Catholic Council of Thailand for Development (CCTD) that formally set up in 1978. The CCTD is one of pioneer NGOs to make much of cultural approach for development. After 1976, NGOs was forced underground. The coordinating body, The Thai Development Support Committee (TDSC) was established in 1982, helping a large number of NGOs to communicate each other. A major seminar on, "Rural Development in Thailand" was held in 1984. This meeting was remarkable in a critical assessment of the government development.

As you know, Thai rural development NGOs were unhappy in the 1970s, such as the government often has suspicion that NGO workers are communists. NGOs, then, come to work with helping with the government each other. The government has regarded NGOs as one part of Government Organizations (GOs). It was derived from that both GOs and NGOs promote the likely projects; forming of saving groups, rice bank, 'buffalo bank, training occupation, and others through the idea of self-reliance, Village Institution Promotion (VIP) and Rural Development Documentation Centre (RUDOC) combined to be coalitional NGO, called Thai Institute for Rural Development (THIRD), in 1988. The THIRD was said one of the most valuable NGOs. The leader of this organization is Seri Phongphit who edited to publish some popular books; *Back to the Root, Religion in the Changing Society,* and *Turning Point of Thai Peasants.* His idea and these books are widely influencing NGO workers. He may be said to be one of idealistic leaders of Thai NGOs.

Nowadays, the characteristics of NGOs are as the followings. NGO workers were apt to value rural development rather than the others. Most of NGO workers tried to develop by making much of the Buddhist idea. The monks participate with rural development above all. They thus cooperate with GOs in development processes. They respect natural environment due to the world wide NGOs. Finally, they are interested in the natural problems: i.e. the conservation of natural environment in the place of social problems.

Types of the Projects of Rural Development NGOs

We will class types of rural development NGOs. First, according to Dr. Puey, they are summarized as follows:

(1) Rural community organization and community development work.

(2) Support for the role of community leaders (teachers or monks) in community development work.

(3) Community leaders and youth training for development.

(4) Children's development projects (nutrition, day-care centers, child labor, mass media for children, progressive education, etc.)

(5) Primary health care work.

(6) Campaign work on human rights issues and social problems. (?) Appropriate technology projects and service.

(8) Projects and campaigns on women's issues.

(9) Training of development workers, provision of volunteers.

(10) Coordination of activities among development organizations.

Moreover, we will reclassify the types of aims in the case of Foundation for Agricultural and Rural Management (FARM) which was established in 1980. For example, the community development projects of the FARM are divided into buffalo bank, village medicines bank, rice bank, fertilizer bank, water resource improvement, integrated agricultural promotion, school lunch program, *Samlow* (tricycle) cooperation, and women vocational training program to prevent a lot of prostitutes, urban project such as supporting poor people in slum, and hill tribe projects. The types of the FARM projects can be classed in six types. One type is to form a group such as a rice bank, a buffalo bank, a savings group etc. Second is concerning to the circumstance-friendly agriculture like integrated or organic agriculture. Third is the project for women concerning to a vocational women training to learn some techniques or prevent women from becoming prostitutes. Fourth is for students, e.g. a school lunch program, a scholarship, and constructing a little library or pre-school day care center etc. Fifth is to improve community-based goods like water resource. Sixth is to prevail the idea of Buddhism for monks interested in development work. Besides, there is a type of project that cannot be found in the projects of the FARM. That project is to promote the Buddha's teachings, namely Dhamma, to solve some cultural problems.

Issues of the Rural Development NGOs' Activities

Dr. Puey summarized the issues of NGOs are as follows:

(1) Lack of stability, recognition, and public support.

(2) Lack of competent and experienced manpower.

(3) Inadequate self-development and learning through experience.

(4) Lack of common direction.

(5) Problems concerning political climate.

NGO coordinating committee indicates that the issues are as follows. First, it is the lack of exchange of information and techniques of experienced workers to coordinate. Second, it is the lack of technical and financial supports concerning the organization and management of villagers' movements. These are concerning (2) and (3) which Dr. Puey addressed. Third, NGO workers criticize that a rice bank introduces the economic system of laissez-faire into the villages. Finally, it is related to the idea of Buddhist rural development.

First, we cannot have the view that the peasants should product for their consumption. This idea is true in one side, because the peasants will not be able to subsist if they do not produce cash crops for free market. In short, the peasants need to produce crops not only for self-consumption but also for market. Concerning the integrated farming in which some NGOs encourage, it is significant to criticize the attitude of self-consumption. However, as you has seen, you should not consider that NGO workers have contributed to introduce the economic system of laissez-faire into the villages through a rice bank or a saving group. It is a way for villagers to assemble capital at a short time, pretending themselves from rich men, as they cannot help renting from rich men in high interest. But there-are some problems in that poor villagers are almost not member in rice banks or saving groups. Namely, poor villagers are excluded from them. Furthermore, the farmers of middle class are mainly leaders among the villagers. The problem is, accordingly, a method of making a group. However, it is difficult to practice the integrated farming, because the peasants will not be able to subsist enough without partly dependent on free market.

Second, in the case of Apichart, it is the problem that the village can be regarded to be autonomous. As Keyes said, a village is a natural community in northeastern Thailand. On the contrary, a village is not somehow a natural community in northern Thailand. Then, as Potter said, the Thai village structure is not the same throughout Thailand. A village structure is different between the northeastern and the northern region.

Third, rural development NGO such as the CCTD, at present, start to take a cultural approach. From the perspective of cultural approach, the concept of self-reliance cannot be interpreted as the independent. The concept implies the collective rather than the individualistic, for the Thai people pay respect to helping each other *(chuai kan),* being interdependent. The villagers are really ego-centric, factious, and cooperative. NGO workers have to understand a community culture before doing activities in advance. But it is important to notice that the villagers put respect to their culture. If the labors derived from rural area know their culture, they could come back to help for their home. Moreover, the villagers could work to help among others for themselves. It is important for NGO workers to develop the cultural identity of villagers.

Fourth, a large number of NGOs adopted the Buddhist idea as an ideal purpose. This idea includes the case that monks are leaders. Buddhism is regarded to be a basis of the Thai traditional culture. This fourth type has different character from the third type. It is important to divide these two types. The Buddhist development NGOs have respect for spiritualism rather than materialism or consumerism. This type is called an alternative development in the sense.

Issues of Buddhist Rural Development NGOs' Activities

Buddhist rural development NGOs value Thai traditional culture. To grasp this aspect we will take up the case of Foundation for Education and Development of Rural Areas (FE-DRA), one of the most famous NGOs in the northern region. The FEDRA was set up in 1974, and was registered in

1975. The office is at the temple called Pa Dara Bhirom in Chi-angmai Province, which Gohlert referred to. The FEDRA's main purposes are to encourage agriculture, to encourage education, to promote religion, and to develop local areas. First and second principles are solutions for material problems. But the third is a solution for spiritual problem. The FEDRA hold diligence, frugality, self-sacrifice, and unity in Buddha's teachings in great account.

Four principles of diligence, frugality, self-sacrifice, and unity are held in esteem. The unique activity of the FEDRA is that the monks participate in developing the village: the project is Sangha Promotion Program for Rural Development. Vanpen analyzed the history and activities of FEDRA in his book in detail. Vanpen estimated the projects of GO as well as those of NGOs, e.g. the FEDRA.

For example, villagers participate in the cases of GOs more than NGO. The other hand, the FEDRA not only carries out the integrated agriculture, but also supports the villagers to product a cash crop. It arranges to supply the villagers some types of production at the same time: i.e. for .self-consumption and nearly and remote markets.

As is well known, Sluk is one of the most famous NGOs' leaders. He criticized government development as a materialism, quantitative and consumerism in the some aspects. Then he gives weight to Buddhism as the Thai traditional culture. He esteems spirit rather than material, quality rather than quantity, diligence rather than greed for consumption.

By the way, it is well known that he gives importance to the Four Sublime Abodes (Brahma Vihara): loving kindness *(Metta),* compassion *{Karuna),* sympathetic joy *(Mudita),* and Equanimity*(Upekkha)* (Sulak 198K75~78). He has been influenced from the Sarvodaya Shramadana Movement that started as the development movement in Srilanka. So then he respects the four Dhamma, namely sharing*(dana),* pleasant speech *(piyavaca*), constructive action *(atthacariya),* and equality *(samanattata).* The movement might be said Buddhist socialism which goals are love, freedom, liberation, and equality.

Buddhism is nothing but making merits for peasants. However, the Thai people are classed in ruling class and subordinate class. The rulers used Brahmanism and Buddhism for legitimacy of governance. The peasants believe the spirit *(phii)* belief from old times. The Thai religion is syncretic in which indigenous *phii* belief, Brahmanism, and Buddhism mix.

Anyway, one must notice that Buddhism has been used as the instrument of modernization by the Thai royal family and government to dominate the people. In other words, the Thai government has driven the modernization by means of the promotion of the spirit of Buddhism through promoting the modernization.

However, the peasants believe Buddhism only on the surface. In other words, they believe Buddhism to gain merits in the present world through merit-making. The people believe only merit-making and Karma in Buddhism. According to Chuji Tanaka, villagers pray peace of life *(kwaam yuu dii kin dii),* and have the worldview of *saiyasat* from early times. The term *saiyasat* means the people believe the spirits in all natural things; grass, tree, river, rice and so on, and made of syncretism of indigenous animistic belief, Brahmanism, and Buddhism. For instance, Niels Mulder did not use the term *saiyasat,* but use the term *saksit,* while he uses the term *decha* as undomesticated power. The people accepted Buddhism on the basis of *saiyasat*.

By the way, NGO workers tend to have an idea that Buddhism is the traditional cultural order. For example, the Thai intellectual such as . Sulak got this idea. Have they forgotten the fact that Buddhism was controlled under the development plan of the government ? Otherwise, have they forgotten the fact that the people believe only Buddhism in merit-making ? The villagers do not understand the principles of Buddha's teachings, and do not have a disposition of the diligence, frugality, self-sacrifice, and unity through believing Buddhism. The people only hope to be happy by making merits rather than becoming unselfish, diligence, frugality or self-sacrifice, etc. According to Tanaka, the people believe the *sai-ysat,* although Sulak did not refer to the above idea. He should understand the above idea.

Social Structure of Thai Rural Society

The patron-client relations are nuclear characteristic in human relationship of the Thai people. You can see superior-subordinate relations anywhere, as this is the patron-client relationship. In general, patronage makes peasants have dispositions dependent on patron. The patron-client relations have a base of *sakdina* institution and *phrai* institution in the pre-modern regime. According to Tanaka's study, the personality of the Thai people is present-oriented, lack of time perspective, love *fun(sanuk), saiyasat.* As the peasants are ego-centric and love fun, they prevent them cooperating in the long term.

Poor peasants tend to agree with rich men formally in the village meeting in spite of their factual disagreement. Their formal actions prevent rich men from getting angry. As poor peasants are rent from rich peasants, they fear rich peasants; the relationship between rich peasants and poor peasants are the patron-client one.

However, some leaders of NGOs have considered that the Thai villages are themselves an autonomous society with political system, original culture, social or educational system in every village. Every village has a unity, because some researchers understand that the Thai village does not have a unity and cooperation in the village in northern Thai village. But multi-households of kinsmen actually have cooperation everywhere and every time, and some conflicts have broken out in almost villages. There is factionalism prevalent in the villages, as some researchers noted. The factionalism means the patron-client relations. Then there is common wealth in the northeastern Thai village, unlike the northern Thai village.

The Thai village is recently imaged to have an autonomous system. If we explain it concretely, it is well to be said that the government has made the village have a unity through the administrative institution. That is to say, the Thai government made a village headman and a village committee have a prestige in villages, because they progress rural development in rural area and ordered them to dominate villagers through the administrative institution.

The method of government development is materialistic, consumerism, and quantitative rather than qualitative, and then indigenous NGOs work to set store on community participation, a self-reliance, etc. Indigenous NGOs themselves are alternative development. As Gohlert said, the ends do not justify the means. The community participation in the process of decision-making is valuable in itself. The ideas of self-reliance or cultural integrity can be realized through the process of rural development One can say that the means will be more important than the ends; in short, that poor peasants protect themselves from rich men through making a group.

The cultural approach is prevalent in many NGOs. There are no absolute models for the use of the cultural approach. Then the community culture means villagers' identity in that each culture represents the identity of each community. This kind of idea is important for workers in the sense that NGOs carry weight with villagers' identity, local wisdom. To put it into concrete, the community identity is based on everyday life-style, belief, and way of thinking, etc. Thus a cultural approach is a way to work with villagers while understanding the culture as a life-style, way of grouping, way of thinking, and belief, etc.

If NGO workers try to understand the community culture, they will have to understand that they are humor, lazy and with all one's might, selfish and unselfish at the same time.

Then they are individualistic as well as not individualistic. They tend to change their attitude easily due to the conditions. Accordingly, if NGO workers take a cultural approach, they do not have to intend to drive the life-style of villagers change directly. Valuing the community culture is not a goal to directly change the villagers. Then, the villagers consequently change of life-style or the way of thinking through the process of development.

As to the Buddhist rural development NGOs, one must understand two kinds of Buddhism. One is beliefs of the monks or the intellectuals, including the students of university, which give importance to a meditation, a religious precept, unselfishness, liberation of self and so on. Another is belief of the people who ask for an interest in the present world by the merit-making. One can say that the people ask for an interest in the present world by the merit-making. That is to say, there are two kinds of Buddhism between a monk or the intellectual, elite, and the people in Thailand. Buddhist rural development NGO workers often confuse two kinds of Buddhism. These two kinds of Buddhism should be distinguished.

The monks or the intellectuals have made a group seeking for an ideal society in the present world according to the teachings of Buddha. However, the most important thing is that the Thai government has used Buddhism as logic of legitimacy to prevail their domination system. Consequently, Buddhist rural development NGOs spread the idealistic religion to the people, and in short, they manage to permeate the ethics favorable to the government in one side. The diligence, frugality and unity might be said the ethics of legitimacy not only for Buddhism but also for keeping men submitting to the nation. The populace believes the rebirth, namely reincarnation, and Karma, which is a cosmological idea of legitimacy of the present world order. One should not forget that the Thai royal system has been legitimated by Brahmanism and Buddhism. At the same time, one should not forget that the royal system could not easily be collapsed because the Thai people believes Buddhism and respects the royal nowadays.

The Thai people have had the idea of self-reliance, since the villagers have protected themselves by themselves, but the nation has not protected them. The government set local every temple in a system of national Buddhist hierarchy, and one can say that the government has dominated local villagers through systematizing the Sangha (organization of monks). The people have not originally had the idea of Buddhism, Consequently, we cannot help saying that the community culture is not based on Buddhism. It might be said that the government compelled Buddhism into the traditional culture by political power. Contrary to Sulak's intention, one must consider the traditional culture like the above. Notwithstanding, it might be said that Sulak tried to make Thai society into an ideal one.

References

Bobsbawm E. & Ranger T. (eds.) (1983). *The Invention of Tradition* .Cambridge: The University Press of Cambridge.

Heim, Franz G., Akin Rabibhadana and Chirmsak Pinthong, (1983). *How to Work with Peasants-A Manual for Field Workers,* Khon Kaen: RDI, Khon Kaen University.

Mulder, Niels, (1979). *Inside Thai Society: An Interpretation of Everyday Life,* Bangkok: Editions Duang Kamol.

Oakley, P. and Marsden, D., (1984). *Approaches to Participation in Rural Development,* Geneva: International Labour Office.

Seri Phongphit and Robert Bennoun (eds), (1988). *Turning Point of Thai Peasants: Village and Self-Reliance in a Thai Context,* Bangkok: THIRD.

Vanpen Surarerks, (1988). *Issues and Experiences in the Use of Community Participation by Government and Private Organizations in Rural Development Programs in Thailand,* Chiangmai: Chiangmai University.

15

Participatory Rural Development in Vietnam

Vietnam is a long and narrow territory – 2,000 km in length from north to south, but the width from west to east is only about 60 km at the narrowest place. Despite the fact that the country is rapidly changing towards industrialization and modernization, agriculture is still dominant and nearly 75 percent of population live in rural areas. And, the contribution of this area to GDP is quite large – about 30-40 percent. After the revolution in 1975, Vietnam has changed significantly and created conditions for developing the economy and the society; standard of living also has been improved rapidly. Moreover, the consumption demand of the society, particularly in rural areas, is increasing at a rate.

All of the above-mentioned achievements have been based on the development of communes. Commune is the basic cell of Vietnamese rural society. These communities established since the early days of Vietnamese nation, about 3,000 years ago. And they have created a history. In the past, Vietnam had to fight long wars. The country used to be a colony of China over 1,000 years, and was under rule of France for nearly 100 years. However, nation's characteristics still remain, although the culture from outside had been imposed and disseminated strongly by Empires. This shows the power of "commune communities". Even though the enemy has occupied the country, the communes protected their own characteristics, so the great national traditions, which were there for thousands of years, had been maintained and conserved. However, in order to develop further and to improve rural social face, Vietnamese Government is employing novel strategics and policies while conserving and making use of the age-old traditions. In this development process local communities and institutions play a major role.

Administrative Organization of Local Communities

Vietnamese administrative organization has four levels:

- Central (Trung uong);
- Province or city (Tinh, Thanh);
- District (Quan, Huyen); and
- Commune (Lang, Xa).

Under the commune is the hamlet (*ap*), but it is not considered as an administrative unit as it does not have a separate budget.

Vietnam has 61 provinces and cities. Each province or city has 10-20 districts, 10-15 communes belong to each district, and 5-10 hamlets are in each commune. Population of a province or city usually is 0.5-1.5 million, except for Ha Noi (2.5 million) and Ho Chi Minh city (5.2 million). Each district has several hundred thousand people. The population of a commune is about 10,000-30,000. In Ho Chi Minh city, some communes have more than 50,000 people.

Ho Chi Minh City's Administrative Organization

Being a big city in both area and population wise, Ho Chi Minh city has 22 districts and an area of 2,093 km. Ha Noi, the capital of Vietnam is located 1,700 km south of Ho Chi Minh. Except for districts that are established based on administrative boundaries, the city also has departments relate to the scope of society, economy, defense, politics, security, etc. Organizations and associations related to rural development in Ho Chi Minh city are as follows:

- Service of Education and Training;
- Service of Agriculture and Rural Development;
- Service of Planning and Investment;
- Service of Technology, Science and Environment;
- Institute of Economy;
- Service of Communication and Public Works;
- Farmer's Association;

- Women's Association;
- Horticulture Association; and
- Youth's Association, etc.

In addition, some central institutions (related to rural development) are also established in Ho Chi Minh city. Few examples are given below:

- University for Agricultural and Forestry
- Institute of Southern Agricultural Science
- Institute of Forestry Science
- Institute of Oil Plant
- Institute of Forest Investigation and Planning.

Local Communities and Integrated Rural Development

Community development should adopt an integrated approach and address such activities as: improving production; employment generation; restoring traditional professions in the society; education; family planning; infrastructure development, etc. Functions and roles of institutions dealing with these different subjects of rural development will differ to each other.

Local governments should be dealing with Integrated Rural Development (IRD). The annual plan of a commune has short-, medium- and long-term objectives set up by Ho ChiMinh city's government (or by the Center). Local communities have to cooperate with concerning institutions.

Service of Education and Training

State management is concerned about improving cultural knowledge, eradicating illiteracy of people who did not have the opportunity to go to school. In each district, Educational Division has a unit to help people committees to accomplish such objectives. For eradicating illiteracy, associations such as farmers', women's and youth's organizations and the NGOs play a significant role.

Service of Planning and Investment

Service of Planning and Investment is an organization managed by the State. Its function is to approve plans and distribute the budget to related work via projects. Planning Division belongs to district's people committee and it is a unit involved in implementation.

Service of Technology Science and Environment

Service of Technology Science and Environment also an organization managed by the State. It belongs to city's people committee. Its duty is to help identify and apply new technology, science and solve environmental problems (if any) of development projects.

Institute of Economy

This is to organize research and to set up policies related to rural areas and to develop agriculture. In order to do these effectively, there should be a set of suitable policies to stimulate production and to improve rural life.

Service of Communication and Public Works

This is also an organization managed by the State for building infrastructure, treating waste, etc.

Service of Agricultural and Rural Development

This is also a State-managed organization for developing agriculture, rural areas and communities. It always cooperate with others to promote IRD. It has many specific units and the whole service has about 800 cadres.

Center for Technology Science and Agricultural Extension

With 200 cadres in three levels; city, district and commune; this center has the following main functions:

i. To organize research on forestry, agriculture, fisheries, animal husbandry, irrigation, etc.

ii. To transfer new technology (plant, animal) and new farming systems to farmers to increase the yield of plants and animals.

iii. To develop and implement rural development projects.

In order to perform such tasks, the center conduct research, receive technical and scientific knowledge/achievements from within and outside the country, select appropriate knowledge/information/technology and transfer them to farmers via training courses, seminars and field visits, etc. In addition, it develops cadre networks of agricultural extension at commune level. Each commune has one cadre that belongs to the district station. These comprised of progressive farmers, local cadres (association and government). And, they participate in planning and help in the development of projects for the community. Practically, agricultural extension service in Ho Chi Minh city, and in the whole country, is effectively engaged in community development activities.

Besides this center, the "Service of Agriculture and Rural Development" also has other institutions such as:

- Center for Water and Rural Environment Hygiene;
- Branch of Immigration and New Economic Area Development; and
- Branch of Plant Protection, etc.

All of these institutions help in the establishment and implementation of projects such as those linked to the supply of clean water to rural people, environmental hygiene (like treating waste, dirty water, building suitable W.C., etc) and contribute to improve the standard of living of people. The above-mentioned units have 50-100 cadres each.

Associations

These are social/politic units. They have four levels; from central to commune. Therefore, they have formed a system, which is strong enough to participate in implementing the projects of IRD to help farmers to promote production.

Other Institutes and the University

These belong to the Ministry of Agricultural and Rural Development, and Ministry of Education and Training, respectively. However, their offices are located in Ho Chi Minh city. Their main duties are to organize research on farming systems, new seeds, animals and technologies and, transfer them to farmers in Ho Chi Minh city and provinces in the south. Each institute has few hundreds of officers, researchers and several sub-units.

Future Directions of Integrated Rural Development

IRD based on commune must help enhance production, promote economic effectiveness and improve the standard of living of the rural people in Ho Chi Minh city. When changing to market mechanism, Vietnamese Government knew that the gap between the rich and the poor would be widened. The rich has had good conditions to become richer. It is inevitable. But, if appropriate policies are established and suitable sponsors and programs from central, local government, and international organizations are directed through local people's committees and institutions, the poor will not become poorer. Central and city government must adequately invest on poor communities. For Ho Chi Minh city, in the next five years, the following projects are proposed:

1. Six Models of Rural Environmental Hygiene in 6 Districts: Nha Be, Binh Chanh, Cu Chi, Hoc Mon, Can Gio and District 2

The project's contents include: reformation of breeding cage; W.C.; treatment of waste; building environmental hygiene and construction; using suitable chemical fertilizers and

chemical plant protection; dissemination of information on good health; and environment protection information via television, broadcast, brochures, etc. Project has been conducting by Center for Water and Rural Environment Hygiene, in collaboration with people committees of six districts, Service of Technology, Science and Environment, Center for Technology, Science and Agricultural Extension.

2. Social and Economic Development of 20 Poor Communes in 4 Districts: Can Gio, Nha Be, Binh Chanh, District 9

The main aspects of this project are as follows:

- Support to develop traditional professions.
- Guide the poor to become rich via programs of agriculture, forestry, industry, etc.
- Building infrastructure in communes.

The Center for Technology, Science and Agricultural Extension and the branch of Immigration and New Economic Area Development have the responsibility for setting up and implementing this project. Using organic fertilizers to replace chemical fertilizers in agricultural farming at Phuoc Vinh An commune, Cu Chi district is conducted by the Center for Technology, Science and Agricultural Extension. In addition, there are activities to help farmers to change old farming systems. These include demonstrations, training courses and seminars. Projects also pay attention to eradicate illiteracy, increase cultural and environmental knowledge, improve the role of women in community development, improving health, etc. It is concluded that local community organizations and institutions have to play an extremely important role in changing the pace of rural society and economy. They are the bridge between local people and government in identifying demand, developing plans, searching resources for investment (local and international) and in implementing projects.

References

Center for Technology, Science and Agricultural Extension, (2001). Project on "Using Organic Fertilizers in Agricultural Farming for Sustainable Production at Phuoc Vinh An Commune, Cu Chi District, Ho Chi Minh City".

Ho Chi Minh City Service of Agricultural and Rural Development, (2002). Project on "Social, Economic Development at 20 of Poor Communes".

Kramer, R., (1987). *Voluntary Agencies in the Welfare State*, University of California Press, Berkeley.

Service of Agricultural and Rural Development, (2001). "Project of Six Models of Rural Environmental Hygiene", Ho Chi Minh City.

Yogo, Toshihiro, (2000). "Local Communities in Development Process – An Analytical Framework", *Local Social Development*, APO, Tokyo.

Bibliography

Abueva, Jose V., (1969). "Local Government, Community Development, and Political Stability", in J. V. Abueva and Raul P. de Guzman (eds.) *Foundations and Dynamics of Filipino Government and Politics*, pp.468-475, Bookmark, Manila

Acharya, Umesh, (2001). *Decentralization and Local Governance.*

Agrawal, A. and K. Gupta (2005) 'Decentralization and Participation: The Governance of Common Pool Resources in Nepal's Terai'. *World Development,* Vol. 33, No. 7, pp. 1101–1114.

Agricultural Bank of Islamic Republic of Iran, (1998). *Role of Agricultural Bank in Rural Development.* APERI, 1996. *Iran Agriculture at a Glance.*

Ahmed, Junaid, (2007), Local Governments: International Experiences, paper presented to National Workshop on Strengthening of Local Government Institutions, Dhaka, National Institute of Local Government.

Antiporta, D. B., (1999). *Agriculture and Rural Sector in Regional Perspectives: Growth, Food Security and Poverty Alleviation*, M.C. 5 series of 1999, DAR.

APO, (1999). *Role of Institutions in Rural Community Development*, proceedings of the Study Meeting on Role of Institutions in Rural Community Development, 21-29 September 1998 held in Colombo, APO, Tokyo

Aryal, Bojendra, (2003)."Approaches and Methods of Rural Development" *Sociology of Rural Development.* Dikchayanta Pulication, Kritipur.

Asian Productivity Organization, (2001). Proceedings of the Seminar on Effective Decentralization for Community Development, 23-31 March 2001, Sri Lanka

Bista, Kumar, (2000)."An Alternative strategy". Rural Dvelopment in Nepal, Udya Books, KTM.

Blessing, Garcia-Glova. *Local Governance and Agrarian Reform: A Focus on Two Municipalities.*

Bobsbawm E. & Ranger T. (eds.) (1983). *The Invention of Tradition* .Cambridge: The University Press of Cambridge.

Center for Technology, Science and Agricultural Extension, (2001). Project on "Using Organic Fertilizers in Agricultural Farming for Sustainable Production at Phuoc Vinh An Commune, Cu Chi District, Ho Chi Minh City".

Central Bank of Sri Lanka, (2001). *Annual Report of the Central Bank*, Colombo, Sri Lanka.

Cernea, Michel M., (1997). *NGOs and Community Development*, translated version by Gholam H. Salleh Nassb, Ministry of Jihad, 1376.

Choudhury, R. C. and S. Rajakutty, (2000). "Rural Development Charging Focus of Strategy", *The Survey of Indian Agriculture 2000*, pp.213-215, the Hindu, Chennai.

Cooke, B. and U. Kothari, eds. (2001) *Participation: The New Tyranny?* London: Zed Books.

Dahlen, A., (1992). *Comparative Evaluation Study of the Sri Lanka Integrated Development Program*, Ministry of Policy Planning and Implementation, Colombo, Sri Lanka.

Day, Graham, (1998). "Working with the Grain? Towards Sustainable Rural and Community Development", *Journal of Rural Studies* 14(1): 89-105.

Ekka, Alexius, (1999). Country paper in Dr. Prachanda Pradhan (ed.) *Role of Institutions in Rural Community Development*, pp.154-167, APO, Tokyo.

Ellis, F. (2000) *Rural Livelihoods and Diversity in Developing Countries.* Oxford: Oxford University Press.

ESCAP (2007) *Persistent and Emerging Issues in Rural Poverty Reduction.* Bangkok: ESCAP

Fisher, R. J., Hukum Bahadur Singh, Deepak Raj Pandey and Helmut Lang, (1990). *The* Management of Forest Resources in Sindhu Palchok and Kabhre Palanchok Districts *of Nepal*, Mountain Populations and Employment Discussion Paper Series 8, ICIMOD, Kathmandu.

Francis, P. (2001) 'Participatory Development at the World Bank: The Primacy of Process'. Chapter 5 in Cooke and Kothari, 2001, pp. 72-87.

Gelal, Mani Ram, (2002). *Participatory Rural Infrastructure Development in Nepal.*

Gunarathne, L., (1987). *The Poorest and the Poor in Sri Lanka and the Alleviation of Poverty in Sri Lanka*, Central Bank of Sri Lanka, Colombo.

Hanumantha Rao, C. H., (2001). "Changing Economic Structure of the Rural Economy in Asia and the Pacific" in Dr. C. H. Hanumantha Rao (ed), *Rural Transformation in Asia and the Pacific*, pp.66-80, APO, Tokyo.

Heck, B, van (2003) *Participatory Development: Guidelines on Beneficiary Participation in Agricultural and Rural Development.* Second edition. Rome: FAO.

Heim, Franz G., Akin Rabibhadana and Chirmsak Pinthong, (1983). *How to Work with Peasants-A Manual for Field Workers,* Khon Kaen: RDI, Khon Kaen University.

Ho Chi Minh City Service of Agricultural and Rural Development, (2002). Project on "Social, Economic Development at 20 of Poor Communes".

Hossain, Zillur Rahman (2001), *Actors and Roles, Community Capacities and Local Governance;* Dhaka: Power and Participatory Research Centre.

IBRD, (1987). *World Bank Experience with Rural Development, 1965-1986*, Washington D.C.

Jabbari, Habib, (1997). "NGOs: Concepts and Practices", *Municipalities Magazine*, Vol.6, 1376.

Khan Zarina R. and Akther Hussain (2001), *Review/Stocktaking in Local Governance,* University of Dhaka.

Kramer, R., (1987). *Voluntary Agencies in the Welfare State*, University of California Press, Berkeley.

Kramer, R., (1987). *Voluntary Agencies in the Welfare State*, University of California Press, Berkeley.

Lipsky, M. and S. R. Smith, (1990). "Nonprofit Organizations, Government, and the Welfare State", *Publican Science Quarterly* 104(4): 625-648.

Manzuri, Ghazala and Vijayendra Rao. (2004). *Community-Based and -Driven. Development: A Critical Review.* World Bank Policy Research Working Paper 3209.

Messerschmidt, Donald A., (1984). *Using Human Resources in Natural Resource Management Innovations in Himalayan Development*, Working Paper WSM I/1, ICIMOD, Kathmandu.

Ministry of Finance, Planning, Ethnic Affairs and National Integration, (1995). *Integrated Rural Development Program: 15 Years Experience in Sri Lanka*, Regional Development Division, Sri Lanka.

Ministry of Interior, (2001). *Symposium on the Role and Status of NGOs*, in national and international version, first print, Tehran, 1380.

Morapaya, R. B., (1986). *Integrated Rural Development in Sri Lanka*, Sterling Publishers Ltd., New Delhi.

Mulder, Niels, (1979). *Inside Thai Society: An Interpretation of Everyday Life,* Bangkok: Editions Duang Kamol.

National Institute of Rural Development (NIRD), (2001). S. P. Jain (ed) *Emerging Institutions for Decentralized Rural Development*, Vol. I and II, pp. 1-982.

National Reconstruction Bureau, (2000). *Local Government Plan,* Chief Executive Secretariat, Government of Pakistan.

Nepal Australia Forestry Project, (1990). *Gaunle Ko Ban Byavastha: Indigenous Forest Management in Nepal*, film produced by Worldview International Foundation, Nepal for NAFP.

Oakley, P. and Marsden, D., (1984). *Approaches to Participation in Rural Development,* Geneva: International Labour Office.

Pakistan Academy for Rural Development, (1990). Local Government for Rural Development in Pakistan.

Patnam, Robert, (2001). *Democracy and Civil Traditions*, translated version by M. Taghi Delforouz, Ministry of Interior, first print, 1380.

PDDP, (2000). *Making A Difference*, PDDP Impact Series: 01/2000.

Peter Oakley. (1988). *The Monitoring and Evaluation of Participation in Rural Development*, by FAO, Rome.

Planning Commission, (2001-2002). *Progress Report on PSDP Projects*, Government of Pakistan.

Pradhan, Prachanda, (1999). "Role of Institutions in Rural Community Development" in Dr. Prachanda Pradhan (ed), *Role of Institutions in Rural Community Development*, pp.27-49, APO, Tokyo.

Ramakrisnan, P. S., (1987). *Some Aspects of the Integrated Rural Development in Sri Lanka – Past Experiences and Further Perspectives*, Regional Development Division, Ministry of Plan Implementation, Colombo, Sri Lanka.

Roling, N. G., and J. Jiggins, (1998). "The Ecological Knowledge System", in N. G. Roling and M. Wagemakers (eds.) *Facilitating Sustainable Agriculture*, p..283-311, Cambridge University Press.

Sen, Amatay (1999), *Development as Freedom.* London: Oxford University Press.

Seri Phongphit and Robert Bennoun (eds), (1988). *Turning Point of Thai Peasants: Village and Self-Reliance in a Thai Context,* Bangkok: THIRD.

Service of Agricultural and Rural Development, (2001). "Project of Six Models of Rural Environmental Hygiene", Ho Chi Minh City.

Shigetomi, Shinichi, (1998). *Cooperation and Community in Rural Thailand: An Organizational Analysis of Participatory Rural Development*, Institute of Developing Economies, Tokyo

Shotton, Roger (ed), (2004), *Local Government Initiative: Pro-Poor Infrastructure and Service Delivery in Rural Asia – A Synthesis of Case Studies,* NY: UNCDF, 2004.

Singh, Katar. (1999). "Rural Development Policies and Strategies". *Rural Development Principles, Policies and Management*. Sage Publication, India.

Soemardjan, Selo and Kenon Breaseale, (1993). *Cultural Change in Rural Indonesia: Impact of Village Development*, Sebelas Maret University Press, Surakarta

Sosmeña, Guadioso, Jr., (1991). *Decentralization and Empowerment*, Local Government Foundation, Manila.

Taha, M., Om Prakash, (1989). *Integrated Rural Development in India*, Center for Integrated Rural Development for Asia and the Pacific, Dhaka.

Tapales, Proserpina D., (1992). "History and Evolution of Philippine Local Government Administration", in *Strengthening Local Administration and Accelerating Local Development*, UP College of Public Administration, Quezon City.

UNDP and NORAD, (1998). *Putting People First, The Year in Review*

Uphoff, Norman, (1986). *Local Institutional Development: An Analytical Sourcebook with Cases*, Kumarian Press, West Hartford, CT.

____ and C. M. Wijayaratna, (2000). "Demonstrated Benefits from Social Capital: The Productivity of Farmer Organizations in Gal Oya, Sri Lanka, 2000", *World Development*, No. 28, Vol. 11, November 2000.

Valsan, E. H., (1970). *Community Development Programs and Rural Local Development: Comparative Case Studies of India and the Philippines*, Praeger Publications, New York.

Vanpen Surarerks, (1988). *Issues and Experiences in the Use of Community Participation by Government and Private Organizations in Rural Development Programs in Thailand,* Chiangmai: Chiangmai University.

Villarin, Thomas S., (1994). *KAISAHAN*, Occasional Paper No. 94-02.

Wijayaratna, C. M., (1985). "Involvement of Farmers in Water Management in Gal Oya, Sri Lanka" in *Participatory Experiences in Irrigation Water Management: Proceedings of the Expert Consultation on Irrigation Water Management* held in Yogyakarta and Bali, Indonesia, 16-22 July 1984, 117-32, FAO.

Williams, M; Keith McLean, and Graham Kerr (1998), D*ecentralization and Rural Development: Characterizing Efforts in 19 Selected Countries*, World Bank, September.

Wolf, T., (1990). *Managing a Nonprofit*, Prentice-Hall Press, New York.

World Bank, (1996). Report No. 11956 – IRN/*Islamic Republic of Iran, Services for Agricultural and Rural Development.*

World Bank. (2004). *World Development Report 2004: Making Services Working for Poor People.* Oxford University Press.

Yogo, Toshihiro, (2000). "Local Communities in Development Process – An Analytical Framework", *Local Social Development*, APO, Tokyo.

Index